Computational Biology

Computational Biology

Mitchell Spencer

SYRAWOOD
PUBLISHING HOUSE

New York

Published by Syrawood Publishing House,
750 Third Avenue, 9th Floor,
New York, NY 10017, USA
www.syrawoodpublishinghouse.com

Computational Biology
Mitchell Spencer

International Standard Book Number: 978-1-64740-014-9 (Hardback)

Cataloging-in-Publication Data

Computational biology / Mitchell Spencer.
    p. cm.
Includes bibliographical references and index.
ISBN 978-1-64740-014-9
1. Computational biology. 2. Bioinformatics. 3. Systems biology.
4. Biology. I. Spencer, Mitchell.
QH324.2 .C66 2020
570.285--dc23

TABLE OF CONTENTS

PREFACE

Computational biology is a field that deals with the development and application of data-analytical and theoretical methods for studying various behavioral, ecological, biological and social systems. It also uses mathematical modeling and computational simulation techniques. It is closely related to the field of bioinformatics where computers are used for storing and processing biological data. Computational biology is an interdisciplinary field that applies concepts from biology, mathematics, biochemistry, chemistry, biophysics, molecular biology and computer science. There are various sub-fields of computational biology such as computational anatomy, computational biomodeling, computational genetics, computational neuroscience, pharmacology, evolutionary biology and computational neuropsychiatry. This textbook provides significant information of this discipline to help develop a good understanding of computational biology and related fields. It is a valuable compilation of topics, ranging from the basic to the most complex theories and principles in this field. This book is an essential guide for both academicians and those who wish to pursue this discipline further.

Given below is the chapter wise description of the book:

Chapter 1- The branch of biology which seeks to use biological data in order to develop algorithms for studying biological systems and relationships is known as computational biology. A few of its sub-fields are computational anatomy, computational neuroscience and computational genomics. This chapter has been carefully written to provide an easy understanding of the varied facets of these sub-fields of computational biology.

Chapter 2- Systems biology refers to the mathematical and computational modeling and analysis of complex biological systems. Some of the areas where systems biology is applied are protein structure prediction and medical research. This chapter discusses in detail the principles and applications of system biology.

Chapter 3- Phylogenetics refers to the study of the evolutionary history and relationships between individuals or groups of living beings. The application of computational algorithms, methods and programs for phylogenetic analyses is known as computational phylogenetics. The diverse applications of computational phylogenetics as well as phylogenetic networks have been thoroughly discussed in this chapter.

Chapter 4- The branch of science which is involved in developing methods and software tools in order to understand biological data is referred to as bioinformatics. It is used in sequence analysis and gene prediction. The topics elaborated in this chapter will help in gaining a better perspective about the different techniques and processes associated with bioinformatics.

Chapter 5- Databases are an integral part of bioinformatics research and applications. Some of the software used in bioinformatics are Clustal, MUSCLE, Bowtie and HMMER. The topics elaborated in this chapter will help in gaining a better perspective about these software as well as the different types of databases such as primary and secondary databases.

Indeed, my job was extremely crucial and challenging as I had to ensure that every chapter is informative and structured in a student-friendly manner. I am thankful for the support provided by my family and colleagues during the completion of this book.

Mitchell Spencer

Chapter 1

Introduction to Computational Biology

The branch of biology which seeks to use biological data in order to develop algorithms for studying biological systems and relationships is known as computational biology. A few of its sub-fields are computational anatomy, computational neuroscience and computational genomics. This chapter has been carefully written to provide an easy understanding of the varied facets of these sub-fields of computational biology.

Computational biology is a branch of biology involving the application of computers and computer science to the understanding and modeling of the structures and processes of life. It entails the use of computational methods (e.g., algorithms) for the representation and simulation of biological systems, as well as for the interpretation of experimental data, often on a very large scale.

The beginnings of computational biology essentially date to the origins of computer science. British mathematician and logician Alan Turing, often called the father of computing, used early computers to implement a model of biological morphogenesis (the development of pattern and form in living organisms) in the early 1950s, shortly before his death. At about the same time, a computer called MANIAC, built at the Los Alamos National Laboratory in New Mexico for weapons research, was applied to such purposes as modeling hypothesized genetic codes. (Pioneering computers had been used even earlier in the 1950s for numeric calculations in population genetics, but the first instances of authentic computational modeling in biology were the work by Turing and by the group at Los Alamos.)

By the 1960s, computers had been applied to deal with much more-varied sets of analyses, namely those examining protein structures. These developments marked the rise of computational biology as a field, and they originated from studies centred on protein crystallography, in which scientists found computers indispensable for carrying out laborious Fourier analyses to determine the three-dimensional structure of proteins.

Starting in the 1950s, taxonomists began to incorporate computers into their work, using the machines to assist in the classification of organisms by clustering them based on similarities of sets of traits. Such taxonomies have been useful particularly for phylogenetics (the study of evolutionary relationships). In the 1960s, when existing techniques were extended to the level of DNA sequences and amino acid sequences of proteins and combined with a burgeoning knowledge of cellular processes and protein structures, a whole new set of computational methods was developed in support of molecular phylogenetics. These computational methods entailed the creation of increasingly sophisticated techniques for the comparison of strings of symbols that benefited from the formal study of algorithms and the study of dynamic programming in particular. Indeed, efficient algorithms always have been of primary concern in computational biology, given the scale of data available, and biology has in turn provided examples that have driven much advanced research in computer science. Examples include graph algorithms for genome mapping (the process of locating fragments of DNA on chromosomes) and for certain types of DNA and peptide sequencing methods, clustering algorithms for gene expression analysis and phylogenetic reconstruction, and pattern matching for various sequence search problems.

Beginning in the 1980s, computational biology drew on further developments in computer science, including a number of aspects of artificial intelligence (AI). Among these were knowledge representation, which contributed to the development of ontologies (the representation of concepts and their relationships) that codify biological knowledge in "computer-readable" form, and natural-language processing, which provided a technological means for mining information from text in the scientific literature. Perhaps most significantly, the subfield of machine learning found wide use in biology, from modeling sequences for purposes of pattern recognition to the analysis of high-dimensional (complex) data from large-scale gene-expression studies.

Applications of Computational Biology

Initially, computational biology focused on the study of the sequence and structure of biological molecules, often in an evolutionary context. Beginning in the 1990s, however, it extended increasingly to the analysis of function. Functional prediction involves assessing the sequence and structural similarity between an unknown and a known protein and analyzing the proteins' interactions with other molecules. Such analyses may be extensive, and thus computational biology has become closely aligned with systems biology, which attempts to analyze the workings of large interacting networks of biological components, especially biological pathways.

Biochemical, regulatory, and genetic pathways are highly branched and interleaved, as well as dynamic, calling for sophisticated computational tools for their modeling and analysis. Moreover, modern technology platforms for the rapid, automated (high-throughput) generation of biological data have allowed for an extension from traditional hypothesis-driven experimentation to data-driven analysis, by which computational experiments can be performed on genome-wide databases of unprecedented scale. As a result, many aspects of the study of biology have become unthinkable without the power of computers and the methodologies of computer science.

Computational Biology

Another way computers have reshaped biology is by introducing statistics and data analysis methods. A good example is understanding how mutational processes shape genomes. Mutational processes—be it cigarette smoke, sunlight, or defects in homologous recombination—are not visible in individual mutations but only in their global patterns. How often is a C turned into a T? How does this frequency vary depending on the neighbours of the mutated base? How much of this frequency is explained by other features of the genome, like replication timing? Answering these questions helps us to understand basic properties of the mutational processes active in cells, and it is only possible by statistical techniques that identify patterns and correlations.

These types of analyses need large data collections, and thus the success of computational biology is closely linked to the success of large-scale efforts to gather genotypes and phenotypes of model organisms and humans. One of the first examples highlighting the power of computational approaches was sequencing the human genome, which showed how efficiently computational alignment and scaffolding methods were able to assemble the DNA fragments produced during shotgun sequencing, and modern Next Generation Sequencing techniques completely rely on advances in computational biology to analyze huge amounts of short sequence reads. DNA sequencing was once a Nobel Prize–worthy development. Now, computational biology is leading the way in turning it into a widely available and practical approach for both basic biology and medical research, which is currently revolutionizing what we know about tissues and single cells.

Computational Biology Provides an Atlas of Life

By combining large data collections with databases and statistics, computational biology is providing a reference map for biology—an atlas of life that holds together individual insights. This map is not at the level of resolution provided by Google Street View, rather, it is a map like the one used by Columbus, Magellan, or Vasco da Gama—intrepid explorers in search of adventure. The map provides a general outline, but many areas are sketchy, and some important parts might even be missing and waiting for discovery. "Here be dragons," it just says. But even with all these shortcomings, the map is still an indispensable guide: the atlas of life provided by computational biology forms the background for planning, executing, and interpreting all focussed small-scale experiments that probe the uncharted areas and push out the boundaries of biological knowledge.

Computational Biology Turns Ideas into Hypotheses

Finally, computers reshaped biology by making fuzzy concepts rigorous and testable. Here is one example from my own research: for decades, cancer researchers have discussed the idea that genetic heterogeneity between cells in the same tumour helps to make a cancer resistant to therapy. It is a simple idea: the more diverse the cell population is, the more likely it is that a subset of the cells is resistant to therapy and can regrow the tumour after all other cells were killed.

But how exactly can you measure "genetic heterogeneity," and how big is its influence on resistance development? To answer these questions, we had to turn the idea into a testable hypothesis. We used genomic approaches to measure changes in cancer genomes at different sites in a patient and then defined quantitative measures of heterogeneity, which could be compared statistically to clinical information on treatment resistance. And indeed, we found evidence supporting the initial idea that heterogeneity determines resistance.

This is just one of many examples in which a quantitative computational approach was needed to turn a fuzzy idea into a testable hypothesis. Computational biology excels at distilling huge amounts of complex data into something testable in the wet lab, thus, shaping and directing experimental follow-up.

Sub-fields of Computational Biology

Bioinformatics: This is the most well-known field of computational biology. This field deals with the development and creation of databases or other methods of storing, retrieving, and analyzing biological data (originally starting with genes) through mathematical and computing algorithms. Bioinformatics employs both mathematics and an ever-increasing variety of computing languages to ease the storage and analysis of biological data. Databases themselves have made way for sprouting research fields such as data mining.

Computational Biology: Computational biology has become a broad term that refers to the application of mathematical models, computing algorithms and programs, and simulation tools to aid in various biological research such as genetics, molecular biology, biochemistry, ecology, and neuroscience among many others. Computational biology research encompasses many disciplines such as health informatics, comparative genomics and proteomics, protein modelling, neuroscience, etc.

Mathematical Biology: This field is an amalgamation of biology and a various fields of mathematics. Often times, some computational biology topics are more math-based (computing) than computer science-based. Various mathematics used in mathematical biology research include discrete mathematics, topology (also useful for computational modeling), Bayesian statistics (such as for biostatistics), Linear Algebra, Logic, Boolean algebra, and many other higher level mathematics. This field is also often called theoretical biology due to its focus on equations, algorithms, and theoretical models.

Systems Biology: This field deals with the interactions between various biological systems ranging from the cellular level to entire populations with the goal of discovering emergent properties. Systems biology usually involves networking cell signalling or metabolic pathways. Systems biology often employs computational techniques and biological modelling to study these complex interactions at cellular levels.

Computational Anatomy

Computational anatomy (CA) is the mathematical study of anatomy I in I = I(alpha) o G, an orbit under groups of diffeomorphisms (i.e., smooth invertible mappings) g in G of anatomical exemplars I(alpha) in I. The observable images are the output of medical imaging devices. There are three components that CA examines:

i) Constructions of the anatomical submanifolds,

ii) Comparison of the anatomical manifolds via estimation of the underlying diffeomorphisms g in G defining the shape or geometry of the anatomical manifolds, and

iii) Generation of probability laws of anatomical variation P(.) on the images I for inference and disease testing within anatomical models.

Computational Pharmacology

Computational pharmacology is a sub branch of computational biology where the effects of genomic data is studied inorder to find links between genotypes and diseases and then screening of drug data. There are several data sets available and researchers and scientists are developing computational methods to analyze these data sets. Computational pharmacology tries to bridge the gap between strcture and function via dynamics.

Computational Methods in Drug Discovery

Computer-aided drug discovery/design methods have played a major role in the development of therapeutically important small molecules for over three decades. These methods are broadly classified as either structure-based or ligand-based methods. Structure-based methods are in principle analogous to high-throughput screening in that both target and ligand structure information is imperative. Structure-based approaches include ligand docking, pharmacophore, and ligand design methods.

Position of Computer-aided Drug Design in the Drug Discovery Pipeline

CADD is capable of increasing the hit rate of novel drug compounds because it uses a much more targeted search than traditional HTS and combinatorial chemistry. It not only aims to explain the molecular basis of therapeutic activity but also to predict possible derivatives that would improve activity. In a drug discovery campaign, CADD is usually used for three major purposes: (1) filter large compound libraries into smaller sets of predicted active compounds that can be tested experimentally; (2) guide the optimization of lead compounds, whether to increase its affinity or optimize drug metabolism and pharmacokinetics (DMPK) properties including absorption, distribution, metabolism, excretion, and the potential for toxicity (ADMET); (3) design novel compounds, either by "growing" starting molecules one functional group at a time or by piecing together fragments into novel chemotypes. Figure below illustrates the position of CADD in drug discovery pipeline.

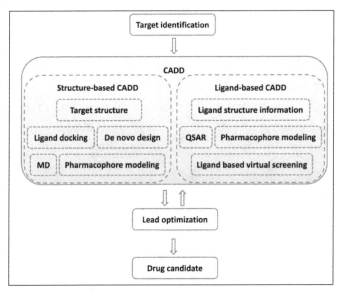

Figure above discribe CADD in drug discovery/design pipeline. A therapeutic target is identified against which a drug has to be developed. Depending on the availability of structure information, a structure-based approach or a ligand-based approach is used. A successful CADD campaign will allow identification of multiple lead compounds. Lead identification is often followed by several cycles of lead optimization and subsequent lead identification using CADD. Lead compounds are tested in vivo to identify drug candidates.

CADD can be classified into two general categories: structure-based and ligand-based. Structure-based CADD relies on the knowledge of the target protein structure to calculate interaction energies for all compounds tested, whereas ligand-based CADD exploits the knowledge of known active and inactive molecules through chemical similarity searches or construction of predictive, quantitative structure-activity relation

(QSAR) models. Structure-based CADD is generally preferred where high-resolution structural data of the target protein are available, i.e., for soluble proteins that can readily be crystallized. Ligand-based CADD is generally preferred when no or little structural information is available, often for membrane protein targets. The central goal of structure-based CADD is to design compounds that bind tightly to the target, i.e., with large reduction in free energy, improved DMPK/ADMET properties, and are target specific, i.e., have reduced off-target effects. A successful application of these methods will result in a compound that has been validated in vitro and in vivo and its binding location has been confirmed, ideally through a cocrystal structure.

One of the most common uses in CADD is the screening of virtual compound libraries, also known as virtual high-throughput screening (vHTS). This allows experimentalists to focus resources on testing compounds likely to have any activity of interest. In this way, a researcher can identify an equal number of hits while screening significantly less compounds, because compounds predicted to be inactive with high confidence may be skipped. Avoiding a large population of inactive compounds saves money and time, because the size of the experimental HTS is significantly reduced without sacrificing a large degree of hits. Note that the first mention of vHTS was in 1997 and chart an increasing rate of publication for the application of vHTS between 1997 and 2010. They also found that the largest fraction of hits has been obtained for G-protein-coupled receptors (GPCRs) followed by kinases.

vHTS comes in many forms, including chemical similarity searches by fingerprints or topology, selecting compounds by predicted biologic activity through QSAR models or pharmacophore mapping, and virtual docking of compounds into target of interest, known as structure-based docking . These methods allow the ranking of "hits" from the virtual compound library for acquisition. The ranking can reflect a property of interest such as percent similarity to a query compound or predicted biologic activity, or in the case of docking, the lowest energy scoring poses for each ligand bound to the target of interest. Often initial hits are rescored and ranked using higher level computational techniques that are too time consuming to be applied to full-scale vHTS. It is important to note that vHTS does not aim to identify a drug compound that is ready for clinical testing, but rather to find leads with chemotypes that have not previously been associated with a target. This is not unlike a traditional HTS where a compound is generally considered a hit if its activity is close to 10 μM. Through iterative rounds of chemical synthesis and in vitro testing, a compound is first developed into a "lead" with higher affinity, some understanding of its structure-activity-relation, and initial tests for DMPK/ADMET properties. Only after further iterative rounds of lead-to-drug optimization and in vivo testing does a compound reach a clinically appropriate potency and acceptable DMPK/ADMET properties. For example, the literature survey performed by Ripphausen et al. revealed that a majority of successful vHTS applications identified a small number of hits that are usually active in the micromolar range, and hits with low nanomolar potency are only rarely identified.

The cost benefit of using computational tools in the lead optimization phase of drug development is substantial. Development of new drugs can cost anywhere in the range of 400 million to 2 billion dollars, with synthesis and testing of lead analogs being a large contributor to that sum. Therefore, it is beneficial to apply computational tools in hit-to-lead optimization to cover a wider chemical space while reducing the number of compounds that must be synthesized and tested in vitro. The computational optimization of a hit compound can involve a structure-based analysis of docking poses and energy profiles for hit analogs, ligand-based screening for compounds with similar chemical structure or improved predicted biologic activity, or prediction of favorable DMPK/ADMET properties. The comparably low cost of CADD compared with chemical synthesis and biologic characterization of compounds make these methods attractive to focus, reduce, and diversify the chemical space that is explored.

De novo drug design is another tool in CADD methods, but rather than screening libraries of previously synthesized compounds, it involves the design of novel compounds. A structure generator is needed to sample the space of chemicals. Given the size of the search space (more than 1060 molecules) heuristics are used to focus these algorithms on molecules that are predicted to be highly active, readily synthesizable, devoid of undesirable properties, often derived from a starting scaffold with demonstrated activity, etc. Additionally, effective sampling strategies are used while dealing with large search spaces such as evolutionary algorithms, metropolis search, or simulated annealing. The construction algorithms are generally defined as either linking or growing techniques. Linking algorithms involve docking of small fragments or functional groups such as rings, acetyl groups, esters, etc., to particular binding sites followed by linking fragments from adjacent sites. Growing algorithms, on the other hand, begin from a single fragment placed in the binding site to which fragments are added, removed, and changed to improve activity. Similar to vHTS, the role of de novo drug design is not to design the single compound with nanomolar activity and acceptable DMPK/ADMET properties but rather to design a lead compound that can be subsequently improved.

Ligand Databases for Computer-aided Drug Design

Virtual HTS uses high-performance computing to screen large chemical data bases and prioritize compounds for synthesis. Current hardware and algorithms allow structure-based screening of up to 100,000 molecules per day using parallel processing clusters. To perform a virtual screen, however, a virtual library must be available for screening. Virtual libraries can be acquired in a variety of sizes and designs including general libraries that can be used to screen against any target, focused libraries that are designed for a family of related targets, and targeted libraries that are specifically designed for a single target.

General libraries can be constructed using a variety of computational and combinatorial tools. Early systems used molecular formula as the only constraint for structure generation, resulting in all possible structures for a predetermined limit in the number of atoms. As comprehensive computational enumeration of all chemical space is and will remain infeasible, additional restrictions are applied. Typically, chemical entities difficult to synthesize or known/expected to cause unfavorable DMPK/ADMET properties are excluded. Fink et al. proposed a generation method for the construction of virtual libraries that involved the use of connected graphs populated with C, N, O, and F atoms and pruned based on molecular structure constraints and the removal of unstable structures. The final data base proposed with this method is called the GDB (Generated a DataBase) and contains 26.4 million chemical structures that have been used for vHTS. A more recent variation of this data base called GDB-13 includes atoms C, N, O, S, and Cl (F is not included in this variation to accelerate computation) and contains 970 million compounds.

Most frequently, vHTS focuses on drug-like molecules that have been synthesized or can be easily derived from already available starting material.

Target Data Bases for Computer-aided Drug Discovery/Design

The knowledge of the structure of the target protein is required for structure-based CADD. The Protein Data Bank (, established in 1971 at the Brookhaven National Laboratory, and the Cambridge Crystallographic Data Center, are among the most commonly used data bases for protein structure. PDB currently houses more than 81,000 protein structures, the majority of which have been determined using X-ray crystallography and a smaller set determined using NMR spectroscopy. When an experimentally determined structure of a protein is not available, it is often possible to create a comparative model based on the experimental structure of a related protein. Most frequently the relation is based in evolution that introduced the term "homology model." The Swiss-Model server is one of the most widely used web-based tools for homology modeling. Initially, static protein structures were used for all structure-based design methods. However, proteins are not static structures but rather exist as ensembles of different conformational states. The protein fluctuates through this ensemble depending on the relative free energies of each of these states, spending more time in conformations of lower free energy.

Ligands are thought to interact with some conformations but not others, thus stabilizing conformational populations in the ensemble. Therefore, docking compounds into a static protein structure can be misleading, as the chosen conformation may not be representative of the conformation capable of binding the ligand. Recently, it has become state of the art to use additional computational tools such as molecular dynamics and molecular mechanics to simulate and evaluate a protein's conformational space. Conformational sampling provides a collection of snapshots that can be used in place of a single structure that reflect the breadth of fluctuations the ligand may encounter in vivo. This approach was proven to be invaluable in CADD by Schames et al. in the 2004 identification of novel HIV integrase inhibitors. Some methods, such as ROSETTALIGAND, are capable of incorporating protein flexibility during the actual docking procedure, omitting the need for snapshot ensembles.

The collection of events that occurs when a ligand binds a receptor extends far beyond the noncovalent interactions between ligand and protein. Desolvation of ligand and binding pocket, shifts in the ligand and protein conformational ensembles, and reordering of water molecules in the binding site all contribute to binding free energies. Consideration of water molecules as an integral part of binding sites is necessary for key mechanistic steps and binding. These water molecules shift the free energy change of ligand binding by either facilitating certain noncovalent interactions between the ligand and protein or by being displaced into more favorable direct interactions between the ligand and protein, causing an overall change in free energy upon binding. Improvements in computational resources allow inclusion of better representations of physiochemical interactions in computational methods to increase their accuracies.

Benchmarking Techniques of Computer-aided Drug Design

Effective benchmarks are essential for assessment of performance and accuracy of CADD algorithms. Design of the benchmark in terms of number and type of target proteins, size, and composition of active and inactive chemicals, and selection of quality measures play a key role when comparing new CADD methods with existing ones. Scientific benchmarks usually involve screening a library of compounds that include a subset of known actives combined with known inactive compounds and then evaluating the number of known actives that were identified by the CADD technique used.

Performance is commonly reported by correlating predicted activities with experimentally observed activities through the use of receiver operating characteristic curves. These curves plot the number of true positive predictions on the y-axis versus the false-positive predictions on the x-axis. A random predictor would result in a plot of a line with a slope of 1, whereas curves with high initial slopes above this line represent increasing performance scores for the method tested. Receiver operating characteristic curves are therefore analyzed by determining the area under the curve, positive predictive value—the ratio of true positives in a subset selected in a vHTS screen, or enrichment—a benchmark that normalizes positive predictive value by the background ratio of positives in the dataset.

For structure-based CADD, it is now common also to include decoy molecules that further test a technique's ability to discern actives from inactives at high resolution. Irwin et al. created the Directory of Useful Decoys (DUD) dataset designed for high-resolution benchmarking. It includes experimental data for approximately 3000 ligands covering up to 40 different targets and a set of carefully chosen decoys. These decoys were designed to resemble positive ligands physically but not topologically. These decoys, however, are not experimentally validated and are only postulated to be "inactive" against the targets. Good and Oprea developed clustered versions of DUD with added datasets from sources such as WOMBAT to avoid challenges in enrichment comparisons between methods due to different parameters and limited diversity.

The present review covers various established structure-based and ligand-based CADD methods followed by a section on CADD methods in ADMET profile prediction. The applications of various methods discussed in the manuscript are illustrated with recent studies. We prioritize studies that concluded in compounds that were at least tested in vivo and often entered clinical trials.

Computational Neuroscience

Computational neuroscience is the only field that can help you understand, how you're able to think and process information in your brain. Even by the time you finished this sentence, there will be a good number of actions happening inside your brain which can be decoded by the study of neurons. The ultimate goal of computational neuroscience is to explain how electrical and chemical signals are used in the brain to represent and process information. It explains the biophysical mechanisms of computation in neurons, computer simulations of neural circuits, and models of learning.

Over the last few years, we've been seeing advancements in Neural Networks which are completely inspired by this "Computational neuroscience". The algorithms or models which are used in several areas of Neural Networks/Computer Vision are derived by a theoretical understanding of neuroscience. All we know about our brains is, they are fast, intelligent, they take in input from the environments and some chemical reactions/fusions happen and finally, they give us the solution or the output.

Neuroscience

The term 'Computational neuroscience' was coined by Eric L. Schwartz, at a conference to provide a review of a field, which until that point was referred to by a variety of names, such as Neural modeling, Brain theory, and Neural Networks. Later, Hubel & Wiesel discovered the working of neurons across the retina, in the primary visual cortex (the first cortical area). This is explained in section 3. Further, with the rise in computational power, most computational neuroscientists collaborate closely with experimentalists in analyzing different data and synthesizing new models of biological phenomena.

Theoretical Neuroscience

Neuroscience encompasses approaches ranging from molecular and cellular studies to human psychophysics and psychology. The aim of computational neuroscience is to describe how electrical and chemical signals are used in the brain to interpret and process information. This intention is not new, but much has changed in the last decade. More is known now about the brain because of advances in neuroscience, more computing power is available for performing realistic simulations of neural systems, and new insights are being drawn from the study of simplified models of large networks of neurons.

Understanding the brain is a challenge that is attracting a growing number of scientists, from many disciplines. Although there has been an explosion of discoveries over the last several decades concerning the structure of the brain at the cellular and molecular levels, we do not yet understand how the nervous system enables us to see, hear, learn, remember and plan certain actions. But there are numerous fields that depend on computational neuroscience, a few are listed below:

- Deep Learning, Artificial Intelligence and Machine Learning

- Human psychology

- Medical sciences

- Mental models

- Computational anatomy

- Information theory

Neural Cells, Anatomy and Electrical Personality of Neurons

So, to get a clear understanding of how the brain works and how we're able to perceive the world around us, let's look at the primary part of the brain, namely the neurons. These are the computational units of human brain.

The brain can be broken down into individual discrete parts called neurons. There're many neuronal shapes possible, say, in the visual cortex, the neuron is pyramidal, and in the cerebellum, they are called the Purkinje cells.

Structure of Neurons

A neuron consists of three main parts namely Soma, Dendrites, and Axon. Soma is the cell body. Dendrites are the input ends of the neurons whereas the axon is the output end. So, the input is received by the dendrites from the axons of the adjacent neuron. These inputs give rise to an Excitatory Post-Synaptic Potential (EPSP), and when taken as a combination from several other neurons, it provides an Action Potential or a Spike. This spiking happens only when the input reaches a certain threshold.

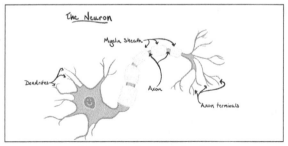

Structure of neuron (src).

Peeking Inside

Interestingly, neurons can be defined as a "leaky bag of charged liquid."So, all of a sudden, how have chemicals cropped up? It's a crucial thing which many of us aren't aware of. Neurons deal entirely with chemicals, and chemical reactions drive all the spikes and synapses. We indeed have Na^+, Cl^-, K^+, et al. in our brains. Fascinating, isn't it?

Contents of a neuron are enclosed within a lipid bilayer, and the lipid is "fat" in simple terms. This bilayer is impermeable to charged ions, such as Na^+, K^+, Cl- et al. So, how do these chemicals move among the neurons? To answer this, let's deep dive into Ionic channels.

Ionic Channels

The "Ionic Channels" allow the transmission of these ions, i.e., to pass in and out of the neurons. This results in a Potential Difference which exists between the insides and the outer part of the neuron, the inside potential is -70mv relative to the outside.

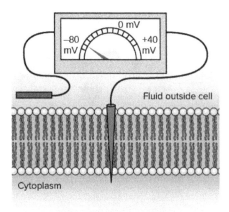

Membrane potential (src).

We have Na^+, Cl- on the outside, whereas K^+, Organic Anion- are present in the inside of a neuron. Vice-versa is possible too, but the ionic concentrations are lower in this case as depicted in the below figure.

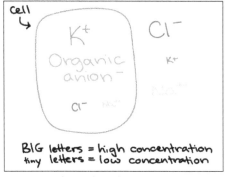

Types of ions found in neurons (src).

So, how's the potential always -70mv? This is maintained by pumping the ions in and out of the neurons, i.e., by expelling Na^+ out and allowing K^+ in. Ionic channels permit only specific neurons to pass and can be classified into three gated channels:

- Voltage-Gated — Probability of opening the channel depends on membrane voltage.

- Chemically Gated — Binding to a chemical causes the channel to open.

- Mechanically Gated — Pressure or stretch influences the channel to open/close.

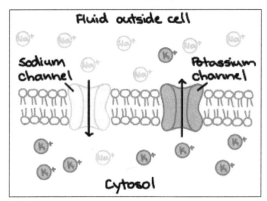

Ionic passage across the neuron membrane (src).

Neuronal Signaling

Neuronal signaling is the interaction that happens among the neurons by the transmission of the signals. The gated channels discussed above allow for neuronal signaling, let's see how:

- Firstly, the inputs from other neurons activate the chemically gated channels, i.e open the channels, which lead to changes in the local membrane potential.

- Next, this leads to the opening/closing of voltage-gated channels resulting in Depolarization(a positive change in voltage) and Hyperpolarization(a negative change in voltage). Repolarization is where the cell is brought back to the actual potential.

- A strong enough depolarisation will lead to the spike or the action potential.

- This indeed opens the Na^+ channels(voltage-gated), followed by rapid Na^+ influx(out to in) which drives more channels to open until they inactivate.

- When slowly the Na^+ channels start to inactivate, K^+ outflux(in to out) restores membrane potential or the K^+ channels open, reducing the spike. This is Repolarization.

- Thereafter, the cell is made more negative as the K⁺ channels stay open and continue to let the positive ions exit the neuron. This is termed as Hyperpolarization.

- As the potassium channels close, the sodium-potassium pump works to reestablish the resting state again.

- After the spike is generated, it is propagated along the axon.

- Along the axon, Na⁺ channels open first, causing the rise of the Action Potential, followed by the closing of the Na⁺ channels and the opening of the K⁺ channels, which lead to the fall of Action Potential.

Graphically, this is how membrane potential is recorded as the time varies,

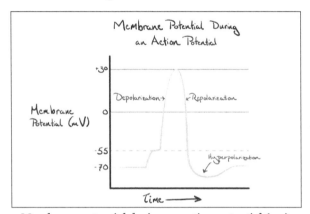

Membrane potential during an action potential (src).

Velocity

Signals travel real quick along the axon mainly due to 2 reasons; size and Myelin Sheath. It's an insulating substance which doesn't allow ions to pass.

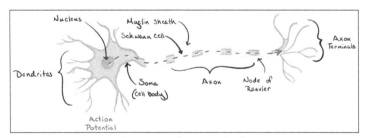

Anatomy of neuron (src).

The Node of Ranvier as depicted in the above neuron, are the spaces which are present in between the myelin sheath wrappings around the axon. In the peripheral nervous system, myelin is found in Schwann cell membranes. In the central nervous system, oligodendrocytes are responsible for insulation.

Peripheral Nervous System is made up of nerves and ganglia outside of the brain and the spinal cord. Central Nervous System consists of the brain and the spinal cord.

When action potential traverses through the axon, there are chances where it might get lost, so, the presence of myelin preserves it.

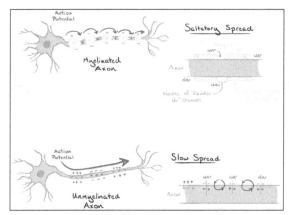

Myelinated vs. Unmyelinated Axon (src).

A myelin sheath decreases the capacitance of the neuron in the area it covers. So, the neurons get a lot of agitated negative ions which need to be balanced out. Hence, they spread out to the end of the membrane, in a hope to find the positive ions. The positive ions then approach these to calm them down. This, in turn, leads to the formation of thin layers of positive ions on the outside and the negative ions on the inside. When myelin is wrapped around the axon, fewer negative ions accumulate at the myelin wrapped parts of the axon, since then, they won't be able to access the positive ions with ease. This means that, as the action potential comes rushing by, it is easier to depolarize (a positive change in voltage) the areas that are sheathed because there are fewer negative ions to counteract.

The nodes of ranvier have these positive gated voltage channels, where the positive ions form a swarm since they are the uncovered areas. So, the negative ions in the axons want to reach the nodes of ranvier to balance themselves. This propagation of the action potential looks like a signal jumping from node to node, termed as "Saltatory Conduction".

This also explains the shape of the spike, where it increases to a certain extent and then decreases.

Understanding Brain

Now that we have seen how neurons are structured and how they compute by sending signals and generating chemicals, it's now time to group a set of neurons to understand the brain. Understanding the brain is always a tricky question, sometimes we can't predict how people/brains react in a few scenarios, in spite of them indulging in routine activities. They store a lot of information inside neurons based on the actions they keep triggering. So the question here is, how do we need to interpret the information? There are three computational models to understand brains which explain the three questions, "What, How, and Why". These models are named as Descriptive, Mechanistic, and Interpretive models respectively. Now let's discuss in brief about these:

Descriptive Models: This model answers the question "What are the neuronal responses to external stimuli?" They review large amounts of experimental data, thereby characterizing what neurons and neural circuits do. These models may be based loosely on Biophysical, Anatomical, and Physiological findings, but their primary purpose is to describe phenomena, not to explain them.

The two main properties of descriptive models are:

- They define qualitatively how to describe a scene or data by Neural Encoding.

- They also define how we can extract information from neurons by Neural Decoding techniques.

Mechanistic Models: Mechanistic models, on the other hand, address the question of "How nervous systems operate by known anatomy, physiology, and circuitry". Such models often form a bridge among descriptive models at different levels.

The two main properties of mechanistic models are:

- How can we simulate the behaviour of a single neuron on a computer?

- How do we simulate a network of neurons?

Interpretive Models: These use computational and information-theoretic principles to explore the behavioral and cognitive significance of various aspects of nervous system functionality, addressing the question of "Why nervous systems operate as they do".

The two main properties of interpretive models are:

- Why do brains operate the way they do?

- What are the computational principles underlying them?

Applications of Computational Neuroscience

The goal of computational neuroscience is to understand how brains generate behaviors using computational approaches. Computational models of the brain explore how populations of highly interconnected neurons are formed during development and how they represent, process, store, act upon, and become altered by information present in the body and the environment. Techniques from physics, computer science, and mathematics are used to simulate and analyze these computational models and provide links between the wide range of levels that brains are investigated, from molecular interactions to large-scale systems. Models are also used for interpreting experimental data and providing a conceptual framework for the dynamical properties of neural systems, which should lead to more comprehensive theories of brain function.

Biological neurosystems provide the data against which the modelled systems are measured for their accuracy and correctness. Modelling predominantly focuses on particular facets of biological systems, such as specific chemical and molecular interactions or the effects of neuron physiologies.

The field of computational neuroscience demonstrates that by reducing the levels of complexity found in biology to mathematical and computational models, biologically useful insights can be achieved. For example, detailed compartmental membrane models of neurons can be accurately simulated by software packages such as GENESIS and NEURON.

Computational Genomics

Computational Genomics uses the latest sequencing technology and advanced computational methods to study problems in biology and human health, including how genes cause disease, how genomes evolve, and how gene expression changes in response to different conditions within the cell. Bridging the fields of biomedical engineering, computer science, biology, and biostatistics, computational genomicists are designing novel algorithms that can handle the enormous data sets generated by modern sequencing experiments.

Genome assembly refers to the process of putting nucleotide sequence into the correct order. Assembly is required, because sequence read lengths – at least for now – are much shorter than most genomes or even most genes. Genome assembly is made easier by the existence of public databases,. Just as it is much easier to assemble a picture puzzle if you know what the picture looks like, it is much easier to assemble genes and genomes if you have a good idea of the sequence order. In the human genome, genes occur in the same physical location on the chromosome, but there can be different numbers of copies and variable numbers of repeated sequence that complicate assembly. Although bacterial genomes are much smaller, genes are not necessarily in the same location and multiple copies of the same gene may appear in different locations on the genome. Therefore even with the availability of commercial software and ever growing reference databases, the process of genome assembly can take considerably longer than the time to obtain actual sequence.

Computational and Statistical Genetics

The interdisciplinary research field of Computational and Statistical Genetics uses the latest approaches in genomics, quantitative genetics, computational sciences, bioinformatics and statistics to develop and apply computationally efficient and statistically robust methods to sort through increasingly rich and massive genome wide data sets to identify complex genetic patterns, gene functionalities and interactions, disease and phenotype associations involving the genomes of various organisms. This field is also often referred to as computational genomics. This is an important discipline within the umbrella field computational biology.

Haplotype Phasing

During the last two decades, there has been a great interest in understanding the genetic and genomic makeup of various species, including humans primarily aided by the different genome sequencing technologies to read the genomes that has been rapidly developing. However, these technologies are still limited, and computational and statistical methods are a must to detect and process errors and put together the pieces of partial information from the sequencing and genotyping technologies.

A haplotype is defined the sequence of nucleotides (A,G,T,C) along a single chromosome. In humans, we have 23 pairs of chromosomes. Another example is maize which is also a diploid with 10 pairs of chromosomes. However, with current technology, it is difficult to separate the two chromosomes within a pair and the assays produce the combined haplotype, called the genotype information at each nucleotide. The objective of haplotype phasing is to find the phase of the two haplotypes given the combined genotype information. Knowledge of the haplotypes is extremely important and not only gives us a complete picture of an individuals genome, but also aids other computational genomic processes such as Imputation among many significant biological motivations.

For diploid organisms such as humans and maize, each organism has two copies of a chromosome - one each from the two parents. The two copies are highly similar to each other. A haplotype is the sequence of nucleotides in a chromosome. the haplotype phasing problem is focused on the nucleotides where the two homologous chromosomes differ. Computationally, for a genomic region with K differing nucleotide sites, there are $2^K - 1$ possible haplotypes, so the phasing problem focuses on efficiently finding the most probable haplotypes given an observed genotype.

Prediction of SNP Genotypes by Imputation

Although the genome of a higher organism (eukaryotes) contains millions of single nucleotide polymorphisms (SNPs), genotyping arrays are pre- determined to detect only a handful of such markers. The missing markers are predicted using imputation analysis. Imputation of un-genotyped markers has now become an essential part of genetic and genomic studies. It utilizes the knowledge of linkage disequilibrium (LD) from haplotypes in a known reference panel (for example, HapMap and the 1000 Genomes Projects) to predict genotypes at the missing or un-genotyped markers. The process allows the scientists to accurately perform analysis of both the genotyped polymorphic markers and the un-genotyped markers that are predicted computationally. It has been shown that downstream studies benefit a lot from imputation analysis in the form of improved the power to detect disease-associated loci. Another crucial contribution of imputation is that it also facilitates combining genetic and genomic studies that used different genotyping platforms for their experiments. For example although 415 million common and rare genetic variants exist in the human genome,the current genotyping arrays such as Affymetrix and Illumina microarrays can only assay up to 2.5 million SNPs. Therefore, imputation analysis is an important research direction and it is important to identify methods and platforms to impute high quality genotype data using existing genotypes and reference panels from publicly available resources, such as the International HapMap Project and the 1000 Genomes Project. For humans, the analysis has successfully generated predicted genotypes in many races including Europeans and African Americans. For other species such as plants, imputation analysis is an ongoing process using reference panels such as in maize.

A number of different methods exist for genotype imputation. The three most widely used imputation methods are - Mach, Impute and Beagle. All three methods utilize hidden markov models as the underlying basis for estimating the distribution of the haplotype frequencies. Mach and Impute2 are more computationally intensive compared with Beagle. Both Impute and Mach are based on different implementations of the product of the conditionals or PAC model. Beagle groups the reference panel haplotypes into clusters at each SNP to form localized haplotype-cluster model that allows it to dynamically vary the number of clusters at each SNP making it computationally faster than Mach and Impute2.

Genome-wide Association Analysis

Over the past few years, genome-wide association studies (GWAS) have become a powerful tool for investigating the genetic basis of common diseases and has improved our understanding of the genetic basis of many complex traits. Traditional single SNP (single-nucleotide polymorphism) GWAS is the most commonly used method to find trait associated DNA sequence variants - associations between variants and one or more phenotypes of interest are investigated by studying individuals with different phenotypes and examining their genotypes at the position of each SNP individually. The SNPs for which one variant is statistically more common in individuals belonging to one phenotypic group are then reported as being associated with the phenotype. However, most complex common diseases involve small population-level contributions from multiple genomic loci. To detect such small effects as genome-wide significant, traditional GWAS rely on increased sample size e.g. to detect an effect which accounts for 0.1% of total variance, traditional GWAS needs to sample almost 30,000 individuals. Although the development of high throughput SNP genotyping technologies has lowered the cost and improved the efficiency of genotyping. Performing such a large scale study still costs considerable money and time. Recently, association analysis methods utilizing gene-based tests have been proposed that are based on the fact that variations in protein-coding and adjacent regulatory regions are more likely to have functional relevance. These methods have the advantage that they can account for multiple independent functional variants within a gene, with the potential to greatly increase the power to identify disease/trait associated genes. Also, imputation of ungenotyped markers using known reference panels(e.g. HapMap and the 1000 Genomes Project) predicts genotypes at the missing or untyped markers thereby allowing one to accurately evaluate the evidence for association at genetic markers that are not directly genotyped (in addition to the typed markers) and has been shown to improve the power of GWAS to detect disease associated loci.

Statistical Disease Related Interaction Analysis

In this era of large amount of genetic and genomic data, accurate representation and identification of statistical interactions in biological/genetic/genomic data constitutes a vital basis for designing interventions and curative solutions for many complex diseases. Variations in human genome have been long known to make us susceptible to many diseases. We are hurtling towards the era of personal genomics and personalized medicine that require accurate predictions of disease risk posed by predisposing genetic factors. Computational and statistical methods for identifying these genetic variations, and building these into intelligent models for diseaseassociation and interaction analysis studies genome-wide are a dire necessity across many disease areas. The principal challenges are:

(1) most complex diseases involve small or weak contributions from multiple genetic factors that explain only a minuscule fraction of the population variation attributed to genetic factors.

(2) Biological data is inherently extremely noisy, so the underlying complexities of biological systems (such as linkage disequilibrium and genetic heterogeneity) need to be incorporated into the statistical models for disease association studies.

The chances of developing many common diseases such as cancer, autoimmune diseases and cardiovascular diseases involves complex interactions between multiple genes and several endogenous and exogenous environmental agents or covariates. Many previous disease association studies could not produce significant results because of the lack of incorporation of statistical interactions in their mathematical models explaining the disease outcome. Consequently much of the genetic risks underlying several diseases and disorders remain unknown. Computational methods such as to model and identify the genetic/genomic variations underlying disease risks has a great potential to improve prediction of disease outcomes, understand the interactions and design better therapeutic methods based on them.

Genomic Analysis

Genome analysis entails the prediction of genes in uncharacterized genomic sequences. The 21st century has seen the announcement of the draft version of the human genome sequence. Model organisms have been sequenced in both the plant and animal kingdoms.

However, the pace of genome annotation is not matching the pace of genome sequencing. Experimental genome annotation is slow and time consuming. The demand is to be able to develop computational tools for gene prediction.

Computational Gene prediction is relatively simple for the prokaryotes where all the genes are converted into the corresponding mRNA and then into proteins. The process is more complex for eukaryotic cells where the coding DNA sequence is interrupted by random sequences called introns.

Some of the questions which biologists want to answer today are:

- Given a DNA sequence, what part of it codes for a protein and what part of it is junk DNA.

- Classify the junk DNA as intron, untranslated region, transposons, dead genes, regulatory elements etc.

- Divide a newly sequenced genome into the genes (coding) and the non-coding regions.

The importance of genome analysis can be understood by comparing the human and chimpanzee genomes. The chimp and human genomes vary by an average of just 2% i.e. just about 160 enzymes. A complete genome analysis of the two genomes would give a strong insight into the various mechanisms responsible for the differences.

Given below is a table listing down the estimated sizes of certain genomes and the number of genes in them.

Species	Genome size (Mb)	Number of genes
Mycoplasma genitalium	0.58	500
Streptococcus pneumoniae	2.2	2300
Escherichia coli	4.6	4400
Saccharomyces cerevisiae	12	5800
Caenorhabditi elegans	97	19,000
Arabidopsis thaiana	125	25,500
Drosophila melanogaster	180	13,700
Oryza sativa	466	45-55,000
Mus musculus	2500	29,000
Homo sapiens	3300	27,000

Arabidopsis and Humans have the same number of genes, though the Arabidopsis genome is around 250 times smaller than humans. How is that ?

The human genome has a lot of junk DNA, specifically transposons and mobile genetic elements. This increases the size of the human genome, though the number of genes is only 27,000.

However, the number of protein products in humans is significantly higher. Many of the sequenced human genes have alternative splice products. In addition, several other processes (e.g. signal transduction) proceed via further protein modifications, such as Glycosylation. Therefore, the number of human protein products could far exceed the number of genes.

Why do plants have such bulky genomes when they are not as complex as some of the higher eukaryotes?

This is mostly due to two factors: the ability of plants to duplicate their genomes in order to reproduce (a process known as polyploidization) and the susceptibility of plants to mobile genetic elements.

- Polyploidization allows plants to more easily form hybrids when pollen and ova from different species come together. The result of such hybridization events are plants with genomes that are the sum of the two parent genome sizes (as opposed to half of one parent's genome and half of the other parent's genome as in normal sexual reproduction.

- Also, in case of plants, it is fairly common to observe insertion of transposable elements in intergenic regions. This also explains the difference in the sizes of plant genomes among themselves as well.

Metabolic Control Analysis

Metabolic control analysis (MCA) provides a quantitative description of substrate flux in response to changes in system parameters of complex enzyme systems. Medical applications of the approach include the following: understanding the threshold effect in the manifestation of metabolic diseases; investigating the gene dose effect of aneuploidy in inducing phenotypic transformation in cancer; correlating the contributions of individual genes and phenotypic characteristics in metabolic disease (e.g., diabetes); identifying candidate enzymes in pathways suitable as targets for cancer therapy; and elucidating the function of "silent" genes by identifying metabolic features shared with genes of known pathways. MCA complements current studies of genomics and proteomics, providing a link between biochemistry and functional genomics that relates the expression of genes and gene products to cellular biochemical and physiological events. Thus, it is an important tool for the study of genotype–phenotype correlations. It allows genes to be ranked according to their importance in controlling and regulating cellular metabolic networks. We can expect that MCA will have an increasing impact on the choice of targets for intervention in drug discovery.

References

- Computational-biology, science: britannica.com, Retrieved 2 April, 2019

- The-sub-fields-of-computational-biology: wordpress.com, Retrieved 10 February, 2019

- Computational-pharmacology: omicsonline.org, Retrieved 13 July, 2019

- Introduction-to-computational-neuroscience-part: towardsdatascience.com, Retrieved 3 January, 2019

- Computational-neuroscience, computer-science: sciencedirect.com, Retrieved 14 June, 2019

- Computational-genomics: bme.jhu.edu, Retrieved 8 August, 2019

- Genome-assembly, agricultural-and-biological-sciences: sciencedirect.com, Retrieved 17 March, 2019

- Computational Genetics and Genomics - Springer. Link.springer.com. 2005. doi:10.1007/978-1-59259-930-1. ISBN 978-1-58829-187-5, Retrieved 9 May, 2019

- Genomeanalysis: scfbio-iitd.res.in, Retrieved 12 January, 2019

Chapter 2

Systems Biology

Systems biology refers to the mathematical and computational modeling and analysis of complex biological systems. Some of the areas where systems biology is applied are protein structure prediction and medical research. This chapter discusses in detail the principles and applications of system biology.

Systems biology is the study of the interactions and behaviour of the components of biological entities, including molecules, cells, organs, and organisms.

The organization and integration of biological systems has long been of interest to scientists. Systems biology as a formal, organized field of study, however, emerged from the genomics revolution, which was catalyzed by the Human Genome Project and the availability to biologists of the DNA sequences of the genomes of humans and many other organisms. The establishment of the field was also influenced heavily by the general recognition that organisms, cells, and other biological entities have an inherently high degree of complexity. Two dominant themes of modern biology are rooted in that new outlook: first, the view that biology is fundamentally an informational science—biological systems, cells, and organisms store and transfer information as their most-fundamental processes—and second, the emergence of new technologies and approaches for studying biological complexity.

Biological organisms are very complex, and their many parts interact in numerous ways. Thus, they can be considered generally as integrated systems. However, whereas an integrated complex system such as that of a modern airliner can be understood from its engineering design and detailed plans, attempting to understand the integrated system that is a biological organism is far more difficult, primarily because the number and strengths of interactions in the system are great and they must all be inferred after the fact from the system's behaviour. In the same manner, the blueprint for its design must be inferred from its genetic material. That "integrated systems" point of view and all the associated approaches for the investigation of biological cells and organisms are collectively called systems biology.

Complexity and Emergent Properties

Many of the most-critical aspects of how a cell works result from the collective behaviour of many molecular parts, all acting together. Those collective properties—often called "emergent properties"—are critical attributes of biological systems, as under-standing the individual parts alone is insufficient to understand or predict system be-haviour. Thus, emergent properties necessarily come from the interactions of the parts of the larger system. As an example, a memory that is stored in the human brain is an emergent property because it cannot be understood as a property of a single neuron or even many neurons considered one at a time. Rather, it is a collective property of a large number of neurons acting together.

One of the most-important aspects of the individual molecular parts and the complex things they constitute is the information that the parts contain and transmit. In biology information in molecular structures—the chemical properties of molecules that enable them to recognize and bind to one another—is central to the function of all processes. Such information provides a framework for understanding biological systems, In other words, life is defined in terms of interactions, relationships, and collective properties of many molecular systems and their parts.

The central argument concerning information in biology can be seen by considering the heredity of information, or the passing on of information from one generation to the next. For a given species, the information in its genome must persist through reproduc-tion in order to guarantee the species' survival. DNA is passed on faithfully, enabling a species' genetic information to endure and, over time, to be acted on by evolution-ary forces. The information that exists in living things today has accumulated and has been shaped over the course of more than 3.4 billion years. As a result, focusing on the molecular information in biological systems provides a useful vantage point for under-standing how living systems work.

That the emergent properties derived from the collective function of many parts are the key properties of biological systems has been known since at least the first half of the 20th century. They have been considered extensively in cell biology, physiology, developmental biology, and ecology. In ecology, for example, debate regarding the im-portance of complexity in ecological systems and the relationship between complexity and ecological stability began in the 1950s. Since then, scientists have realized that complexity is a general property of biology, and technologies and methods to under-stand parts and their interactive behaviours at the molecular level have been devel-oped. Quantitative change in biology, based on biological data and experimental meth-ods, has precipitated profound qualitative change in how biological systems are viewed, analyzed, and understood. The repercussions of that change have been immense, re-sulting in shifts in how research is carried out and in how biology is understood.

A comparison with systems engineering can provide useful insight into the nature of systems biology. When engineers design systems, they explore known components that can be put together in such a way as to create a system that behaves in a prescribed fashion, according to the design specifications. When biologists look at a system, on the other hand, their initial tasks are to identify the components and to understand the properties of individual components. They then attempt to identify how interactions between the components ultimately create the system's observable biological behaviours. The process is more closely aligned with the notion of "systems reverse engineering" than it is with systems design engineering.

The Human Genome Project contributed broadly to that revolution in biology in at least three different ways: (1) by acquiring the genetics "parts list" of all genes in the human genome; (2) by catalyzing the development of high-throughput technology platforms for generating large data sets for DNA, RNA, and proteins; and (3) by inspiring and contributing to the development of the computational and mathematical tools needed for analyzing and understanding large data sets. The project, it could be argued, was the final catalyst that brought about the shift to the systems point of view in biology.

Evolution in Systems Biology

Ukrainian American geneticist and evolutionist Theodosius Dobzhansky noted in the 20th century that "nothing makes sense in biology except in the light of evolution." Understanding evolution is essential to systems biology, but understanding where the information in the system came from and how it became complex also provides a focus for evolutionary thought. In a series of evolutionary transitions, biological systems have acquired remarkable mechanisms for storing, handling, and deploying information in the living world. The fundamental parts for storage and transmission are RNA and DNA. A striking insight that emerged from the study of those parts is that the evolution of developmental and physiological systems has involved basic components of gene-regulatory networks, including transcription factors (a class of proteins that regulate gene expression) and transcription factor-binding cis-regulatory elements in DNA. Gene-regulatory networks are coupled in turn to other networks that have profound effects on the function of systems and thereby determine evolutionary possibilities.

Networks and Information

Engineers and mathematicians have provided valuable insights into the nature of information, particularly related to communications, and biologists have adapted some of those insights to the study of biological systems. A significant area of research in biology centres on the question of whether higher-order biological processes can be represented from an information perspective. The conceptual tools for looking at biological phenomena are based on mathematical ideas about information and computing, but significant further development is required before a satisfactory theoretical basis is realized. For example, a key aspect of describing and measuring biological information is the context in which the information operates, which has been difficult to represent in a clear and useful way. An example of the type of challenge that researchers face is the process of gene expression, which involves the production of a specific protein molecule from genetic information. A number of factors impinge on the expression of any one gene—from the type of cell involved to the external signals received by and the metabolic state of the cell to preexisting states of gene expression. Efforts to under-stand those factors form a major area of research in modern biology.

Although some small networks, such as certain metabolic networks in bacteria or yeast, are relatively well characterized, more-complex networks, such as developmental net-works, remain only partially understood. Mathematical concepts relevant to the study of both types of networks have been developed and implemented. Still, few biological systems have been characterized sufficiently to enable researchers to model them as networks. Examples include the lactose- and galactose-utilization systems in certain bacteria, such as Escherichia coli and Streptococcus. However, wider interactions of those networks are comparatively less well understood. The early embryonic devel-opment of the sea urchin is another system that has been effectively modeled. Models offer unique insight into biological development and physiology, and scientists have envisioned a future when models will become available for most biological systems. Indeed, quantitative models could ultimately come to embody hypotheses about the structure and function of any biological system in question.

Ideas about biological systems have the potential to transform agriculture, animal husbandry, nutrition, energy, and other industries and fields of research. By the ear-ly 21st century, the practice of medicine had already begun to move from reactive treatment of patients' symptoms to proactive and personalized care because of im-proved understanding of the functions of the complex systems that are human cells and organs.

Main Principles of Systems Biology Approaches to Research

The field of systems biology revolves around the principle that the phenotype of any individual living organism is a reflection of the simultaneous multitude of molecular in-teractions from various levels occurring at any one time, combined in a holistic manner to produce such a phenotype. Consequently, against the standard concept of reduction-ist approach where dysregulations in isolated molecular components are studied, data from dysregulations of multiple key molecular players from varying cellular levels of activity are pooled and studied in their entirety, for the purpose of identifying distinct changes in the pattern of intermolecular relationships, vis a vis the organism's investi-gated phenotypes. The methods applied as the principal research tools vary, depending on the nature of the molecular level being investigated and also on the volumes of data generated; therefore, nowadays most self-sufficient systems biology research groups are composed of research scientists with a discernable knowledge of experimental in-vestigation for most molecular level research and/or are unique experts in their own specific research field.

Consequently, systems biology is very much an interdisciplinary field of research, requiring the technology platforms and research expertise of individuals from a spectrum of scientific research niche. However, the measurement of all molecular parts of an organ or even bio-medical pathway is far from routinely achievable, and great efforts to improve sensitivity of analysis and to make the output data possess a quantitative significance are starting to improve through implementation of field standards. Given current constraints, Boolean approaches are assisting with production of 1st generation systems biology models. A main difference between systems biology and systems medicine is that the former assumes the data to be correct and useable as often wet-lab data generation expertise is not the main goal but is assumed to be correct and useable. Systems medicine (sometimes referred to as systems healthcare) promises to lead with clinical and molecular know-how to produce exquisite datasets that are employed to generate pathway models and treatment and will hopefully directly contribute to stratified medicine en-route to personalized healthcare.

In addition to performing function as an interdisciplinary research field, systems biology research methods rely heavily on the bioinformatics/computational and mathematical modeling components for achieving answers to the specific research questions. Such informatics technology utilization can be twofold in system biology, namely, the implementation of a hypothesis driven "top-down" approach or experimental data driven "bottom-up" approaches.

The bottom-up, data driven approach initiates from the collection of large volume datasets derived through a spectrum of omics-based experimental procedures, followed by thorough mathematical modeling analyses to combine the relationships between key molecular players from the varying omics data results obtained. One of the primary methodologies employed by the bottom-up systems biology conceptual approach is network modeling. A typical biological network model is composed of multiple nodes interacting with each other through edges, whereby nodes are classified as individual key molecular players from any omics level (such as genes, noncoding RNA family members, and proteins) and the edges represent experimentally validated molecular interactions. Both the nature and detail of the nodes and edges within any particular biological network may vary. In addition, highly active nodes interacting in a close-knit network are defined as hubs. Hubs can be further subdivided into two categories, namely, "party" hubs and "date" hubs. Party hubs represent nodes which commonly interact with multiple other molecular partners in a simultaneous manner, whereas date hubs are much more dynamic since they interact with other molecular partners across multiple timeframes and within varying locations.

Conversely to the bottom-up experimental methodologies, the hypothesis driven top-down approach relies heavily on mathematical modeling for conducting studies on small-scale molecular interactions for a specific biological condition or phenotype. The dynamical modeling employed for such purpose involves the translation of molecular pathway interactions present in the studied organism into defined mathematical formats, such as ordinary differential equations (ODEs) and partial differential equations (PDEs) that can be analysed and probed within a "dry lab" environment . Such a method can be utilized since most intermolecular activities occur with specific kinetics that can be mimicked (e.g., Michaelis-Menten kinetics) by appropriate mathematical derivations. However, dynamical modeling can only be effective if specific assumptions are imposed regarding the biomolecular interactions taking place, such as the selection of defined reaction rate kinetics occurring within the studied biomolecular interactions.

In summary, there are four main phases to develop accurately functioning dynamical modeling, namely, model design to identify the pillar intermolecular activities, model construction of such molecular interactions into representative differential equations, model calibration to identify and modulate nonspecific kinetics of individual biomolecular components of the model for the purpose of fine tuning the mathematical model to the experimental format, and model validation by inferring distinct predictions that can be verified in a "wet-lab" experimental scenario.

Interestingly, there can also be a third approach to systems biology research models that implement both the top-down and bottom-up methodologies, namely, the middle-out (rational) approach.

Human Genome Project

Human Genome Project (HGP) is an international collaboration that successfully determined, stored, and rendered publicly available the sequences of almost all the genetic content of the chromosomes of the human organism, otherwise known as the human genome.

The Human Genome Project (HGP), which operated from 1990 to 2003, provided researchers with basic information about the sequences of the three billion chemical base pairs (i.e., adenine [A], thymine [T], guanine [G], and cytosine [C]) that make up human genomic DNA (deoxyribonucleic acid). The HGP was further intended to improve the technologies needed to interpret and analyze genomic sequences, to identify all the genes encoded in human DNA, and to address the ethical, legal, and social implications that might arise from defining the entire human genomic sequence.

Timeline of the HGP

Prior to the HGP, the base sequences of numerous human genes had been determined through contributions made by many individual scientists. However, the vast majority of the human genome remained unexplored, and researchers, having recognized the necessity and value of having at hand the basic information of the human genomic sequence, were beginning to search for ways to uncover this information more quickly. Because the HGP required billions of dollars that would inevitably be taken away from traditional biomedical research, many scientists, politicians, and ethicists became involved in vigorous debates over the merits, risks, and relative costs of sequencing the entire human genome in one concerted undertaking. Despite the controversy, the HGP was initiated in 1990 under the leadership of American geneticist Francis Collins, with support from the U.S. Department of Energy and the National Institutes of Health (NIH). The effort was soon joined by scientists from around the world. Moreover, a series of technical advances in the sequencing process itself and in the computer hardware and software used to track and analyze the resulting data enabled rapid progress of the project.

Technological advance, however, was only one of the forces driving the pace of discovery of the HGP. In 1998 a private-sector enterprise, Celera Genomics, headed by American biochemist and former NIH scientist J. Craig Venter, began to compete with and potentially undermine the publicly funded HGP. At the heart of the competition was the prospect of gaining control over potential patents on the genome sequence, which was considered a pharmaceutical treasure trove. Although the legal and financial reasons remain unclear, the rivalry between Celera and the NIH ended when they joined forces, thus speeding completion of the rough draft sequence of the human genome. The completion of the rough draft was announced in June 2000 by Collins and Venter. For the next three years, the rough draft sequence was refined, extended, and further analyzed, and in April 2003, coinciding with the 50th anniversary of the publication that described the double-helical structure of DNA, written by British biophysicist Francis Crick and American geneticist and biophysicist James D. Watson, the HGP was declared complete.

Science Behind the HGP

To appreciate the magnitude, challenge, and implications of the HGP, it is important first to consider the foundation of science upon which it was based—the fields of classical, molecular, and human genetics. Classical genetics is considered to have begun in the mid-1800s with the work of Austrian botanist, teacher, and Augustinian prelate Gregor Mendel, who defined the basic laws of genetics in his studies of the garden pea (Pisum sativum). Mendel succeeded in explaining that, for any given gene, offspring inherit from each parent one form, or allele, of a gene. In addition, the allele that an offspring inherits from a parent for one gene is independent of the allele inherited from that parent for another gene.

Mendel's basic laws of genetics were expanded upon in the early 20th century when molecular geneticists began conducting research using model organisms such as Drosophila melanogaster (also called the vinegar fly or fruit fly) that provided a more comprehensive view of the complexities of genetic transmission. For example, molecular genetics studies demonstrated that two alleles can be codominant (characteristics of both alleles of a gene are expressed) and that not all traits are defined by single genes; in fact, many traits reflect the combined influences of numerous genes. The field of molecular genetics emerged from the realization that DNA and RNA (ribonucleic acid) constitute the genetic material in all living things. In physical terms, a gene is a discrete stretch of nucleotides within a DNA molecule, with each nucleotide containing an A, G, T, or C base unit. It is the specific sequence of these bases that encodes the information contained in the gene and that is ultimately translated into a final product, a molecule of protein or in some cases a molecule of RNA. The protein or RNA product may have a structural role or a regulatory role, or it may serve as an enzyme to promote the formation or metabolism of other molecules, including carbohydrates and lipids. All these molecules work in concert to maintain the processes required for life.

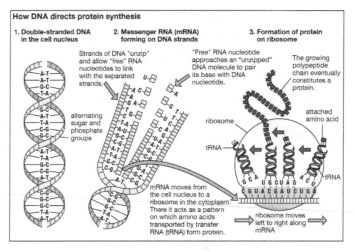

Molecular genetics emerged from the realization that DNA and RNA constitute the genetic material of all living organisms. (1) DNA, located in the cell nucleus, is made up of nucleotides that contain the bases adenine (A), thymine (T), guanine (G), and cytosine (C). (2) RNA, which contains uracil (U) instead of thymine, transports the genetic code to protein-synthesizing sites in the cell. (3) Messenger RNA (mRNA) then carries the genetic information to ribosomes in the cell cytoplasm that translate the genetic information into molecules of protein.

Studies in molecular genetics led to studies in human genetics and the consideration of the ways in which traits in humans are inherited. For example, most traits in humans and other species result from a combination of genetic and environmental influences. In addition, some genes, such as those encoded at neighbouring spots on a single chromosome, tend to be inherited together, rather than independently, whereas other genes, namely those encoded on the mitochondrial genome, are inherited only from the mother, and yet other genes, encoded on the Y chromosome, are passed only from fathers to sons. Using data from the HGP, scientists have estimated that the human genome contains anywhere from 20,000 to 25,000 genes.

Advances based on the HGP

Advances in genetics and genomics continue to emerge. Two important advances include the International HapMap Project and the initiation of large-scale comparative genomics studies, both of which have been made possible by the availability of databases of genomic sequences of humans, as well as the availability of databases of genomic sequences of a multitude of other species.

The International HapMap Project is a collaborative effort between Japan, the United Kingdom, Canada, China, Nigeria, and the United States in which the goal is to identify and catalog genetic similarities and differences between individuals representing four major human populations derived from the continents of Africa, Europe, and Asia. The identification of genetic variations called polymorphisms that exist in DNA sequences among populations allows researchers to define haplotypes, markers that distinguish specific regions of DNA in the human genome. Association studies of the prevalence of these haplotypes in control and patient populations can be used to help identify potentially functional genetic differences that predispose an individual toward disease or, alternatively, that may protect an individual from disease. Similarly, linkage studies of the inheritance of these haplotypes in families affected by a known genetic trait can also help to pinpoint the specific gene or genes that underlie or modify that trait. Association and linkage studies have enabled the identification of numerous disease genes and their modifiers.

In contrast to the International HapMap Project, which compares genomic sequences within one species, comparative genomics is the study of similarities and differences between different species. In recent years a staggering number of full or almost full genome sequences from different species have been determined and deposited in public databases such as NIH's Entrez Genome database. By comparing these sequences, often using a software tool called BLAST (Basic Local Alignment Search Tool), researchers are able to identify degrees of similarity and divergence between the genes and genomes of related or disparate species. The results of these studies have illuminated the evolution of species and of genomes. Such studies have also helped to draw attention to highly conserved regions of noncoding sequences of DNA that were originally thought to be nonfunctional because they do not contain base sequences that are translated into protein. However, some noncoding regions of DNA have been highly conserved and may play key roles in human evolution.

Impacts of the HGP

Impact on Medicine

The public availability of a complete human genome sequence represented a defining moment for both the biomedical community and for society. In the years since completion of the HGP, the human genome database, together with other publicly available resources such as the HapMap database, has enabled the identification of a variety of genes that are associated with disease. This, in turn, has enabled more objective and accurate diagnoses, in some cases even before the onset of overt clinical symptoms. Association and linkage studies have identified additional genetic influences that modify the development or outcome for both rare and common diseases. The recognition that human genomes may influence everything from disease risk to physiological response to medications has led to the emergence of the concept of personalized medicine—the idea that knowledge of a patient's entire genome sequence will give health care providers the ability to deliver the most appropriate and effective care for that patient. Indeed, continuing advances in DNA sequencing technology promise to lower the cost of sequencing an individual's entire genome to that of other, relatively inexpensive, diagnostic tests.

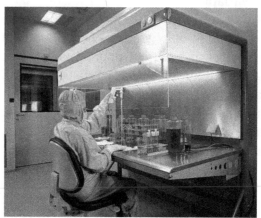

Researchers working in laboratories can determine the genetic composition of an individual's genome.

Impact on Law and the Social Sciences

The HGP affects fields beyond biomedical science in ways that are both tangible and profound. For example, human genomic sequence information, analyzed through a system called CODIS (Combined DNA Index System), has revolutionized the field of forensics, enabling positive identification of individuals from extremely tiny samples of biological substances, such as saliva on the seal of an envelope, a few hairs, or a spot of dried blood or semen. Indeed, spurred by high rates of recidivism (the tendency of a previously convicted criminal to return to prior criminal behaviour despite punishment or imprisonment), some governments have even instituted the policy of banking DNA samples from all convicted criminals in order to facilitate the identification of perpetrators of future crimes. While politically controversial, this policy has proved highly effective. By the same token, innocent men and women have been exonerated on the basis of DNA evidence, sometimes decades after wrongful convictions for crimes they did not commit.

Comparative DNA sequence analyses of samples representing distinct modern populations of humans have revolutionized the field of anthropology. For example, by following DNA sequence variations present on mitochondrial DNA, which is maternally inherited, and on the Y chromosome, which is paternally inherited, molecular anthropologists have confirmed Africa as the cradle of the modern human species, Homo sapiens, and have identified the waves of human migration that emerged from Africa over the last 60,000 years to populate the other continents of the world. Databases that map DNA sequence variations that are common in some populations but rare in others have enabled so-called molecular genealogists to trace the continent or even subcontinent of origin of given families or individuals. Perhaps more important than helping to trace the roots of humans and to see the differences between populations of humans, DNA sequence information has enabled recognition of how closely related one population of humans is to another and how closely related humans are to the multitude of other species that inhabit Earth.

Modelling Biological Systems

Modelling biological systems is a significant task of systems biology and mathematical biology. Computational systems biology aims to develop and use efficient algorithms, data structures, visualization and communication tools with the goal of computer modelling of biological systems. It involves the use of computer simulations of biological systems, including cellular subsystems (such as the networks of metabolites and enzymes which comprise metabolism, signal transduction pathways and gene regulatory networks), to both analyze and visualize the complex connections of these cellular processes.

Artificial life or virtual evolution attempts to understand evolutionary processes via the computer simulation of simple (artificial) life forms.

An unexpected emergent property of a complex system may be a result of the interplay of the cause-and-effect among simpler, integrated parts (see biological organisation). Biological systems manifest many important examples of emergent properties in the complex interplay of components. Traditional study of biological systems requires reductive methods in which quantities of data are gathered by category, such as concentration over time in response to a certain stimulus. Computers are critical to analysis and modelling of these data. The goal is to create accurate real-time models of a system's response to environmental and internal stimuli, such as a model of a cancer cell in order to find weaknesses in its signalling pathways, or modelling of ion channel mutations to see effects on cardiomyocytes and in turn, the function of a beating heart.

By far the most widely accepted standard format for storing and exchanging models in the field is the Systems Biology Markup Language (SBML). The SBML.org website includes a guide to many important software packages used in computational systems biology. A large number of models encoded in SBML can be retrieved from BioModels. Other markup languages with different emphases include BioPAX and CellML.

Particular Tasks

Cellular Model

Creating a cellular model has been a particularly challenging task of systems biology and mathematical biology. It involves the use of computer simulations of the many cellular subsystems such as the networks of metabolites and enzymes which comprise metabolism, signal transduction pathways and gene regulatory networks to both analyze and visualize the complex connections of these cellular processes.

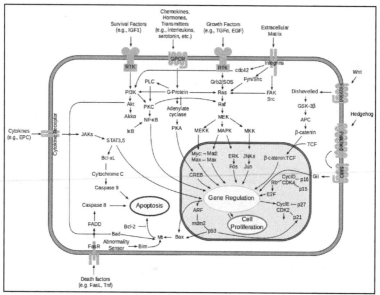

Part of the cell cycle.

The complex network of biochemical reaction/transport processes and their spatial organization make the development of a predictive model of a living cell a grand challenge for the 21st century, listed as such by the National Science Foundation (NSF) in 2006.

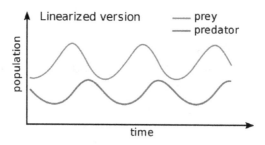

A sample time-series of the Lotka–Volterra model.

A whole cell computational model for the bacterium *Mycoplasma genitalium*, including all its 525 genes, gene products, and their interactions, was built by scientists from Stanford University and the J. Craig Venter Institute and published on 20 July 2012 in Cell.

A dynamic computer model of intracellular signaling was the basis for Merrimack Pharmaceuticals to discover the target for their cancer medicine MM-111.

Membrane computing is the task of modelling specifically a cell membrane.

Multi-cellular Organism Simulation

An open source simulation of C. elegans at the cellular level is being pursued by the OpenWorm community. So far the physics engine Gepetto has been built and models of the neural connectome and a muscle cell have been created in the NeuroML format.

Protein Folding

Protein structure prediction is the prediction of the three-dimensional structure of a protein from its amino acid sequence—that is, the prediction of a protein's tertiary structure from its primary structure. It is one of the most important goals pursued by bioinformatics and theoretical chemistry. Protein structure prediction is of high importance in medicine (for example, in drug design) and biotechnology (for example, in the design of novel enzymes). Every two years, the performance of current methods is assessed in the CASP experiment.

Human Biological Systems

Brain Model

The Blue Brain Project is an attempt to create a synthetic brain by reverse-engineering the mammalian brain down to the molecular level. The aim of this project, founded in May 2005 by the Brain and Mind Institute of the *École Polytechnique* in Lausanne, Switzerland, is to study the brain's architectural and functional principles. The project is headed by the Institute's director, Henry Markram. Using a Blue Gene supercomputer running Michael Hines's NEURON software, the simulation does not consist simply of an artificial neural network, but involves a partially biologically realistic model of neurons. It is hoped by its proponents that it will eventually shed light on the nature of consciousness. There are a number of sub-projects, including the Cajal Blue Brain, coordinated by the Supercomputing and Visualization Center of Madrid (CeSViMa), and others run by universities and independent laboratories in the UK, U.S., and Israel. The Human Brain Project builds on the work of the Blue Brain Project. It is one of six pilot projects in the Future Emerging Technologies Research Program of the European Commission, competing for a billion euro funding.

Model of the Immune System

The last decade has seen the emergence of a growing number of simulations of the immune system.

Virtual Liver

The Virtual Liver project is a 43 million euro research program funded by the German Government, made up of seventy research group distributed across Germany. The goal is to produce a virtual liver, a dynamic mathematical model that represents human liver physiology, morphology and function.

Tree Model

Electronic trees (e-trees) usually use L-systems to simulate growth. L-systems are very important in the field of complexity science and A-life. A universally accepted system for describing changes in plant morphology at the cellular or modular level has yet to be devised. The most widely implemented tree generating algorithms are described in the papers "Creation and Rendering of Realistic Trees", and Real-Time Tree Rendering.

Ecological Models

Ecosystem models are mathematical representations of ecosystems. Typically they simplify complex foodwebs down to their major components or trophic levels, and quantify these as either numbers of organisms, biomass or the inventory/concentration of some pertinent chemical element (for instance, carbon or a nutrient species such as nitrogen or phosphorus).

Models in Ecotoxicology

The purpose of models in ecotoxicology is the understanding, simulation and prediction of effects caused by toxicants in the environment. Most current models describe effects on one of many different levels of biological organization (e.g. organisms or populations). A challenge is the development of models that predict effects across biological scales. Ecotoxicology and models discusses some types of ecotoxicological models and provides links to many others.

Modelling of Infectious Disease

It is possible to model the progress of most infectious diseases mathematically to discover the likely outcome of an epidemic or to help manage them by vaccination. This field tries to find parameters for various infectious diseases and to use those parameters to make useful calculations about the effects of a mass vaccination programme.

Cellular Model

Cellular model systems represent approximations of healthy and diseased tissues or organs present in animals or humans. By virtue of the culture conditions in artificial tissue cultures over a period of time, these cellular systems suffer from a number of shortcomings in comparison to tissues in organisms, such as a lack of blood supply, lymphatic clearance, innervation, and hormonal regulation. Therefore, cell models can only capture a number of characteristics of tissue physiology. The better the models are in representing a particular tissue state, the more the key parameters can be represented in the models. It is, therefore, of crucial importance to understand the complexity of tissue and organ biology, in order to define the conditions that need to be established in culture. The appropriate cell types and their relative and spatial orientation belong to these conditions, as well as extracellular matrix (ECM) components, medium composition, and additives. A similar challenge exists for the establishment of disease models. Not only do we need to understand disease mechanisms, we also need to recognize what cellular and molecular consequences arise on normal tissue when the disease is present. Replication of such complex relationships is a very demanding task.

There are several ways to assess healthy and diseased tissue states in a culture. One comprises the cultivation of healthy or diseased tissues directly isolated from healthy individuals or animals as well as from patients or disease animal models in culture for a certain period of time. Such cultures will subsequently be referred to as "normal" or "disease" explant cultures. One of the advantages of explant cultures is that the composition of cells in their natural environment fully reflects the in vivo situation, at least at the start of the cultivation. It is important for such cultures that the cultivation conditions allow the perpetuation of the healthy or disease state for as long as possible over the required duration of an experiment. Another approach is co-cultivating cells in a defined manner, resembling normal tissue architecture (e.g., human 3D dermo-epidermal skin equivalents). Here, a simplified dermal compartment is represented by normal human primary fibroblasts embedded in a collagen matrix, whereas a simplified epidermal compartment is substituted by normal human primary keratinocytes, which are allowed to stratify in an air–liquid interphase (ALI). To convert such reconstituted "healthy" cultured tissue into a disease model, disease stimuli need to be introduced in a disease-specific manner, as further addressed below. Yet another approach involves a combination of reconstructed models consisting of cells from healthy individuals and from diseased tissues. In the simplest version, cells from healthy individuals and from patients are compared with each other for a certain biological function upon cultivation. For models with higher complexity, cells from healthy individuals are used to generate 3D skin models, in which patient-derived cells harvested from diseased tissue are subsequently introduced to study the effects of diseased cells on tissue function, thus constituting in vitro disease models.

Protein Structure Prediction

Protein structure prediction methods attempt to determine the native, *in vivo* structure of a given amino acid sequence. To do so, knowledge of protein structure determinants are critical: the hydrophobicity and hydrophilicity of residues, electrostatic interactions, hydrogen and covalent bonds, van der Waals interactions, bond angle stresses, and enthalpy and entropy.

There are two important facts about the determinants mentioned: First, information about them, and thus a protein's structure, is contained entirely within the sequence (in addition to knowledge of the solvent). Second, they are all measurements of physical properties (energies, actually). Assuming a protein can take its native conformation in solvent, without the aid of protein chaperones, we have enough information to predict protein structures *ab initio* (from basic principles). However, many of the determinants are not known precisely enough, or may be too compute-intensive (computationally non-tractable).

In the absence of feasible *ab initio* methods, protein structure prediction has turned to knowledge-based methods: homology modeling and protein fold recognition methods being the two major and complementary approaches taken.

The low amount of accuracy (usually ranging 50-70%) is a disadvantage for both methods. Another disadvantage for both is that known structures have to be available. The methods would fail when predicting the structure of a novel protein. Additionally, they tend to fail in predicting structures which are particularly sensitive to sequence differences, such as with random coils.

Homology Modeling

For homology modeling, the amino acid sequence of a protein with unknown structure is aligned against sequences of proteins with known structures. High degrees of homology (very similar sequences across and between the proteins) can be used to determine the global structure of the protein with unknown structure and place it into a certain fold category. Lower degrees of homology may still be used to determine local structures, an example being the Chou-Fasman method for predicting secondary structure. An advantage for homology modeling methods is the lack of dependence on the knowledge of physical determinants.

Fold Recognition

Fold recognition methods take a complementary approach. With these, structures, not sequences, are aligned. With the method called "threading," the sequence of a protein with unknown structure is forced to take the conformation of the backbone (protein sans side chains) of a protein with known structure. The better the physical determinants measure for each attempt, the better the score for the alignment. These methods tend to be more compute-intensive than homology modeling methods, but they give more confidence in the physical viability of the results.

Network and Systems Biology

Network analysis seeks to understand the relationships within biological networks such as metabolic or protein–protein interaction networks. Although biological networks can be constructed from a single type of molecule or entity (such as genes), network biology often attempts to integrate many different data types, such as proteins, small molecules, gene expression data, and others, which are all connected physically, functionally, or both.

Systems biology involves the use of computer simulations of cellular subsystems (such as the networks of metabolites and enzymes that comprise metabolism, signal transduction pathways and gene regulatory networks) to both analyze and visualize the complex connections of these cellular processes. Artificial life or virtual evolution attempts to understand evolutionary processes via the computer simulation of simple (artificial) life forms.

Molecular Interaction Networks

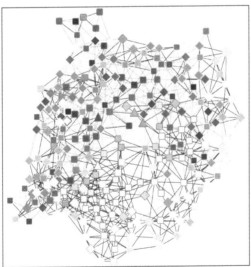

Interactions between proteins are frequently visualized and analyzed using networks.
This network is made up of protein–protein interactions from Treponema
pallidum, the causative agent of syphilis and other diseases.

Tens of thousands of three-dimensional protein structures have been determined by X-ray crystallography and protein nuclear magnetic resonance spectroscopy (protein NMR) and a central question in structural bioinformatics is whether it is practical to predict possible protein–protein interactions only based on these 3D shapes, without performing protein–protein interaction experiments. A variety of methods have been developed to tackle the protein–protein docking problem, though it seems that there is still much work to be done in this field.

Other interactions encountered in the field include Protein–ligand (including drug) and protein–peptide. Molecular dynamic simulation of movement of atoms about rotatable bonds is the fundamental principle behind computational algorithms, termed docking algorithms, for studying molecular interactions.

Applications

Systems biology has been responsible for some of the most important developments in the science of human health and environmental sustainability. It is a holistic approach to deciphering the complexity of biological systems that starts from the understanding that the networks that form the whole of living organisms are more than the sum of their parts. It is collaborative, integrating many scientific disciplines – biology, computer science, engineering, bioinformatics, physics and others – to predict how these systems change over time and under varying conditions, and to develop solutions to the world's most pressing health and environmental issues.

This ability to design predictive, multiscale models enables our scientists to discover new biomarkers for disease, stratify patients based on unique genetic profiles, and target drugs and other treatments. Systems biology, ultimately, creates the potential for entirely new kinds of exploration, and drives constant innovation in biology-based technology and computation.

Because systems biology requires constant attention to a very complex, very human social experiment, ISB fosters the kind of financial, social and psychological environment in which the world's best scientists, technologists, engineers and mathematicians can collaborate and do their best work.

Systems Biology

ISB's Innovation Engine

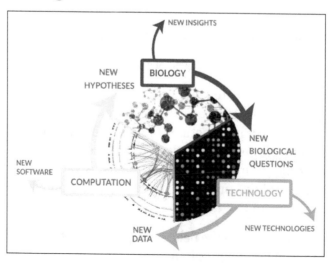

A fundamental tenet of systems biology is that solving challenging biological problems always requires the development of new technologies in order to explore new dimensions of data space. New data types require novel analytical tools. This virtuous cycle of biology driving technology driving computation can exist only in a cross-disciplinary environment where biologists, chemists, computer scientists, engineers, mathematicians, physicists, physicians and others can come together in teams to tackle grand challenges. This is ISB. And this describes what we call the "innovation engine" (depicted below) that drives our ability to develop intellectual property, which we share through open-access platforms or by spinning out companies.

Cross-disciplinary Teams

In describing systems biology and the distinguishing characteristics of ISB's approach, we always emphasize how our lab groups are intentionally and necessarily cross-disciplinary. One of our labs, for example, includes molecular biologists, microbiologists, geneticists, engineers, oceanographers, and even an astrophysicist. The complexity of biology in this age of "big data" requires diverse teams in order tackle such vast amounts of data and to make sense of it all. New technologies that crunch data faster and more efficiently also permit researchers to re-analyze existing datasets, a process which often reveals undiscovered information. Complementary skills empower any of our groups of researchers to better understand biological or environmental challenges from different perspectives and to arrive at shareable insights more quickly. Our interdisciplinary teams have contributed notable advances to everything from ocean acidification to neurodegenerative diseases and tuberculosis to multiple cancers.

Network of Networks

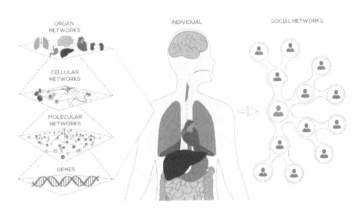

With networks, we can organize and integrate information at different levels. Social networks have transformed communications in the 21st Century, democratizing our platforms for communications. At ISB we are also concerned with networks. One of the tenets of systems biology we often refer to is the "Network of Networks." On a biological level, our bodies are made up of many networks that are integrated at and communicating on multiple scales. From our genome to the molecules and cells that makeup the organs in our bodies all the way out to ourselves in our world: we are fundamentally a network of networks. Systems biology looks at these networks across scales to integrate behaviors at different levels, to formulate hypotheses for biological function and to provide spatial and temporal insights into dynamical biological changes. It is not enough to understand only one part of a system when studying the complexity of biology. Therefore the framework of the "Network of Networks" provides meaningful insight into understanding how systems biology's approach is different, more integrated and more capable of analyzing and predicting state transitions in biological systems.

Multiscale Modeling

Whether we explicitly recognize it or not, multiscale phenomena are part of our daily lives. We organize our time in days, months and years, as a result of the multiscale dynamics of the solar system. Our society is organized in a hierarchical structure, from towns to states, countries and continents. The human body is a complex machine, with many little parts that work by themselves or with other parts to perform specific functions. Organelles inside each cell in our bodies interact with one another to maintain a healthy functioning cell that moves, differentiates and dies. These subcellular organelles and their processes govern each cell's signalling mechanism to interact with its neighboring cells, and form multi-cellular systems called tissues (e.g. epithelial tissue, muscular tissue). Two or more types of tissues work together to form an organ that performs a specific task (e.g. mouth, stomach, liver). Two or more organs work together to form organ systems, such as the digestive system and the nervous system, that perform more complex tasks. All these organ systems interact with each other to enable a healthy functioning organism. Traditional approaches to modeling real world systems focus on a single scale that imparts a limited understanding of the system. The pace at which biotechnology has grown has enabled us to collect large volumes of data capturing behavior at multiple scales of a biological system. Genetic as well as environmental alterations to the DNA, expression levels of RNAs, expression of genes and synthesis of proteins – all this is measurable now within a matter of days at a rapidly declining cost. So, it is really up to scientists and data analysts to make use of this variety of data types and build integrative models that enable a comprehensive understanding of the system under study. Multiscale models do just that. By integrating models at different scales and allowing flow of information between them, multiscale models describe a system in its entirety, and as such, are intrinsic to the principles of systems biology.

Single Cell Analysis

It is well known that there is no "average" patient. Therefore, in clinical trials encompassing large groups of patients, one needs to consider the characteristics of each patient, including each person's individual genetic propensity to respond to a drug in a particular way. The statistical analysis of population averages suppresses valuable individual-specific information. The consideration of population heterogeneity due to inevitable patient-to-patient variability is called "stratification" and is at the heart of personalized medicine. Such stratification will allow a proper impedance match against appropriate and effective drugs. Each cell in a cell population of apparently identical cells is a distinct individual. There is no "average" cell even within a population of cells of the very same cell type. Just as one can look at individual patients in a population and identify subtypes of diseases, one can identify "quantized" or "discrete" cell-subtypes in a cell population. The quantized subtypes perform different functions and form a network – much like a social network in human populations. So understanding how an organ works will require understanding the coordinated integration of the functioning of all the quantized cell types. Because of such cellular heterogeneity, even the most potent target-selective drug will kill only a fraction of tumor cells – explaining the inexorable drug resistance in malignant tumors. This new insight on cellular heterogeneity calls for the measurement of all molecular profiles in individual cells. Tissues must be seen not as an amorphous mass but analyzed as dynamical populations of cells and at single-cell resolution.

Understanding Proteomics

If DNA is the blueprint for life, then proteins are the bricks. The genes in DNA are translated into proteins, strings of amino acids that fold into three-dimensional structures. The type and order of the amino acids in a protein will change its shape and determine its special function. Proteins are the molecules that make life happen: they are the powerplants that turn food into energy, the machines that make cells move, and even the computers that read DNA and make more proteins. The information to build every protein in an organism is contained in the DNA, but not every protein is produced at once or in the same amount. Think of a cell in your liver and a cell in your retina – both cells contain identical DNA, but very different subsets of proteins are being produced in order to give each cell its special function. Proteomics is the discipline of identifying and quantifying the proteins present in an organism. At ISB, we use state-of-the-art scientific instruments and cutting edge computational techniques to detect thousands of proteins at once, giving us a systems-level view of the molecular machinery of life.

The Value of Family Genomics

The Family Genomics Group at the Institute for Systems Biology is an interdisciplinary group that researches human disease and wellness using next generation whole genome sequencing and computational genomics in the context of family pedigrees. The team is interested in examining the diversity of the human genome over the entirety of the human population. Researchers utilize public genomes, such as those from the Thousand Genomes Project, a carefully curated selection of variants from our private genomes, and compilations of human variation to generate resources that allow them to examine this in further detail. Family genomics is a powerful and precise method for identifying sequencing errors, disease-causing gene mutations and genetic relationships between individuals.

References

- Evolution-in-systems-biology, systems-biology, science: britannica.com, Retrieved 14 March, 2019

- Human-Genome-Project: britannica.com, Retrieved 29 July, 2019

- Tavassoly, Iman; Goldfarb, Joseph; Iyengar, Ravi (2018-10-04). "Systems biology primer: the basic methods and approaches". Essays in Biochemistry. 62 (4): 487–500. doi:10.1042/EBC20180003. ISSN 0071-1365. PMID 30287586, Retrieved 11 April, 2019

- Cellular-model, medicine-and-dentistry: sciencedirect.com, Retrieved 20 February, 2019

- Protein-structure-prediction: bioinformatics.org, Retrieved 25 June, 2019

- Hall, L.O. (2010). Finding the right genes for disease and prognosis prediction. System Science and Engineering (ICSSE),2010 International Conference. pp. 1–2. doi:10.1109/ICSSE.2010.5551766. ISBN 978-1-4244-6472-2, Retrieved 15 March, 2019

- What-is-systems-biology: systemsbiology.org, Retrieved 5 May, 2019

Chapter 3
Computational Phylogenetics

Phylogenetics refers to the study of the evolutionary history and relationships between individuals or groups of living beings. The application of computational algorithms, methods and programs for phylogenetic analyses is known as computational phylogenetics. The diverse applications of computational phylogenetics as well as phylogenetic networks have been thoroughly discussed in this chapter.

Phylogenetics

In biology Phylogenetics is the the study of the ancestral relatedness of groups of organisms, whether alive or extinct.

The Tree of Life

Ancestral relationships among species are commonly represented as phylogenetic trees (also called cladograms or dendrograms). A cladogram is a physical diagrammatic representation of a hypothesis of inferred relationship between species. The evolutionary relatedness between species is reflected by branching pattern of the tree and the relative distance between species on the tree. Any two species will have a common ancestor at the point where their respective branches are traced back to intersect. The more recent a common ancestor to humans, the more closely related it is to humans. For example, the common ancestor of modern humans and Neanderthals would be traced back to approximately 500,000 years ago. Similarly, the common ancestor of humans/Neanderthals and chimpanzees existed approximately 6.5 million years ago. Thus, since humans and Neanderthals share a common ancestor not shared by chimpanzees, we have reason to believe that humans are more closely related to Neanderthals than to chimpanzees. Similar retracing can be done farther and farther back on the branches of the tree of life to connect the common ancestry humans have with unicellular species some billions of years ago.

Estimating Relatedness

Cladograms can be constructed with the aid of technologies that estimate molecular divergences in key sequences of DNA or protein amino acids. Similar to the progress seen in estimating the age of organic substances with the use of radioactive decay technologies and carbon dating, the advent of molecular biological technologies in the later half of the 20th century have increasingly allowed scientists to more accurately estimate the degree of evolutionary relatedness at the genetic level. Taking two homologous DNA sequences in different species, one can estimate evolutionary distance by measuring the number of nucleotide substitutions that have occurred over time. Alternatively, using protein products of DNA expression, one can measure the number of amino acid substitutions that have occurred between homologous protein sequences.

Substitution Model

In biology, a substitution model describes the process from which a sequence of symbols changes into another set of traits. For example, in cladistics, each position in the sequence might correspond to a property of a species which can either be present or absent. The alphabet could then consist of "0" for absence and "1" for presence. Then the sequence 00110 could mean, for example, that a species does not have feathers or lay eggs, does have fur, is warm-blooded, and cannot breathe underwater. Another sequence 11010 would mean that a species has feathers, lays eggs, does not have fur, is warm-blooded, and cannot breathe underwater. In phylogenetics, sequences are often obtained by firstly obtaining a nucleotide or protein sequence alignment, and then taking the bases or amino acids at corresponding positions in the alignment as the characters. Sequences achieved by this might look like AGCGGAGCTTA and GCCGTAGACGC.

Substitution models are used for a number of things:

1. Constructing evolutionary trees in phylogenetics or cladistics.

2. Simulating sequences to test other methods and algorithms.

Neutral, Independent, Finite Sites Models

Most substitution models used to date are neutral, independent, finite sites models.

Neutral

Selection does not operate on the substitutions, and so they are unconstrained.

Independent

Changes in one site do not affect the probability of changes in another site.

Finite Sites

There are finitely many sites, and so over evolution, a single site can be changed multiple times. This means that, for example, if a character has value 0 at time 0 and at time t, it could be that no changes occurred, or that it changed to a 1 and back to a 0, or that it changed to a 1 and back to a 0 and then to a 1 and then back to a 0, and so on.

The Molecular Clock and the Units of Time

Typically, a branch length of a phylogenetic tree is expressed as the expected number of substitutions per site; if the evolutionary model indicates that each site within an ancestral sequence will typically experience x substitutions by the time it evolves to a particular descendant's sequence then the ancestor and descendant are considered to be separated by branch length x.

Sometimes a branch length is measured in terms of geological years. For example, a fossil record may make it possible to determine the number of years between an ancestral species and a descendant species. Because some species evolve at faster rates than others, these two measures of branch length are not always in direct proportion. The expected number of substitutions per site per year is often indicated with the Greek letter mu (μ).

A model is said to have a strict molecular clock if the expected number of substitutions per year μ is constant regardless of which species' evolution is being examined. An important implication of a strict molecular clock is that the number of expected substitutions between an ancestral species and any of its present-day descendants must be independent of which descendant species is examined.

Note that the assumption of a strict molecular clock is often unrealistic, especially across long periods of evolution. For example, even though rodents are genetically very similar to primates, they have undergone a much higher number of substitutions in the estimated time since divergence in some regions of the genome. This could be due to their shorter generation time, higher metabolic rate, increased population structuring, increased rate of speciation, or smaller body size. When studying ancient events like the Cambrian explosion under a molecular clock assumption, poor concurrence between cladistic and phylogenetic data is often observed. There has been some work on models allowing variable rate of evolution.

Models that can take into account variability of the rate of the molecular clock between different evolutionary lineages in the phylogeny are called "relaxed" in opposition to "strict". In such models the rate can be assumed to be correlated or not between ancestors and descendants and rate variation among lineages can be drawn from many distributions but usually exponential and lognormal distributions are applied. There is a special case, called "local molecular clock" when a phylogeny is divided into at least two partitions (sets of lineages) and a strict molecular clock is applied in each, but with different rates.

Time-reversible and Stationary Models

Many useful substitution models are time-reversible; in terms of the mathematics, the model does not care which sequence is the ancestor and which is the descendant so long as all other parameters (such as the number of substitutions per site that is expected between the two sequences) are held constant.

When an analysis of real biological data is performed, there is generally no access to the sequences of ancestral species, only to the present-day species. However, when a model is time-reversible, which species was the ancestral species is irrelevant. Instead, the phylogenetic tree can be rooted using any of the species, re-rooted later based on new knowledge, or left unrooted. This is because there is no 'special' species, all species will eventually derive from one another with the same probability.

A model is time reversible if and only if it satisfies the property.

$$\pi_i Q_{ij} = \pi_j Q_{ji}$$

or, equivalently, the detailed balance property,

$$\pi_i P(t)_{ij} = \pi_j P(t)_{ji}$$

for every $i, j,$ and t.

Time-reversibility should not be confused with stationarity. A model is stationary if Q does not change with time. The analysis below assumes a stationary model.

The Mathematics of Substitution Models

Stationary, neutral, independent, finite sites models (assuming a constant rate of evolution) have two parameters, π, an equilibrium vector of base (or character) frequencies and a rate matrix, Q, which describes the rate at which bases of one type change into bases of another type; element Q_{ij} for $i \neq j$ is the rate at which base i goes to base j. The diagonals of the Q matrix are chosen so that the rows sum to zero:

$$Q_{ii} = - \sum_{\{j | j \neq i\}} Q_{ij},$$

The equilibrium row vector π must be annihilated by the rate matrix Q:

$$\pi Q = 0.$$

The transition matrix function is a function from the branch lengths (in some units of time, possibly in substitutions), to a matrix of conditional probabilities. It is denoted $P(t)$. The entry in the ith column and the jth row, $P_{ij}(t)$, is the probability, after time t, that there is a base j at a given position, conditional on there being a base i in that position at time 0. When the model is time reversible, this can be performed between any two sequences, even if one is not the ancestor of the other, if you know the total branch length between them.

The asymptotic properties of $P_{ij}(t)$ are such that $P_{ij}(0) = \delta_{ij}$, where δ_{ij} is the Kronecker delta function. That is, there is no change in base composition between a sequence and itself. At the other extreme, $\lim_{t \to \infty} P_{ij}(t) = \pi_j$ or, in other words, as time goes to infinity the probability of finding base j at a position given there was a base i at that position originally goes to the equilibrium probability that there is base j at that position, regardless of the original base. Furthermore, it follows that $\pi P(t) = \pi$ for all t.

The transition matrix can be computed from the rate matrix via matrix exponentiation:

$$P(t) = e^{Qt} = \sum_{n=0}^{\infty} Q^n \frac{t^n}{n!},$$

where Q^n is the matrix Q multiplied by itself enough times to give its nth power.

If Q is diagonalizable, the matrix exponential can be computed directly: let $Q = U^{-1} \Lambda U$ be a diagonalization of Q with,

$$\Lambda = \begin{pmatrix} \lambda_1 & \cdots & 0 \\ \vdots & \ddots & \vdots \\ 0 & \cdots & \lambda_4 \end{pmatrix},$$

where Λ is a diagonal matrix and where $\{\ \}$ are the eigenvalues of Q, each repeated according to its multiplicity. Then,

$$P(t) = e^{Qt} = e^{U^{-1}(\Lambda t)U} = U^{-1} e^{\Lambda t} U,$$

where the diagonal matrix $e^{\Lambda t}$ is given by,

$$e^{\Lambda t} = \begin{pmatrix} e^{\lambda_1 t} & \cdots & 0 \\ \vdots & \ddots & \vdots \\ 0 & \cdots & e^{\lambda_4 t} \end{pmatrix}.$$

GTR: Generalised Time Reversible

GTR is the most general neutral, independent, finite-sites, time-reversible model possible. It was first described in a general form by Simon Tavaré in 1986.

The GTR parameters for nucleotides consist of an equilibrium base frequency vector, $\vec{\pi} = (\pi_1, \pi_2, \pi_3, \pi_4)$, giving the frequency at which each base occurs at each site, and the rate matrix,

$$Q = \begin{pmatrix} -(x_1 + x_2 + x_3) & x_1 & x_2 & x_3 \\ \dfrac{\pi_1 x_1}{\pi_2} & -\left(\dfrac{\pi_1 x_1}{\pi_2} + x_4 + x_5\right) & x_4 & x_5 \\ \dfrac{\pi_1 x_2}{\pi_3} & \dfrac{\pi_2 x_4}{\pi_3} & -\left(\dfrac{\pi_1 x_2}{\pi_3} + \dfrac{\pi_2 x_4}{\pi_3} + x_6\right) & x_6 \\ \dfrac{\pi_1 x_3}{\pi_4} & \dfrac{\pi_2 x_5}{\pi_4} & \dfrac{\pi_3 x_6}{\pi_4} & -\left(\dfrac{\pi_1 x_3}{\pi_4} + \dfrac{\pi_2 x_5}{\pi_4} + \dfrac{\pi_3 x_6}{\pi_4}\right) \end{pmatrix}$$

Because the model must be time reversible and must approach the equilibrium nucleotide (base) frequencies at long times, each rate below the diagonal equals the reciprocal rate above the diagonal multiplied by the equilibrium ratio of the two bases. As such, the nucleotide GTR requires 6 substitution rate parameters and 4 equilibrium base frequency parameters. Since the 4 frequency parameters must sum to 1, there are only 3 free frequency parameters. The total of 9 free parameters is often further reduced to 8 parameters plus μ, the overall number of substitutions per unit time. When measuring time in substitutions (μ =1) only 8 free parameters remain.

In general, to compute the number of parameters, you count the number of entries above the diagonal in the matrix, i.e. for n trait values per site $\dfrac{n^2 - n}{2}$, and then add n-1 for the equilibrium frequencies, and subtract 1 because μ is fixed. You get,

$$\frac{n^2 - n}{2} + (n-1) - 1 = \frac{1}{2}n^2 + \frac{1}{2}n - 2.$$

For example, for an amino acid sequence (there are 20 "standard" amino acids that make up proteins), you would find there are 208 parameters. However, when studying coding regions of the genome, it is more common to work with a codon substitution model (a codon is three bases and codes for one amino acid in a protein). There are $4^3 = 64c$ codons, resulting in 2078 free parameters, but when the rates for transitions between codons which differ by more than one base are assumed to be zero, then there are only $\dfrac{20 \times 19 \times 3}{2} + 63 - 1 = 632$ parameters.

Mechanistic vs. Empirical Models

A main difference in evolutionary models is how many parameters are estimated every time for the data set under consideration and how many of them are estimated once on a large data set. Mechanistic models describe all substitutions as a function of a number of parameters which are estimated for every data set analyzed, preferably using maximum likelihood. This has the advantage that the model can be adjusted to the particularities of a specific data set (e.g. different composition biases in DNA). Problems can arise when too many parameters are used, particularly if they can compensate for each other. Then it is often the case that the data set is too small to yield enough information to estimate all parameters accurately.

Empirical models are created by estimating many parameters (typically all entries of the rate matrix and the character frequencies) from a large data set. These parameters are then fixed and will be reused for every data set. This has the advantage that those parameters can be estimated more accurately. Normally, it is not possible to estimate all entries of the substitution matrix from the current data set only. On the downside, the estimated parameters might be too generic and do not fit a particular data set well enough.

With the large-scale genome sequencing still producing very large amounts of DNA and protein sequences, there is enough data available to create empirical models with any number of parameters. Because of the problems mentioned above, the two approaches are often combined, by estimating most of the parameters once on large-scale data, while a few remaining parameters are then adjusted to the data set under consideration. The following sections give an overview of the different approaches taken for DNA, protein or codon-based models.

Models of DNA Substitution

Models of DNA evolution were first proposed in 1969 by Jukes and Cantor, assuming equal transition rates as well as equal equilibrium frequencies for all bases. In 1980 Kimura introduced a model with two parameters: one for the transition and one for the transversion rate and in 1981, Felsenstein proposed a four-parameter model in which the substitution rate corresponds to the equilibrium frequency of the target nucleotide. Hasegawa, Kishino and Yano (HKY) unified the two last models to a five-parameter model. In the 1990s, models similar to HKY were developed and refined by several researchers.

For DNA substitution models, mainly mechanistic models (as described above) are employed. The small number of parameters to estimate makes this feasible, but also DNA is often highly optimized for specific purposes (e.g. fast expression or stability) depending on the organism and the type of gene, making it necessary to adjust the model to these circumstances.

Models of Amino Acid Substitutions

For many analyses, particularly for longer evolutionary distances, the evolution is modeled on the amino acid level. Since not all DNA substitution also alter the encoded amino acid, information is lost when looking at amino acids instead of nucleotide bases. However, several advantages speak in favor of using the amino acid information: DNA is much more inclined to show compositional bias than amino acids, not all positions in the DNA evolve at the same speed (non-synonymous mutations are less likely to become fixed in the population than synonymous ones), but probably most important, because of those fast evolving positions and the limited alphabet size (only four possible states), the DNA suffers much more from back substitutions, making it difficult to accurately estimate longer distances.

Unlike the DNA models, amino acid models traditionally are empirical models. They were pioneered in the 1970s by Dayhoff and co-workers, by estimating replacement rates from protein alignments with at least 85% identity. This minimized the chances of observing multiple substitutions at a site. From the estimated rate matrix, a series of replacement probability matrices were derived, known under names such as PAM250. The Dayhoff model was used to assess the significance of homology search results, but also for phylogenetic analyses. The Dayhoff PAM matrices were based on relatively few alignments (since more were not available at that time), but in the 1990s, new matrices were estimated using almost the same methodology, but based on the large protein databases.

Computational Approaches to Phylogeny Inference and Gene Tree Reconciliation

An intricate relationship exists between gene trees and species phylogenies, due to evolutionary processes that act on the genes within and across the branches of the species phylogeny. From an analytical perspective, gene trees serve as character states for inferring accurate species phylogenies, and species phylogenies serve as a backdrop against which gene trees are contrasted for elucidating evolutionary processes and parameters available then (the latter being known as "JTT" matrices).

Multi-locus Analyses and Evolutionary Processes

Species phylogenies and gene trees have an intricate relationship that stems from the evolutionary processes acting within, and sometimes across, species boundaries to shape the gene trees. Three major evolutionary processes are gene duplication, horizontal gene transfer, and hybridization. Gene duplication results in the creation of new copies of genes and thus plays a central role in genome evolution . As these copies acquire genetic differences, their evolutionary fates might differ and result in novel gene functions.

In asexual species, horizontal gene transfer (HGT) shapes the genomic repertoire and imports new genes, sometimes of beneficial consequences, into the host genome. HGT occurs mainly through one of three mechanisms: transformation, which is the uptake of naked DNA from the environment, transduction, which is the transfer of genetic material through a plasmid or bacteriophage, and conjugation, which is the direct transfer of DNA between two cells.

In eukaryotes, the evolutionary histories of various groups of plants and animals have been shown to involve hybridization, which is the production of viable offspring from interspecific mating. Two major outcomes of hybridization are introgression and hybrid speciation. While some parts of the genetic material contributed to the offspring in interspecific mating gets eliminated from the population in later generations, other parts are integrated into the genome, an event that is referred to as introgression. It is important to note that both HGT and introgression leave similar genomic signatures, though the former process occurs in asexual species whereas the latter occurs in sexual species. In some cases, hybridization results in hybrid lineages that become reproductively isolated from the parental species, a phenomenon known as hybrid speciation. Figure below illustrates gene duplication, HGT, and hybridization in three-taxon scenarios.

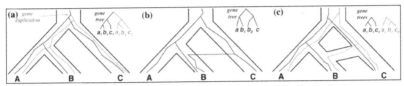

Evolutionary processes within and across species boundaries.

a) A gene duplication event at the most recent common ancestor (MRCA) of all three taxa, results in two copies (red and green) of a gene within the genome, and as the genome undergoes evolution, these copies evolve, diverge, and might have different fates.

b) In prokaryotic organisms, DNA containing genes might be transferred across species boundaries, e.g., from C to B, resulting in a new gene copy. Further, a similar signature might arise in cases of introgression in sexual species.

c) Hybridization between species A and C amounts to individuals from A and B mating and producing viable offspring such that the genetic material in individuals of B can be traced back to two parental species. The gene tree in each case is shown in the inset.

Two of the main tasks of multi-locus analyses are the inference of a species phylogeny and the evolutionary processes that acted upon the individual loci. While species phylogeny inference used to be conducted almost exclusively based on a single gene sampled across species , it is becoming more common to use whole-genome data, or more generally, multiple loci. When gene trees have been inferred for the individual loci, the first task amounts to inferring the species phylogeny from these gene trees. The second task amounts to contrasting, or reconciling, the gene trees with the species phylogeny to elucidate the evolutionary processes that shaped the gene tree and their phenotypic consequences. Multi-locus analyses provide power, in terms of phylogenetic signal, to solve both tasks with high accuracy, yet pose new modeling and computational challenges for phylogenetic inference that mostly stem from a phenomenon known as gene tree incongruence.

Phylogenetic Incongruence: A Signal, Rather than a Problem

As illustrated in figure, each of the evolutionary processes operating on a gene leaves its signature on the gene tree. These processes alone do not necessarily result in signatures in the form of incongruence between gene trees and the species phylogeny.

It is often the evolutionary fates of gene copies that result in such signatures. These evolutionary fates are determined by forces such as mutation, drift, and selection. For example, in figure (a), if the gene copies b1, c1, and a2 are lost, the resulting gene tree differs from the species tree. In figure (b), if the HGT event results in the displacement of the b1 gene copy, then the resulting gene tree differs from the species tree. On the other hand, if the horizontally transferred gene copy, b2, is eventually lost, then the gene tree remains congruent with the species tree. In the case of hybridization, the scenario is dictated by the mode of the evolutionary process. In homoploid hybridization, the offspring has the same ploidy level, or number of chromosomes, as each of the parents in the two hybridizing species. In this case, hybridization is often followed by back-crossing, which is further mating between individuals from the hybrid population and either of the two parental populations. Repeated back-crossing, combined with drift and selection, results in unequal parental genomic contributions in the hybrid offspring and a distribution of differing gene tree topologies across the genomes. In (allo) polypoloid hybridization, the offspring gets the complete sets of chromosomes from the parents, thus having a number of chromosomes that is double that of either of the two parents. While back-crossing does not occur in cases of polyploid hybridization, drift and selection result in unequal parental genomic contributions in the hybrid offspring.

From an inference perspective, these signatures can then be utilized as phylogenetic signal to recover population parameters, evolutionary processes, and the species phylogeny itself. However, it is important to keep in mind several issues that make the inference task very challenging in practice. First, incomplete sampling of gene copies by the practitioner might give rise to artificial signatures that mislead or confound inference tasks. For example, if the practitioner samples only copes a1, b1, and c1 in the scenario given in figure (a), the occurrence of a gene duplication event might not be recovered. Second, multiple occurrences of the same evolutionary process might cancel out or complicate the signature. For example, assuming displacement of gene copy b1 by the HGT event in the scenario of figure (b), a subsequent HGT event from B to A, involving gene copy b2 and the displacement of the original copy of the gene in A, results in a gene tree that is congruent with the species tree (in terms of topology, but not branch lengths). Third, the occurrence of an evolutionary process might not leave a signature on the gene tree topologies. For example, an HGT between two sister taxa does not result in incongruence between the gene and species trees. Fourth, the signature left by an evolutionary process might not be unique to that process. For example, if gene copies b1, c1, and a2 are lost in the scenarios of figures (a) and (c), and the gene copy b1 is lost in the scenario of figure (b), then we end up with the same gene tree topology in all three cases. HGT and introgression might give rise to identical genomic signatures, though they occur in different groups of species. It is crucial that these issues are kept in mind when applying inference methods, developing new ones, or interpreting the results thereof.

It is probably due to these issues, and others, that several genomic studies that are mainly aimed at obtaining the species phylogeny mask signatures by selecting few loci that satisfy stringent criteria so as to eliminate the possibility of incongruence and other studies have strived to do phylogenetic inference despite incongruence. Incongruence is a powerful phylogenetic signal that is "desirable, as it often illuminates previously poorly understood evolutionary phenomena". Fields such as molecular population genetics and phylogenetics have long relied on polymorphism and divergence at the sequence level as signal for inference, and in the post-genomic era, phylogenomics relies on phylogenetic incongruence as the major signal for inference. Therefore, phylogenetic incongruence should not be viewed as a problem to be masked or despite which inference should be made; rather, it should be viewed as a powerful character with a rich set of states to reconstruct and understand evolutionary phenomena, while accounting for the aforementioned issues.

For example, in 1979, Goodman et al. proposed a parsimony-based approach for fitting a gene tree onto a species tree to elucidate gene duplication and loss events from a set of globin sequences. In 1997, Maddison proposed to count the minimum number of branch moves need to convert the species tree into the gene tree, where branch moves do not violate the temporal constraints provided by the trees, as a proxy for the number of HGT or hybridization events. Indeed, if these methods were applied to the scenarios in figure, the true evolutionary events would be uncovered. While these two approaches mainly reveal information about the evolutionary processes themselves, model-based approaches would help elucidate, in addition, knowledge about parameters such as population sizes, divergence times, duplication rates, etc. Further, these reconciliation approaches can be turned into species phylogeny inference approaches by seeking a species phylogeny that, when all gene trees are reconciled with it, achieves some optimality score. In 1997, Maddison surveyed phylogenetic incongruence, and described parsimony and likelihood criteria for various reconciliation and inference problems.

In , Maddison discussed phylogenetic incongruence and the two computational problems of reconciliation and inference. The reconciliation problem seeks a fitting of a given gene tree within, or across, the branches of a given species tree assuming a source of incongruence. That is, every leaf in the gene tree is mapped to a leaf in the species phylogeny, and then internal nodes (which correspond to events of coalescence, duplication, HGT, etc.) in the gene tree are mapped to the branches of the species phylogeny. In this way, the reconciliation reveals the evolutionary processes that acting on the gene, and when model-based approaches are, the reconciliation also reveals information about the timing of these processes, as well as parameters such as population sizes, duplication rates, etc. The inference problem seeks the species tree, given a collection of loci sampled from a set of species. In traditional phylogenetics, the inference problem amounts to estimating a phylogenetic tree from a molecular sequence alignment, often assuming only base-pair mutations. Analogously, in phylogenetic analyses involving multiple loci, the inference problem amounts to estimating a species phylogeny from a collection of gene trees, assuming some of the evolutionary processes discussed above.

For the reconciliation problem, Maddison discussed parsimony approaches for the cases where gene duplication and loss (DL) are both at play and when HGT is at play. In the case of DL, Goodman *et al.* had already proposed a parsimony-based approach for fitting a gene tree onto a species tree to minimize the number of duplications. In this approach, a node x in the gene tree is mapped to the most recent common ancestor (MRCA) of the set of species that contain gene copies descended from node x;. In the case of HGT, Maddison proposed to count the minimum number of branch moves need to convert the species tree into the gene tree, where branch moves do not violate the temporal constraints provided by the trees. This number would constitute a lower bound on the number of HGT events needed to explain the incongruence between the species tree and gene tree; the imbalance in the parental genetic contributions to hybrid offspring, parsimonious detections of hybridization events can be carried out in a similar fashion to that of HGT. In other words, while HGT and hybridization are very different biological processes, their inference under parsimony is very similar, and the same can be said of meiotic recombination. In addition the aforementioned evolutionary processes, Maddison discussed the role that random genetic drift plays in phylogenetic incongruence, a phenomenon we now introduce. Gene trees might disagree with each other, as well as with the species tree, due to random genetic drift acting within the populations, a phenomenon known as incomplete lineage sorting, or ILS ; Unlike gene duplication and loss (DL), HGT, and hybridization, ILS does not introduce new genetic material into genomes; instead, it is a reflection of the inherent stochasticity associated with neutral evolution. Maddison proposed that the same mapping of gene tree nodes to species tree nodes as that employed by would result in a parsimonious reconciliation (one that minimizes the number of "extra" gene lineages) assuming ILS as the source of incongruence. The reconciliations of the gene tree and species tree given in figure below are shown under ILS, DL, and HGT in figure.

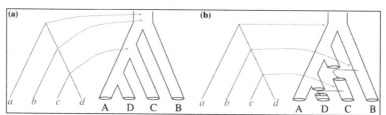

Fitting a gene tree onto a species tree.

Gene trees are drawn with solid lines, and species trees are drawn with tubes.

a) In the case of DL (and ILS), each node x in the gene tree is mapped to (denoted by the green arrows) the most recent common ancestor (MRCA) of the species that contain gene copies descended from node x.

b) In the cases of HGT and hybridization, a smallest set of branch moves (denoted by the purple arrows) that makes the species tree identical to the gene tree and do not violate "a linear time order" is a parsimonious set of HGT or hybridization events that explain the difference between the species tree and gene tree.

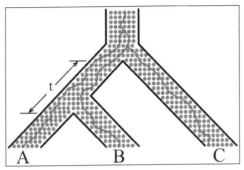

Incomplete lineage sorting.

As the evolution of three sampled alleles (blue solid circles at the bottom) is traced backward in time, alleles from A and B might fail to coalesce in the ancestral population. This result in all three alleles entering the ancestral population of all three species, and the alleles from B and C coalescing first, by chance, giving rise to a gene tree that is incongruent with the species tree. The probability of this event happening in this scenario is a function of the branch length, t, as measured in coalescent units (one coalescent unit equals $2N$ generations, where N is the population size).

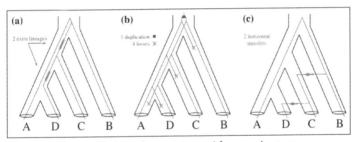

Reconciliation of a gene tree with a species tree.

a) Reconciliation assuming ILS results in two extra lineages, highlighted with thick red lines.

b) Reconciliation assuming DL results in a single duplication event and four losses.

c) Reconciliation assuming HGT (or hybridization) results in two horizontal transfer events, highlighted with red arrows.

These parsimony-based approaches to reconciliation naturally give rise to three parsimony-based criteria for species tree inference: Of all the possible species tree candidates, seek one that minimizes the total number of "extra" gene lineages, duplication events, or HGT events, respectively, when all gene trees in the sample are reconciled with it. Maddison further proposed a maximum likelihood (ML) formulation for the inference problem. However, unlike the case of the parsimony formulations, Maddison considered only deep coalescence (equivalently, ILS) in the case of ML, the reason being that the coalescent theory from population genetics already provided a mechanism for computing the probability of a gene tree, whereas no similar theory existed for computing gene tree probabilities when DL, HGT or hybridization were involved. The ML formulation proposed in assumes a given collection of sequence alignments, each for a sampled locus, and seeks a tree that maximizes the probability of observing these alignments by accounting for mutations within each locus and incongruence across loci.

Progress on Methods that Deal with Individual Processes

As Maddison mentioned, a reconciliation of a gene tree with a species tree under ILS or DL, using the mapping described above, is efficiently computable. Several algorithms have been introduced to compute reconciliations under ILS and DL . In terms of mathematical characterizations, Zhang showed that when the species tree and gene tree have exactly the same leaf-set (i.e., exactly one gene copy from each species is used to infer the gene tree), then the number of extra lineages required to reconcile the trees assuming only ILS equals the number of losses minus twice the number of duplications required to reconcile the same trees assuming only DL. For example, in figure, the number of extra lineages in panel (a) is 2, the number of losses and duplications in panel (b) are 4 and 1 respectively, and we have $2 = 4 - (2 \cdot 1)$. The formula relating the three quantities becomes slightly more involved when the two trees do not necessarily have the same leaf-set . For the inference problem, Maddison and Knowles proposed a heuristic for searching for the species tree that minimizes the number of extra lineages assuming ILS is the sole cause of incongruence. Than and Nakhleh later devised exact algorithms for the problem, including for cases where multiple alleles are sampled . Than and Rosenberg proved that this parsimony criterion of minimizing the number of extra lineages is in fact statistically inconsistent (that is, inference under this criterion might converge on the wrong species tree, even as the number of gene trees used in the inference increases). Bayzid *et al.* devised exact algorithms for inferring a species tree that minimizes the number of duplications and losses.

As for HGT, the field has evolved rapidly so as to deal with complexities not discussed in. The reconciliation problem assuming HGT is very hard algorithmically and, several methods for reconciling a pair of trees were devised; these methods vary in the assumptions and restrictions they make about the trees and reconciliations. Perhaps the issue that challenges Maddison's original proposal most is the concept of a species tree when HGT, or other reticulate evolutionary events, occur. While a species tree in the case of ILS and DL can fit within its branches the evolutionary histories of all genes within the genomes under consideration, that structure would fail to capture adequately the evolutionary histories of genes that are exchanged horizontally. To accommodate reticulate evolutionary histories, phylogenetic networks were introduced as a model of evolutionary histories that capture both vertical and horizontal descent of genetic material. A phylogenetic network extends the notion of phylogenetic trees by allowing for nodes with more than one parent—reticulation nodes. Assuming no ILS or DL, the evolutionary history of each gene in a set of species whose evolutionary history is given by a phylogenetic network N is captured by one of the trees displayed (or, induced) by the phylogenetic network N. A tree is induced by phylogenetic network N if it can be obtained by removing all but one of the parents for each of the reticulation nodes in the network. For example, the four trees induced by the network in figure are (((A,D),C),B), (A,(B,(C,D))), ((A,(C,D)),B), ((A,D),(B,C)). Reconciling a gene tree with a phylogenetic network, excluding ILS and DL, is related to testing whether the gene tree is one of the trees induced by the network, which has been shown to be computationally a very hard problem.

Gene trees within the branches of a phylogenetic network.

The phylogenetic network, drawn with tubes, fits the evolutionary histories of all genes, including those that evolve vertically (e.g., the gene tree drawn with green lines) and those that involved horizontal transfer (e.g., the gene tree drawn with blue lines, and HGT or introgression events highlighted with red arrows).

Not only do phylogenetic networks provide a more adequate model than trees for capturing reticulate evolutionary histories, but they also allow extending Maddison's original proposal from reconciling a pair of trees to a collection of trees. Indeed, in today's phylogenomic analyses, multiple loci are sequenced and multiple gene trees need to be reconciled. Maddison's proposal for reconciling a gene tree with a species tree does not carry over cleanly to a set of gene trees for the inference problem. Introducing the notion of a phylogenetic network, the parsimony version of the inference problem under HGT becomes: find a phylogenetic network with the minimum number of reticulation nodes needed to display all of the gene trees. Several methods have been proposed recently for solving versions of this problem. The progress on likelihood approaches for dealing with gene tree incongruence has been much greater for ILS than the other evolutionary processes, owing mainly to the mature theoretical foundations of the coalescent model that deal with ILS naturally. As we discussed above, the maximum likelihood formulation given in was proposed in the context of ILS alone. Based on that formulation, the likelihood of a species tree is:

$$\prod_{\substack{loci}} \sum_{\substack{gene \\ trees}} [P(sequences \mid gene\ tree)P(gene\ tree \mid species\ tree)].$$

While Maddison used the summation over gene trees, this is to be treated as integration when branch lengths of the gene trees are also considered. The first probability of observing a set of (aligned) sequences given a gene tree depends on the model of sequence evolution and can be computed efficiently. The second probability of observing a gene tree given a species tree is derived from coalescent theory, and methods have been devised for computing it when the gene tree is given only by its topology and when the gene tree is given by its topology and branch lengths. Likelihood methods have been proposed for inference based on this formulation. Advances have been made recently on methods for computing the second probability when only DL is at play was given in. When only reticulation is at play and a parameterized species phylogenetic network is provided, computing the probability of a gene tree is straightforward.

Unifying Processes and Accounting for Error

The fact that much progress has been made on methods that deal with each of the evolutionary processes individually is not to be construed as a statement that these processes do indeed occur in a mutually exclusive manner. As phylogenomic analyses grow in scope to involve more species, individuals, and loci, accounting simultaneously for multiple evolutionary processes becomes essential. Indeed, several studies have highlighted this issue in various groups of organisms. For example, while introgression was hypothesized between Neanderthals and humans, this hypothesis was later dismissed in favor of ILS. Simultaneous patterns of introgression and ILS were reported in 2012 in the house mouse (*Mus musculus*) genome, in the butterfly (*Heliconius melpomene*) genome, in sunflower (*Helianthus*) genomes, and in yeast genomes. Simultaneous patterns of ILS and DL were recently reported in a multi-locus analysis of a group of fungi. Further, simultaneous patterns of DL and reticulation have been reported. Maddison pointed to two challenges facing the development of a "mixed method" that allows all three processes to occur: the algorithmic challenge of conducting reconciliation and inference under multiple processes, and the challenge associated with weighting the three different processes (e.g., should one HGT event be counted as equal to one duplication event?). While the weighting relates mostly to parsimony approaches, its counterpart in a likelihood approach is setting the rates of the various processes (e.g., the rates of duplication, loss, etc.).

As we discussed above, a phylogenetic network provides a more appropriate model of evolutionary relationships than trees when reticulation is involved. It is important to note that a phylogenetic network not only accommodates HGT and hybridization, but treelike evolutionary processes, such as ILS and DL, can be modeled within its branches. For example, figure illustrates how a phylogenetic network simultaneously models hybridization between species and ILS involving gene trees. It further illustrates the generality of the model in terms of accommodating multiple individuals sampled per species or population. when recombination occurs within a locus, even the gene tree is better modeled using a network that is often referred to in the population genetics literature as an ancestral recombination graph.

This position is not to be interpreted as invoking reticulation in every analysis; rather, it is advocates the development of mathematical models and computational methods that utilize the more general model, which is a network rather than a tree, and account for the possibility that in some, or maybe most, cases the inferred network could be a special case that is a tree. The other approach of utilizing a tree as the topological model would exclude the possibility of a reticulate evolutionary history, merely by definition of the model used. Progress on parsimonious reconciliation and inference methods that assume more than a single source of incongruence has been made. Bansal *et al.* recently introduced an efficient algorithm for reconciling a gene tree with a species tree assuming both DL and HGT. Yu *et al.* introduced methods that assume both hybridization and ILS. In particular, the work in provides algorithms for reconciliation as well as search heuristics that explore the space of phylogenetic networks to solve the inference problem. Recently, Stolzer *et al.* introduced a method for reconciling a gene tree with a species tree under DL, HGT, and ILS. While a natural way for integrating all evolutionary processes within a parsimony framework is to optimize a weighted sum of the numbers of events detected, a likelihood approach requires probabilistic models of these processes.

While the coalescent model has provided a natural framework for thinking about ILS, recent studies are beginning to shed light on how to probabilistically model processes including HGT and DL. For integrative likelihood approaches, a method for computing the probability of a gene tree given a species tree assuming both ILS and DL was given in, assuming DL and HGT was given in, and assuming ILS and HGT in a special case was given in. Methods have been developed for computing the probabilities of gene trees under hybridization and ILS in special, limited cases, and then for computing the probabilities in general cases. Marcussen *et al.* recently developed a method for inferring phylogenetic networks in the presence of ILS that is aimed at modeling polyploid hybridization. A salient feature of all phylogenetic analyses, whether they involve a single locus or multiple loci, is the fact that gene trees are estimated from molecular sequences and, consequently, they are likely to be inaccurate. Maddison wrote: "I assume through most of this discussion that the true gene trees are known without error. Of course, there will be errors in practice, and these errors will mean that reconstructed gene trees and species trees will have additional sources of discord." Indeed, Hahn recently showed the effect of error in gene tree estimates on the computed reconciliations and Yang and Warnow showed that methods that explicitly account for error in the gene trees outperform others.

While incongruence caused by evolutionary processes provides a signal for inferring the processes themselves and the species phylogeny, incongruence due to error in the inferred gene trees is a confounding factor that must be accounted for carefully, as it produces topological signatures in the gene trees that can cancel out true evolutionary signals or masquerade as ones. One way to deal with error in the estimates of gene tree topologies is to contract all branches with low support (e.g., as measured by a bootstrap analysis, or posterior probabilities from a Bayesian analysis), and develop methods that can handle non-binary, or multifurcating, trees. In the parsimony setup, a natural way to define the reconciliation of a non-binary gene tree with a species tree is to find the refinement of the polytomies in the gene tree that results in the most parsimonious reconciliation over all possible reconciliations. Indeed, this refinement concept was used in or reconciling non-binary gene and species trees. While the number of refinements is exponential in the degrees of the polytomies (the number of children of a node), Yu *et al.*recently devised polynomial-time, exact algorithms for finding the refinement that results in an optimal reconciliation under ILS. Further, the same ideas were extended to the problem of parsimonious reconciliation of a non-binary gene tree with a phylogenetic network. Under the likelihood approach, it is less clear how to deal with non-binary gene trees. Should the gene tree be refined in a way that maximizes the probability of observing the (binary) gene tree (e.g., as implemented for inference under ILS in)? Or, should the probability of the non-binary gene tree be computed as the average probability of all binary refinements? A different method to handle error in the gene trees is to directly make use of the support values.

The major challenge facing this approach is in translating support values from gene tree branches to support values of reconciliations. Nonetheless, some heuristics were introduced recently based on this approach for reconciliation under HGT. Further, Yu *et al.* incorporated posterior probabilities in methods for reconciling a gene tree with a phylogenetic network under both likelihood and parsimony. Of course, methods that work directly from the sequence alignments of the multiple loci, rather than from estimated gene trees, account implicitly for error. The Bayesian methods of for inference under ILS, and the parsimony and likelihood methods of for inferring HGT events follow this approach.

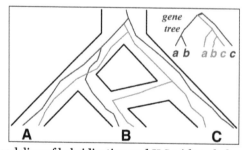

Simultaneous modeling of hybridization and ILS with a phylogenetic networks.

Two individuals are sampled per species, and there is a hybridization event that involves species B and C. Further, ILS patterns complicate the gene genealogy, giving rise to the gene-tree topology shown in the inset. For example, the gene copies in green coalesce with the ancestral copy of the genes in red from A and B, before the latter one coalesces with the copy from C.

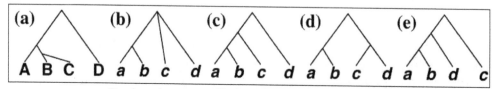

Parsimonious reconciliation of a non-binary gene tree.

(a) A binary species tree. (b) A non-binary gene tree. (c–e) The three possible refinements of the non-binary gene tree. Under parsimony, the refinement in (c) results in the best reconciliation with the species tree, as it results, assuming ILS, DL, or HGT, in 1 extra lineage, 1 duplication and 3 losses, and 1 HGT, respectively.

Other Approaches

Several approaches that do not fit within Maddison's parsimony and likelihood formulations have been proposed. Concatenation is an approach in which the sequences from multiple loci are concatenated, thus resulting in a "super gene," and a phylogenetic tree is inferred from the super gene. This approach was used for example in inferring a phylogenetic tree of a set of yeast species. There are at least three issues with this approach. First, the approach is applicable to loci for which exactly one copy per species is sampled. However, even then, the phylogeny estimated from the concatenated alignment might be wrong. Second, this approach yields, by definition, a phylogenetic tree. Therefore, it masks any signal of reticulate evolution if it exists. Third, the method does not allow for inference of the evolutionary processes. The democratic vote approach amounts to taking the gene tree with the highest frequency as a proxy for the species tree. Applicability of this approach when a small sample of loci is used or when duplication and loss events are involved is questionable. Even when a large number of loci is used and each has exactly a single copy sampled per species, this method produces a misleading phylogeny in the "anomaly zone". Finally, it is not clear how to interpret the gene tree with the highest frequency when the species evolutionary history is reticulate. The majority-rule consensus is a third approach to produce a phylogenetic tree given a set of conflicting gene tree topologies. This approach often results in a phylogenetic tree with a very low degree of resolution. Further, the approach is not well defined for cases where the incongruence is due to DL. Third, like the previous two approaches, this approach always produces a tree, even when the evolutionary history is reticulate.

Mossel and Roch recently introduced a distance-based method for inferring a species tree from pairwise distances computed from multiple loci. This method requires accurate estimates of the distances, and is applicable to neither DL nor reticulate evolutionary events. Bayesian approaches for inferring species trees under ILS were also recently introduced. These methods differ from all the methods discussed above in that they work directly with sequence alignments and perform simultaneous inference of gene and species trees. They have been shown to produce very good results, yet to be inefficient computationally. Further, these Bayesian approaches currently do not handle DL or reticulate evolutionary events. Methods for inferring HGT events based on an assumed species tree and sequence alignments of genes were proposed based on the maximum parsimony and maximum likelihood criteria. These methods do not account for ILS or DL, and assume knowledge of an underlying species tree. Joly *et al.*showed how to use coalescent-based simulations to detect hybridization; however, their approach was presented for a pair of species only. Last but not least, Holland *et al.* demonstrated how to use consensus networks to detect hybridization in the presence of ILS.

In 1997, Wayne Maddison discussed the intricate relationship between a species tree and the gene trees that grow with, and across, its branches. Further, he discussed parsimony and likelihood approaches to reconciling a gene tree with a species tree, and for the inference of species trees from collections of gene trees. Solving these two tasks would shed light on central issues in evolutionary and molecular biology, including speciation, evolutionary processes acting within and across population, the evolution of morphological characters, and genotype-phenotype relationships. Sixteen years later, the significance of understanding this relationship cannot be overstated, given the ability to sequence hundreds of prokaryotic genomes in a day, and eukaryotic genomes in slightly longer timeframes. Indeed, in less than two decades, the computational biology and bioinformatics communities responded to Maddison's proposal by making significant inroads in establishing mathematical results and devising computational methods for detecting, resolving, and ameliorating incongruence that arise in phylogenomic studies. Still, much more is needed in terms of mathematical and computational developments. While models of incongruence and methods for reconciliation and inference have been developed, computational requirements are still a major bottleneck. Most, if not all, of the methods described above are limited to small- or medium-sized data sets. High-performance computing approaches will definitely be needed if it is desired that these methods apply to thousands of loci and hundreds to thousands of taxa. Currently, these data sets are beyond the capabilities of existing tools. Maddison explicitly stated in that his formulations assumed no recombination within a locus. But what happens if this assumption is violated? Recent work has accounted for recombination within phylogenetic networks.

A recent study showed ignoring recombination within loci might not have a significant effect on the quality of the inferred species tree under ILS. Similar studies do not exist for cases of DL and HGT. Nevertheless, more generally, the availability of whole-genome data allows for defining gene trees as the genealogies built from non-recombining regions, which include coding and non-coding DNA. However, potentially more challenging than recombination are the findings of rearrangements at the sub-level, such as gene fission and fusion, which seem to be ubiquitous in prokaryotic genomes and even in eukaryotic genomes. These findings not only complicate the species-gene evolutionary relationships, but also raise broader questions about orthology, gene families, and the "cloudiness" of the species phylogeny.

Further, Maddison assumed the loci are unlinked and, hence, the fact that gene trees can be reconciled with a species phylogeny independently. Indeed, all methods described above assume unlinked loci and it is currently incumbent upon the practitioner to sample loci from the genomes in such a way that ensures this assumption holds (or that violation thereof is minimal). However, to make full use of whole-genome data, models that incorporate linkage across loci, including functional linkage , must be devised, and methods for inference under such models much be developed. A mathematical model for two linked loci was introduced in . More recently, approaches for modeling ILS while accounting for linkage across loci were introduced. These approaches do not account for DL or reticulation at the species level (they do account for recombination). Further, these methods have been applied to three-species data sets and it would be challenging to achieve scalability of these methods to large data sets. This further emphasizes the need for high-performance computing approaches, as modeling dependence only makes the problem harder. While many methods have been developed for reconciliation, the relative performance of these methods is yet to be investigated thoroughly. This is especially important as the practitioner is faced with a wide array of methods that differ in terms of the assumptions they make and the computational resources they need. While studies are beginning to emerge, more comprehensive studies are still needed. In particular, most performance studies focus on ILS, probably due to the fact that the coalescent theory provides a clean generative model for simulating synthetic data, whereas no such theory exists for DL or HGT. Further, while some methods perform poorly under certain conditions, they might perform well under other conditions. Full characterization of conditions under which a method performs well would be of utmost help to practitioners. Most importantly, measures that reflect these characterizations from real data are needed. For example, the anomaly zone has been established for several methods. However, the question that the practitioners face is: Do their data fall within an anomaly zone for a specific method?

Last but not least, when the evolutionary history is reticulate, it is more appropriate to speak of a phylogenetic, or species, network, rather than a species tree. In the population genetics literature, this issue has long been recognized, and ancestral recombination graphs—a class of phylogenetic networks—have been adopted for modeling genealogies that include recombination. Using phylogenetic networks, and more generally, networks, might help uncover hypotheses that would be undetected otherwise. The different flavors in which phylogenetic networks come might have been confusing to the community of practitioners and, consequently, limited their applicability. Recent monograms have been written to clarify the similarities, differences, and applications of the various types of networks. Developments to address the issues above should be applicable to phylogenetic networks.

Computational Phylogenetics

Computational phylogenetics is the application of computational algorithms, methods, and programs to phylogenetic analyses. The goal is to assemble a phylogenetic tree representing a hypothesis about the evolutionary ancestry of a set of genes, species, or other taxa. For example, these techniques have been used to explore the family tree of hominid speciesand the relationships between specific genes shared by many types of organisms. Traditional phylogenetics relies on morphological data obtained by measuring and quantifying the phenotypic properties of representative organisms, while the more recent field of molecular phylogenetics uses nucleotide sequences encoding genes or amino acid sequences encoding proteins as the basis for classification. Many forms of molecular phylogenetics are closely related to and make extensive use of sequence alignment in constructing and refining phylogenetic trees, which are used to classify the evolutionary relationships between homologous genes represented in the genomes of divergent species. The phylogenetic trees constructed by computational methods are unlikely to perfectly reproduce the evolutionary tree that represents the historical relationships between the species being analyzed. The historical species tree may also differ from the historical tree of an individual homologous gene shared by those species.

Types of Phylogenetic Trees and Networks

Phylogenetic trees generated by computational phylogenetics can be either *rooted* or *unrooted* depending on the input data and the algorithm used. A rooted tree is a directed graph that explicitly identifies a most recent common ancestor (MRCA), usually an imputed sequence that is not represented in the input. Genetic distance measures can be used to plot a tree with the input sequences as leaf nodes and their distances from the root proportional to their genetic distance from the hypothesized MRCA. Identification of a root usually requires the inclusion in the input data of at least one "outgroup" known to be only distantly related to the sequences of interest.

By contrast, unrooted trees plot the distances and relationships between input sequences without making assumptions regarding their descent. An unrooted tree can always be produced from a rooted tree, but a root cannot usually be placed on an unrooted tree without additional data on divergence rates, such as the assumption of the molecular clock hypothesis.

The set of all possible phylogenetic trees for a given group of input sequences can be conceptualized as a discretely defined multidimensional "tree space" through which search paths can be traced by optimization algorithms. Although counting the total number of trees for a nontrivial number of input sequences can be complicated by variations in the definition of a tree topology, it is always true that there are more rooted than unrooted trees for a given number of inputs and choice of parameters.

Both rooted and unrooted phylogenetic trees can be further generalized to rooted or unrooted phylogenetic networks, which allow for the modeling of evolutionary phenomena such as hybridization or horizontal gene transfer.

Coding Characters and Defining Homology

Morphological Analysis

The basic problem in morphological phylogenetics is the assembly of a matrix representing a mapping from each of the taxa being compared to representative measurements for each of the phenotypic characteristics being used as a classifier. The types of phenotypic data used to construct this matrix depend on the taxa being compared; for individual species, they may involve measurements of average body size, lengths or sizes of particular bones or other physical features, or even behavioral manifestations. Of course, since not every possible phenotypic characteristic could be measured and encoded for analysis, the selection of which features to measure is a major inherent obstacle to the method. The decision of which traits to use as a basis for the matrix necessarily represents a hypothesis about which traits of a species or higher taxon are evolutionarily relevant. Morphological studies can be confounded by examples of convergent evolution of phenotypes. A major challenge in constructing useful classes is the high likelihood of inter-taxon overlap in the distribution of the phenotype's variation. The inclusion of extinct taxa in morphological analysis is often difficult due to absence of or incomplete fossil records, but has been shown to have a significant effect on the trees produced; in one study only the inclusion of extinct species of apes produced a morphologically derived tree that was consistent with that produced from molecular data.

Some phenotypic classifications, particularly those used when analyzing very diverse groups of taxa, are discrete and unambiguous; classifying organisms as possessing or lacking a tail, for example, is straightforward in the majority of cases, as is counting features such as eyes or vertebrae. However, the most appropriate representation of continuously varying phenotypic measurements is a controversial problem without a general solution. A common method is simply to sort the measurements of interest into two or more classes, rendering continuous observed variation as discretely classifiable (e.g., all examples with humerus bones longer than a given cutoff are scored as members of one state, and all members whose humerus bones are shorter than the cutoff are scored as members of a second state). This results in an easily manipulated data set but has been criticized for poor reporting of the basis for the class definitions and for sacrificing information compared to methods that use a continuous weighted distribution of measurements.

Because morphological data is extremely labor-intensive to collect, whether from literature sources or from field observations, reuse of previously compiled data matrices is not uncommon, although this may propagate flaws in the original matrix into multiple derivative analyses.

Molecular Analysis

The problem of character coding is very different in molecular analyses, as the characters in biological sequence data are immediate and discretely defined - distinct nucleotides in DNA or RNA sequences and distinct amino acids in protein sequences. However, defining homology can be challenging due to the inherent difficulties of multiple sequence alignment. For a given gapped MSA, several rooted phylogenetic trees can be constructed that vary in their interpretations of which changes are "mutations" versus ancestral characters, and which events are insertion mutations or deletion mutations. For example, given only a pairwise alignment with a gap region, it is impossible to determine whether one sequence bears an insertion mutation or the other carries a deletion. The problem is magnified in MSAs with unaligned and nonoverlapping gaps. In practice, sizable regions of a calculated alignment may be discounted in phylogenetic tree construction to avoid integrating noisy data into the tree calculation.

Distance-matrix Methods

Distance-matrix methods of phylogenetic analysis explicitly rely on a measure of "genetic distance" between the sequences being classified, and therefore they require an MSA as an input. Distance is often defined as the fraction of mismatches at aligned positions, with gaps either ignored or counted as mismatches. Distance methods attempt to construct an all-to-all matrix from the sequence query set describing the distance between each sequence pair. From this is constructed a phylogenetic tree that places closely related sequences under the same interior node and whose branch lengths closely reproduce the observed distances between sequences. Distance-matrix methods may produce either rooted or unrooted trees, depending on the algorithm used to calculate them. They are frequently used as the basis for progressive and iterative types of multiple sequence alignments. The main disadvantage of distance-matrix methods is their inability to efficiently use information about local high-variation regions that appear across multiple subtrees.

UPGMA and WPGMA

The UPGMA (*Unweighted Pair Group Method with Arithmetic mean*) and WPGMA (*Weighted Pair Group Method with Arithmetic mean*) methods produce rooted trees and require a constant-rate assumption - that is, it assumes an ultrametric tree in which the distances from the root to every branch tip are equal.

Neighbor-joining

Neighbor-joining methods apply general cluster analysis techniques to sequence analysis using genetic distance as a clustering metric. The simple neighbor-joining method produces unrooted trees, but it does not assume a constant rate of evolution (i.e., a molecular clock) across lineages.

Fitch–Margoliash Method

The Fitch–Margoliash method uses a weighted least squares method for clustering based on genetic distance. Closely related sequences are given more weight in the tree construction process to correct for the increased inaccuracy in measuring distances between distantly related sequences. The distances used as input to the algorithm must be normalized to prevent large artifacts in computing relationships between closely related and distantly related groups. The distances calculated by this method must be linear; the linearity criterion for distances requires that the expected values of the branch lengths for two individual branches must equal the expected value of the sum of the two branch distances - a property that applies to biological sequences only when they have been corrected for the possibility of back mutations at individual sites. This correction is done through the use of a substitution matrix such as that derived from the Jukes-Cantor model of DNA evolution. The distance correction is only necessary in practice when the evolution rates differ among branches. Another modification of the algorithm can be helpful, especially in case of concentrated distances (please report to concentration of measure phenomenon and curse of dimensionality): that modification, described in, has been shown to improve the efficiency of the algorithm and its robustness.

The least-squares criterion applied to these distances is more accurate but less efficient than the neighbor-joining methods. An additional improvement that corrects for correlations between distances that arise from many closely related sequences in the data set can also be applied at increased computational cost. Finding the optimal least-squares tree with any correction factor is NP-complete, so heuristic search methods like those used in maximum-parsimony analysis are applied to the search through tree space.

Using Outgroups

Independent information about the relationship between sequences or groups can be used to help reduce the tree search space and root unrooted trees. Standard usage of distance-matrix methods involves the inclusion of at least one outgroup sequence known to be only distantly related to the sequences of interest in the query set. This usage can be seen as a type of experimental control. If the outgroup has been appropriately chosen, it will have a much greater genetic distance and thus a longer branch length than any other sequence, and it will appear near the root of a rooted tree. Choosing an appropriate outgroup requires the selection of a sequence that is moderately related to the sequences of interest; too close a relationship defeats the purpose of the outgroup and too distant adds noise to the analysis. Care should also be taken to avoid situations in which the species from which the sequences were taken are distantly related, but the gene encoded by the sequences is highly conserved across lineages. Horizontal gene transfer, especially between otherwise divergent bacteria, can also confound outgroup usage.

Maximum Parsimony

Maximum parsimony (MP) is a method of identifying the potential phylogenetic tree that requires the smallest total number of evolutionary events to explain the observed sequence data. Some ways of scoring trees also include a "cost" associated with particular types of evolutionary events and attempt to locate the tree with the smallest total cost. This is a useful approach in cases where not every possible type of event is equally likely - for example, when particular nucleotides or amino acids are known to be more mutable than others.

The most naive way of identifying the most parsimonious tree is simple enumeration - considering each possible tree in succession and searching for the tree with the smallest score. However, this is only possible for a relatively small number of sequences or species because the problem of identifying the most parsimonious tree is known to be NP-hard; consequently a number of heuristic search methods for optimization have been developed to locate a highly parsimonious tree, if not the best in the set. Most such methods involve a steepest descent-style minimization mechanism operating on a tree rearrangement criterion.

Branch and Bound

The branch and bound algorithm is a general method used to increase the efficiency of searches for near-optimal solutions of NP-hard problems first applied to phylogenetics in the early 1980s. Branch and bound is particularly well suited to phylogenetic tree construction because it inherently requires dividing a problem into a tree structure as it subdivides the problem space into smaller regions. As its name implies, it requires as input both a branching rule (in the case of phylogenetics, the addition of the next species or sequence to the tree) and a bound (a rule that excludes certain regions of the search space from consideration, thereby assuming that the optimal solution cannot occupy that region). Identifying a good bound is the most challenging aspect of the algorithm's application to phylogenetics. A simple way of defining the bound is a maximum number of assumed evolutionary changes allowed per tree. A set of criteria known as Zharkikh's rules severely limit the search space by defining characteristics shared by all candidate "most parsimonious" trees. The two most basic rules require the elimination of all but one redundant sequence (for cases where multiple observations have produced identical data) and the elimination of character sites at which two or more states do not occur in at least two species. Under ideal conditions these rules and their associated algorithm would completely define a tree.

Sankoff-morel-cedergren Algorithm

The Sankoff-Morel-Cedergren algorithm was among the first published methods to simultaneously produce an MSA and a phylogenetic tree for nucleotide sequences. The method uses a maximum parsimony calculation in conjunction with a scoring function that penalizes gaps and mismatches, thereby favoring the tree that introduces a minimal number of such events (an alternative view holds that the trees to be favored are those that maximize the amount of sequence similarity that can be interpreted as homology, a point of view that may lead to different optimal trees). The imputed sequences at the interior nodes of the tree are scored and summed over all the nodes in each possible tree. The lowest-scoring tree sum provides both an optimal tree and an optimal MSA given the scoring function. Because the method is highly computationally intensive, an approximate method in which initial guesses for the interior alignments are refined one node at a time. Both the full and the approximate version are in practice calculated by dynamic programming.

MALIGN and POY

More recent phylogenetic tree/MSA methods use heuristics to isolate high-scoring, but not necessarily optimal, trees. The MALIGN method uses a maximum-parsimony technique to compute a multiple alignment by maximizing a cladogram score, and its companion POY uses an iterative method that couples the optimization of the phylogenetic tree with improvements in the corresponding MSA. However, the use of these methods in constructing evolutionary hypotheses has been criticized as biased due to the deliberate construction of trees reflecting minimal evolutionary events. This, in turn, has been countered by the view that such methods should be seen as heuristic approaches to find the trees that maximize the amount of sequence similarity that can be interpreted as homology.

Maximum Likelihood

The maximum likelihood method uses standard statistical techniques for inferring probability distributions to assign probabilities to particular possible phylogenetic trees. The method requires a substitution model to assess the probability of particular mutations; roughly, a tree that requires more mutations at interior nodes to explain the observed phylogeny will be assessed as having a lower probability. This is broadly similar to the maximum-parsimony method, but maximum likelihood allows additional statistical flexibility by permitting varying rates of evolution across both lineages and sites. In fact, the method requires that evolution at different sites and along different lineages must be statistically independent. Maximum likelihood is thus well suited to the analysis of distantly related sequences, but it is believed to be computationally intractable to compute due to its NP-hardness.

The "pruning" algorithm, a variant of dynamic programming, is often used to reduce the search space by efficiently calculating the likelihood of subtrees. The method calculates the likelihood for each site in a "linear" manner, starting at a node whose only descendants are leaves (that is, the tips of the tree) and working backwards toward the "bottom" node in nested sets. However, the trees produced by the method are only rooted if the substitution model is irreversible, which is not generally true of biological systems. The search for the maximum-likelihood tree also includes a branch length optimization component that is difficult to improve upon algorithmically; general global optimization tools such as the Newton-Raphson method are often used.

Bayesian Inference

Bayesian inference can be used to produce phylogenetic trees in a manner closely related to the maximum likelihood methods. Bayesian methods assume a prior probability distribution of the possible trees, which may simply be the probability of any one tree among all the possible trees that could be generated from the data, or may be a more sophisticated estimate derived from the assumption that divergence events such as speciation occur as stochastic processes. The choice of prior distribution is a point of contention among users of Bayesian-inference phylogenetics methods.

Implementations of Bayesian methods generally use Markov chain Monte Carlo sampling algorithms, although the choice of move set varies; selections used in Bayesian phylogenetics include circularly permuting leaf nodes of a proposed tree at each step and swapping descendant subtrees of a random internal node between two related trees. The use of Bayesian methods in phylogenetics has been controversial, largely due to incomplete specification of the choice of move set, acceptance criterion, and prior distribution in published work. Bayesian methods are generally held to be superior to parsimony-based methods; they can be more prone to long-branch attraction than maximum likelihood techniques, although they are better able to accommodate missing data.

Whereas likelihood methods find the tree that maximizes the probability of the data, a Bayesian approach recovers a tree that represents the most likely clades, by drawing on the posterior distribution. However, estimates of the posterior probability of clades (measuring their 'support') can be quite wide of the mark, especially in clades that aren't overwhelmingly likely. As such, other methods have been put forwards to estimate posterior probability.

Model Selection

Molecular phylogenetics methods rely on a defined substitution model that encodes a hypothesis about the relative rates of mutation at various sites along the gene or amino acid sequences being studied. At their simplest, substitution models aim to correct for differences in the rates of transitions and transversions in nucleotide sequences. The use of substitution models is necessitated by the fact that the genetic distance between two sequences increases linearly only for a short time after the two sequences diverge from each other (alternatively, the distance is linear only shortly before coalescence). The longer the amount of time after divergence, the more likely it becomes that two mutations occur at the same nucleotide site. Simple genetic distance calculations will thus undercount the number of mutation events that have occurred in evolutionary history. The extent of this undercount increases with increasing time since divergence, which can lead to the phenomenon of long branch attraction, or the misassignment of two distantly related but convergently evolving sequences as closely related. The maximum parsimony method is particularly susceptible to this problem due to its explicit search for a tree representing a minimum number of distinct evolutionary events.

Types of Models

All substitution models assign a set of weights to each possible change of state represented in the sequence. The most common model types are implicitly reversible because they assign the same weight to, for example, a G>C nucleotide mutation as to a C>G mutation. The simplest possible model, the Jukes-Cantor model, assigns an equal probability to every possible change of state for a given nucleotide base. The rate of change between any two distinct nucleotides will be one-third of the overall substitution rate. More advanced models distinguish between transitions and transversions. The most general possible time-reversible model, called the GTR model, has six mutation rate parameters. An even more generalized model known as the general 12-parameter model breaks time-reversibility, at the cost of much additional complexity in calculating genetic distances that are consistent among multiple lineages. One possible variation on this theme adjusts the rates so that overall GC content - an important measure of DNA double helix stability - varies over time.

Models may also allow for the variation of rates with positions in the input sequence. The most obvious example of such variation follows from the arrangement of nucleotides in protein-coding genes into three-base codons. If the location of the open reading frame (ORF) is known, rates of mutation can be adjusted for position of a given site within a codon, since it is known that wobble base pairing can allow for higher mutation rates in the third nucleotide of a given codon without affecting the codon's meaning in the genetic code. A less hypothesis-driven example that does not rely on ORF identification simply assigns to each site a rate randomly drawn from a predetermined distribution, often the gamma distribution or log-normal distribution. Finally, a more conservative estimate of rate variations known as the covarion method allows autocorrelated variations in rates, so that the mutation rate of a given site is correlated across sites and lineages.

Choosing the Best Model

The selection of an appropriate model is critical for the production of good phylogenetic analyses, both because underparameterized or overly restrictive models may produce aberrant behavior when their underlying assumptions are violated, and because overly complex or overparameterized models are computationally expensive and the parameters may be overfit. The most common method of model selection is the likelihood ratio test (LRT), which produces a likelihood estimate that can be interpreted as a measure of "goodness of fit" between the model and the input data. However, care must be taken in using these results, since a more complex model with more parameters will always have a higher likelihood than a simplified version of the same model, which can lead to the naive selection of models that are overly complex. For this reason model selection computer programs will choose the simplest model that is not significantly worse than more complex substitution models. A significant disadvantage of the LRT is the necessity of making a series of pairwise comparisons between models; it has been shown that the order in which the models are compared has a major effect on the one that is eventually selected.

An alternative model selection method is the Akaike information criterion (AIC), formally an estimate of the Kullback–Leibler divergence between the true model and the model being tested. It can be interpreted as a likelihood estimate with a correction factor to penalize overparameterized models. The AIC is calculated on an individual model rather than a pair, so it is independent of the order in which models are assessed. A related alternative, the Bayesian information criterion (BIC), has a similar basic interpretation but penalizes complex models more heavily.

A comprehensive step-by-step protocol on constructing phylogenetic tree, including DNA/Amino Acid contiguous sequence assembly, multiple sequence alignment, model-test (testing best-fitting substitution models) and phylogeny reconstruction using Maximum Likelihood and Bayesian Inference, is available at *Nature Protocol*.

A non traditional way of evaluating the phylogenetic tree is to compare it with clustering result. One can use a Multidimensional Scaling technique, so called Interpolative Joining to do dimensionality reduction to visualize the clustering result for the sequences in 3D, and then map the phylogenetic tree onto the clustering result. A better tree usually has a higher correlation with the clustering result.

Evaluating Tree Support

As with all statistical analysis, the estimation of phylogenies from character data requires an evaluation of confidence. A number of methods exist to test the amount of support for a phylogenetic tree, either by evaluating the support for each sub-tree in the phylogeny (nodal support) or evaluating whether the phylogeny is significantly different from other possible trees (alternative tree hypothesis tests).

Nodal Support

The most common method for assessing tree support is to evaluate the statistical support for each node on the tree. Typically, a node with very low support is not considered valid in further analysis, and visually may be collapsed into a polytomy to indicate that relationships within a clade are unresolved.

Consensus Tree

Many methods for assessing nodal support involve consideration of multiple phylogenies. The consensus tree summarizes the nodes that are shared among a set of trees. In a strict consensus, only nodes found in every tree are shown, and the rest are collapsed into an unresolved polytomy. Less conservative methods, such as the majority-rule consensus tree, consider nodes that are supported by a given percentage of trees under consideration (such as at least 50%).

For example, in maximum parsimony analysis, there may be many trees with the same parsimony score. A strict consensus tree would show which nodes are found in all equally parsimonious trees, and which nodes differ. Consensus trees are also used to evaluate support on phylogenies reconstructed with Bayesian inference.

Bootstrapping and Jackknifing

In statistics, the bootstrap is a method for inferring the variability of data that has an unknown distribution using pseudoreplications of the original data. For example, given a set of 100 data points, a pseudoreplicate is a data set of the same size (100 points) randomly sampled from the original data, with replacement. That is, each original data point may be represented more than once in the pseudoreplicate, or not at all. Statistical support involves evaluation of whether the original data has similar properties to a large set of pseudoreplicates.

In phylogenetics, bootstrapping is conducted using the columns of the character matrix. Each pseudoreplicate contains the same number of species (rows) and characters (columns) randomly sampled from the original matrix, with replacement. A phylogeny is reconstructed from each pseudoreplicate, with the same methods used to reconstruct the phylogeny from the original data. For each node on the phylogeny, the nodal support is the percentage of pseudoreplicates containing that node.

The statistical rigor of the bootstrap test has been empirically evaluated using viral populations with known evolutionary histories, finding that 70% bootstrap support corresponds to a 95% probability that the clade exists. However, this was tested under ideal conditions (e.g. no change in evolutionary rates, symmetric phylogenies). In practice, values above 70% are generally supported and left to the researcher or reader to evaluate confidence. Nodes with support lower than 70% are typically considered unresolved.

Jackknifing in phylogenetics is a similar procedure, except the columns of the matrix are sampled without replacement. Pseudoreplicates are generated by randomly subsampling the data—for example, a "10% jackknife" would involve randomly sampling 10% of the matrix many times to evaluate nodal support.

Posterior Probability

Reconstruction of phylogenies using Bayesian inference generates a posterior distribution of highly probable trees given the data and evolutionary model, rather than a single "best" tree. The trees in the posterior distribution generally have many different topologies. Most Bayesian inference methods utilize a Markov-chain Monte Carlo iteration, and the initial steps of this chain are not considered reliable reconstructions of the phylogeny. Trees generated early in the chain are usually discarded as burn-in. The most common method of evaluating nodal support in a Bayesian phylogenetic analysis is to calculate the percentage of trees in the posterior distribution (post-burn-in) which contain the node.

The statistical support for a node in Bayesian inference is expected to reflect the probability that a clade really exists given the data and evolutionary model. Therefore, the threshold for accepting a node as supported is generally higher than for bootstrapping.

Step Counting Methods

Bremer support counts the number of extra steps needed to contradict a clade.

Shortcomings

These measures each have their weaknesses. For example, smaller or larger clades tend to attract larger support values than mid-sized clades, simply as a result of the number of taxa in them.

Bootstrap support can provide high estimates of node support as a result of noise in the data rather than the true existence of a clade.

Limitations and Workarounds

Ultimately, there is no way to measure whether a particular phylogenetic hypothesis is accurate or not, unless the true relationships among the taxa being examined are already known (which may happen with bacteria or viruses under laboratory conditions). The best result an empirical phylogeneticist can hope to attain is a tree with branches that are well supported by the available evidence. Several potential pitfalls have been identified:

Homoplasy

Certain characters are more likely to evolve convergently than others; logically, such characters should be given less weight in the reconstruction of a tree. Weights in the form of a model of evolution can be inferred from sets of molecular data, so that maximum likelihood or Bayesian methods can be used to analyze them. For molecular sequences, this problem is exacerbated when the taxa under study have diverged substantially. As time since the divergence of two taxa increase, so does the probability of multiple substitutions on the same site, or back mutations, all of which result in homoplasies. For morphological data, unfortunately, the only objective way to determine convergence is by the construction of a tree – a somewhat circular method. Even so, weighting homoplasious characters does indeed lead to better-supported trees. Further refinement can be brought by weighting changes in one direction higher than changes in another; for instance, the presence of thoracic wings almost guarantees placement among the pterygote insects because, although wings are often lost secondarily, there is no evidence that they have been gained more than once.

Horizontal Gene Transfer

In general, organisms can inherit genes in two ways: vertical gene transfer and horizontal gene transfer. Vertical gene transfer is the passage of genes from parent to offspring, and horizontal (also called lateral) gene transfer occurs when genes jump between unrelated organisms, a common phenomenon especially in prokaryotes; a good example of this is the acquired antibiotic resistance as a result of gene exchange between various bacteria leading to multi-drug-resistant bacterial species. There have also been well-documented cases of horizontal gene transfer between eukaryotes.

Horizontal gene transfer has complicated the determination of phylogenies of organisms, and inconsistencies in phylogeny have been reported among specific groups of organisms depending on the genes used to construct evolutionary trees. The only way to determine which genes have been acquired vertically and which horizontally is to parsimoniously assume that the largest set of genes that have been inherited together have been inherited vertically; this requires analyzing a large number of genes.

Hybrids, Speciation, Introgressions and Incomplete Lineage Sorting

The basic assumption underlying the mathematical model of cladistics is a situation where species split neatly in bifurcating fashion. While such an assumption may hold on a larger scale (bar horizontal gene transfer,), speciation is often much less orderly. Research since the cladistic method was introduced has shown that hybrid speciation, once thought rare, is in fact quite common, particularly in plants. Also paraphyletic speciation is common, making the assumption of a bifurcating pattern unsuitable, leading to phylogenetic networks rather than trees. Introgression can also move genes between otherwise distinct species and sometimes even genera, complicating phylogenetic analysis based on genes. This phenomenon can contribute to "incomplete lineage sorting" and is thought to be a common phenomenon across a number of groups. In species level analysis this can be dealt with by larger sampling or better whole genome analysis. Often the problem is avoided by restricting the analysis to fewer, not closely related specimens.

Taxon Sampling

Owing to the development of advanced sequencing techniques in molecular biology, it has become feasible to gather large amounts of data (DNA or amino acid sequences) to infer phylogenetic hypotheses. For example, it is not rare to find studies with character matrices based on whole mitochondrial genomes (~16,000 nucleotides, in many animals). However, simulations have shown that it is more important to increase the number of taxa in the matrix than to increase the number of characters, because the more taxa there are, the more accurate and more robust is the resulting phylogenetic tree. This may be partly due to the breaking up of long branches.

Phylogenetic Signal

Another important factor that affects the accuracy of tree reconstruction is whether the data analyzed actually contain a useful phylogenetic signal, a term that is used generally to denote whether a character evolves slowly enough to have the same state in closely related taxa as opposed to varying randomly. Tests for phylogenetic signal exist.

Continuous Characters

Morphological characters that sample a continuum may contain phylogenetic signal, but are hard to code as discrete characters. Several methods have been used, one of which is gap coding, and there are variations on gap coding. In the original form of gap coding.

group means for a character are first ordered by size. The pooled within-group standard deviation is calculated and differences between adjacent means are compared relative to this standard deviation. Any pair of adjacent means is considered different and given different integer scores if the means are separated by a "gap" greater than the within-group standard deviation times some arbitrary constant.

If more taxa are added to the analysis, the gaps between taxa may become so small that all information is lost. Generalized gap coding works around that problem by comparing individual pairs of taxa rather than considering one set that contains all of the taxa.

Missing Data

In general, the more data that are available when constructing a tree, the more accurate and reliable the resulting tree will be. Missing data are no more detrimental than simply having fewer data, although the impact is greatest when most of the missing data are in a small number of taxa. Concentrating the missing data across a small number of characters produces a more robust tree.

The Role of Fossils

Because many characters involve embryological, or soft-tissue or molecular characters that (at best) hardly ever fossilize, and the interpretation of fossils is more ambiguous than that of living taxa, extinct taxa almost invariably have higher proportions of missing data than living ones. However, despite these limitations, the inclusion of fossils is invaluable, as they can provide information in sparse areas of trees, breaking up long branches and constraining intermediate character states; thus, fossil taxa contribute as much to tree resolution as modern taxa. Fossils can also constrain the age of lineages and thus demonstrate how consistent a tree is with the stratigraphic record; stratocladistics incorporates age information into data matrices for phylogenetic analyses.

Phylogenetic Comparative Methods

Phylogenetic comparative methods (PCMs) enable us to study the history of organismal evolution and diversification. PCMs comprise a collection of statistical methods for inferring history from piecemeal information, primarily combining two types of data: first, an estimate of species relatedness, usually based on their genes, and second, contemporary trait values of extant organisms. Some PCMs also incorporate information from geological records, especially fossils, but also other gradual and episodic events in the Earth's history (for example, trait data from fossils or the global oxygen concentration as an independent variable). It is important to note at the outset that PCMs are not concerned with reconstructing the evolutionary relationships among species; this has to do with estimating the phylogeny from genetic, fossil and other data, and a separate set of methods for this process makes up the field of phylogenetics. PCMs as a set of methods are distinct from, but are not completely independent of, phylogenetics. PCMs are used to address the questions: how did the characteristics of organisms evolve through time and what factors influenced speciation and extinction?

Phylogenetic Trees

Phylogenetic trees are used to analyze and visualize evolution. However, trees can be imperfect datatypes when summarizing multiple trees. This is especially problematic when accommodating for biological phenomena such as horizontal gene transfer, incomplete lineage sorting, and hybridization, as well as topological conflict between datasets. Additionally, researchers may want to combine information from sets of trees that have partially overlapping taxon sets. To address the problem of analyzing sets of trees with conflicting relationships and partially overlapping taxon sets, we introduce methods for aligning, synthesizing and analyzing rooted phylogenetic trees within a graph, called a tree alignment graph (TAG). The TAG can be queried and analyzed to explore uncertainty and conflict. It can also be synthesized to construct trees, presenting an alternative to supertrees approaches. We demonstrate these methods with two empirical datasets. In order to explore uncertainty, we constructed a TAG of the bootstrap trees from the Angiosperm Tree of Life project. Analysis of the resulting graph demonstrates that areas of the dataset that are unresolved in majority-rule consensus tree analyses can be understood in more detail within the context of a graph structure, using measures incorporating node degree and adjacency support. As an exercise in synthesis (i.e., summarization of a TAG constructed from the alignment trees), we also construct a TAG consisting of the taxonomy and source trees from a recent comprehensive bird study. We synthesized this graph into a tree that can be reconstructed in a repeatable fashion and where the underlying source information can be updated. The methods presented here are tractable for large scale analyses and serve as a basis for an alternative to consensus tree and supertree methods. Furthermore, the exploration of these graphs can expose structures and patterns within the dataset that are otherwise difficult to observe.

The need to visualize and analyze variability among phylogenetic trees has fostered the development of many methods, including consensus trees, cloudograms, concordance analysis, bipartition support, splits graphs, and supertree algorithms. Huson and Scornavacca review a number of phylogenetic network methods that make use of graphs of higher complexity than strictly-bifurcating trees. Many of these attempt to infer a network structure from a sequence alignment instead of aligning source trees into a common structure. Other methods, used to identify hybridization and recombination events, recognize conflict in source trees. However, like network methods, they explicitly assume specific biological events to be the source of the conflict. Although many of these methods continue to be useful in exploring certain events, they do not fully retain the structure of the original source trees in the output statistics or summary networks.

Phylogenies can also be combined to construct a synthetic tree from source trees with partially overlapping taxon sets. Supertree methods are commonly used for this purpose. These methods often produce a tree or trees (the supertree) intended to represent the relationships supported by the input trees. Although this has been demonstrated to be useful in many studies one drawback of supertree methods is that the identifiability of the source trees themselves is lost in the supertree-building process. Furthermore, supertree methods can reconstruct relationships that are not found in any of the input trees making it difficult to interpret the source for such relationships. In addition to these criticisms, supertree methods are not explicitly targeted toward the exploration of variability among the input trees. One recent supertree method makes explicit use of a graph to construct a supertree from source trees that sample nodes from different taxonomic levels. The graph structure in this method functions as an temporary intermediate step. In the Berry et al. graphs, nodes and edges from source trees are mapped in a way that facilitates the extraction of the supertree from the graph, but the semantic identity of nodes and edges is different in the graphs than it is in the source trees (for instance, sibling nodes in source trees are directly connected by edges in the graph). In addition to addressing supertree analyses and bootstrap or posterior probability summaries, the benefit of more generalized data structures for combining trees can simplify practical exercises such as tree grafting and comparisons among trees with fully or partially overlapping tip sets.

Existing solutions to both the tree synthesis and exploration of conflict problems involve analyses that result in a tree or set of trees that contain nodes and edges that are difficult to trace back to the source. Whether because of lack of available database technology or somewhat different goals, the problem of mapping a set of trees, while retaining all of the original information, into a common structure is not often addressed.

We present a set of methods intended to facilitate generalized analyses involving potentially conflicting phylogenetic trees with fully or partially overlapping sets of taxa. These methods address the problem of identifying common nodes and edges across sets of phylogenetic trees and constructing a data structure that efficiently contains this information while retaining original source information. We achieve this with algorithms that align trees into a graph structure called a tree alignment graph (TAG) and stores this information so it can be queried. These methods, which align and identify equivalent nodes across trees or graphs, fall within a class of methods known as graph alignment, and are analogous to the alignment methods of other domains. The goals achieved by aligning trees into a TAG are distinct from the amalgamation of sets of trees into a single tree (e.g. supertree methods), though, in addition to many other analyses, TAGs can be used to facilitate supertree and grafting exercises. As mentioned above, Berry et al. have also examined placing trees into graphs for the specific purpose of constructing supertrees. The methods presented here are intended to be more generally applicable and provide additional means for storing and querying. Other uses of TAGs include mapping uncertainty across trees, synthesis and extraction of a diverse set of summary trees, and more extensive queries that have previously been difficult to address.

Mapping trees into a TAG exploits the fact that rooted phylogenetic trees are in fact a specific type of graph: they are directed, acyclic, and require that each node has, at most, one parent. By relaxing these requirements, we can combine multiple trees into a common graph, while minimizing changes to the semantic interpretations of nodes and edges in the trees. Because they contain nodes and edges directly analogous to those from their source trees, TAGs have the desirable quality of retaining the full identifiability of the original source trees they contain. Additionally, because they are not restricted to the bifurcating model of evolution, TAGs may represent conflict among source trees as reticulations in the graph. Despite having higher complexity than trees, the graphs we present are amenable to fast traversals and straightforward interpretations regarding the evolutionary relationships they imply. In addition to the extraction of synthetic trees by customizable queries, TAGs also support the extraction of the original source trees themselves for the purposes of further analysis or updating.

Here we provide a description of the TAG datatype and some associated analyses. We also demonstrate the alignment of disparate phylogenetic trees with partially overlapping sets of terminal nodes into a graph, the exploration of conflicting and complementary hypotheses of ancestry defined by the input trees, and the extraction of synthesized trees summarizing compatible relationships from multiple input source trees.

TAG Synthesis Techniques

Many operations and queries can be conducted on a graph with trees aligned. One common operation is synthesis of the TAG. By synthesis, we mean the selection of relationships in the graph either by filtering or other procedure to produce a synthetic or composite tree. There are a number of different ways to synthesize the TAG and here we describe a few including (1) preference for specific source trees, (2) preference for more highly supported nodes, and (3) routes with a maximum number of taxa using a branch-and-bound optimization. In figure C, we show the result of one synthetic analysis on the graph where we prefer source trees and specifically (in order) blue, green, and taxonomy source trees.

In each case, synthesis begins by identifying a starting node. For example, this may be a particular clade identified by name or by its set of descendant terminal nodes (i.e. the identification of a LICA). To make a tree from an entire TAG the procedure starts at the root node. From this focal node, it proceeds breadth-first in determining which nodes to include in the synthesis as we traverse the TAG. At each node, the procedure examines the subtending nodes, and determines if any of them conflict. For synthesis, downstream conflict is determined by comparing the LICAs for each child. If the LICAs from nodes subtending the current node overlap, then these descendant subgraphs define incompatible subtrees, and are said to be in conflict. In such cases, the procedure must make a decision about which path to prefer. In figure C, we prefer specific source trees, but there are many criteria that can be used to inform these decisions. The resulting synthetic tree in figure C is a composite of the source trees stored in the TAG. Because of the mapping of the source trees to common graph nodes, the synthetic tree includes the internal node names that originate from the taxonomy. Although we present a tree as the result of synthesis, there is no requirement that the synthetic product be a tree. However, a tree will likely be a more common product.

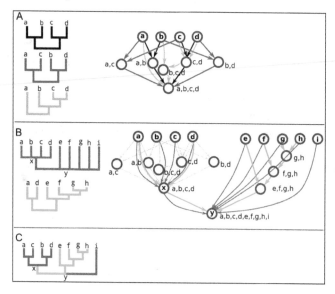

A basic schematic of the results of mapping and synthesis. A) Three source trees with completely overlapping taxon sets (left) mapped into a graph (right). The colored edges in the graph correspond to the source trees on the left, with graph nodes represented as gray circles. Internal graph nodes represent least inclusive common ancestors (LICAs), and are labelled with their descendant terminal taxa. B) A grey taxonomy hierarchy and additional green source tree added to the black, blue, and orange trees from A. The relationships presented in the black, blue, and orange trees are in light grey to cut down on clutter. C) A synthetic tree resulting from preferring source blue, green, and taxonomic source trees.

Preferring Certain Source Trees

One of the simplest but most useful methods for constructing a synthesized tree is to prefer paths from specific source trees included in the graph. This procedure can generate a tree that is entirely congruent with the most-preferred source tree, but which may contain more lineages. In fact, the synthetic tree will contain terminal lineages from all other source trees in the TAG that are compatible with the preferred set. This procedure requires the identification of a preferred list of source trees, sorted by preference. The trees in the preferred list are consulted in order, and any conflicts among them are resolved in favor of those with higher positions in the list. This procedure could easily be extended to use any kind of source tree metadata, such as pre-calculated node support (e.g. posterior probabilities, bootstrap proportions), presence or absence of branch lengths, or other properties.

Preferring Better-supported Nodes

Properties such as node and edge support can also be used to resolve conflict. In the examples below, node support s_q is measured as the proportion of source trees in which the given node is observed. In a TAG constructed from source trees with completely overlapping terminal node sets, the proportion of trees exhibiting a node is the number of outgoing branches (these point to the parent of the specified node). In TAGs containing source trees with incompletely overlapping terminal node sets, node support for a given node q must be corrected to reflect (1) the number of source trees containing any node that may be mapped to q, and (2) the potential that the parent of q in some source tree could have been aligned to more than one LICA. In this case, s_q is the number of source trees associated with the set of outgoing edges of q, divided by the number of source trees containing any terminal node aligned to any descendant of q (these are the source trees that could be aligned to q).

In a support-based tie-breaking procedure, preference is given to the node with the highest support. In datasets with completely overlapping taxon sets, the nodes chosen by this procedure are frequently the same as those chosen by a traditional consensus tree analysis. However, this is a greedy procedure and does not guarantee that the resulting synthetic tree is the best supported tree. Differences between a majority-rule consensus and a best-support synthesis tree will lie mostly in poorly supported areas of a tree.

Preferring Complete Trees using Branch and Bound Optimization

When constructing a synthetic tree from a TAG containing conflict, one challenge lies in maximizing the number of the terminal nodes that will be present in the final synthetic tree. The worst-case for this problem is presented when no additional information is provided to break conflicts. In a general sense, this is related to a classic set cover problem, and is likely to be NP-complete. The solution can be greatly simplified by specifying other properties (such as those mentioned in the previous two sections) with which to break conflicts. In lieu of such specified properties, however, we present a branch-and-bound approach to attempt to maximize the number of terminal nodes in the synthesized tree. There are two implementations of this algorithm: in the first, the bound is based on minimizing cost; in the second, it is based on maximizing scores. The algorithms are presented in the supplemental materials.

Measuring Support and Conflict within a TAG

In simple examples as in figure, conflict and support is easy to observe. For more complex TAGs, such as the angiosperm TAG described below, we can calculate node- and edge-based statistics on the graph Y to describe support and conflict throughout. Node support is calculated as the number of source trees aligned to the focal graph node, scaled by the number of source trees that could be aligned to that node (i.e. contain overlapping taxon sets). Edge support, $S_{q_0|q_1}$ for the edge between the child node q_0 and its parent q_1, is calculated in a similar fashion to node support: it is the number of times that edge is observed (i.e. the number of exactly parallel graph edges between the same parent and child nodes) scaled by the number of source trees in which that edge may be observed.

Complementary to edge-based metrics of support, node-degree (the number of nodes adjacent to a focal node) reflects node-based conflict and uncertainty. As a TAG is a directed graph, we partition node-degree into 1) child- and 2) parent-node relationships. Simple child- or parent-degree counts are not directly informative, as node relationships can be supported to different extents (i.e. by the number of source trees exhibiting the relationships). Because all node relationships from all input source trees are preserved in the graph (even identical relationships), we can instead calculate the *effective* number $\left(\tilde{N}\right)$ of directed node relationships. Consider a focal graph node q with n parent nodes, but $m \geq n$ parent-node relationships (that is, q is present in m source trees, all of which may potentially differ in taxon overlap). Each parent node n_i is supported by some proportion p_i of the m trees. The effective number of parent nodes for q is given by: $\tilde{N}_{parents(q)} = \dfrac{1}{\sum_i^n = p_i^2}$.

The effective number of child nodes $\tilde{N}_{children(q)}$ is calculated similarly, dealing with the number of child nodes and child-node relationships. This metric corresponds to the inverse Simpson diversity index (Simpson, 1949), and is larger when directed node relationships are more evenly supported. For example, a graph node with two parent nodes each supported by 500 trees will have 2 effective parents, whereas another graph node with one parent supported by 999 trees and another parent supported by 1 tree will have 1.002002 effective parents. Note that terminal graph nodes possess no children, and the root graph node has no parent. In general, $\tilde{N}_{children}$ reflects phylogenetic uncertainty (or lack of information), while $_{parents}$ reflects immediate topological conflict (e.g. when a node has 2 or more parent nodes; figure A). In a fully bifurcating TAG, each internal node will have $\tilde{N}_{children} = 2$ and $\tilde{N}_{parents} = 1$. Note that in the tree synthesis procedures above, an overlap of LICA descendants indicates that one or more topological conflicts (that is, $\tilde{N}_{parents} > 1$) resides somewhere within the subtending graph.

While the effective number of parents indicates the degree of immediate topological conflict, it ignores the frequency at which a given node q occurs across a set of source trees. We therefore also define a measure of destabilization, which is the number of effective parents for node pcbi.1003239.s009 scaled by its support:

$$d_q = \tilde{N}_{parents(q)}.S_q$$

Destabilization measures the contribution of a given LICA to the conflict in the neighboring nodes. Graph nodes with high values of d are frequently observed in source trees but rarely in the same topological position. These nodes contribute heavily to the collapse of clades in traditional consensus methods.

For each internal node q in the graph we also calculate the average d for all n descendant nodes,

$$z_q = \frac{\sum_{i=1}^{n} d_i}{n}$$

A z_q value greater than 1 indicates that the subgraph of q contains conflict. This statistic has the useful property of being directly comparable among TAGs constructed from different data sets.

It is also useful to quantify how average downstream conflict z changes with the inclusion of a graph node q and its descendant subgraph. We therefore compute a metric of resolution, which quantifies the difference in average downstream conflict between a node q and its n immediate parent node(s):

$$c_q = s_q.\sum_{i=1}^{n}\left(z_q - z_{r_i}\right).s_{q|r_i}$$

where S_q is the node support for node q, $s_{q|r_i}$ is the edge support connecting node q to its parent node r_i, and z_{r_i} is the average downstream conflict experienced by parent node r_i. High values of c indicate clades that are frequently observed but whose inclusion in the graph contributes heavily to overall conflict within their parent clade.

Phylogenetic Networks

Phylogenetic networks are a generalization of phylogenetic trees that are used to represent non-tree-like evolutionary histories that arise in organisms such as plants and bacteria, or uncertainty in evolutionary histories. An *unrooted* phylogenetic network on a non-empty, finite set X of taxa, or *network*, is a connected, simple graph in which every vertex has degree 1 or 3 and whose leaf set is X. It is called a *phylogenetic tree* if the underlying graph is a tree.

Let X be a finite set with $|X| \geq 1$. An *unrooted phylogenetic network N (on X)* (or *network N (on X)* for short) is a connected, simple graph (V, E) with $X \subseteq V$, every vertex has degree 1 or 3, and the set of degree 1 vertices (or *leaves*) is precisely X. A *phylogenetic tree* on X is a network which is also a tree. Phylogenetic trees and networks are commonly used by biologists to represent the evolution of species; in this setting the set X usually denotes a collection of species. Networks have interesting mathematical and computational properties, and they can be generated from biological data using software packages such as T-REX and Splitstree . In addition, networks have been used to study the genome fusion origin of eukaryotes and as a tool in biogeography studies.

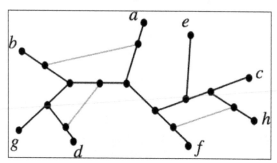

A tree-based network that has been constructed from a phylogenetic tree with leaf set {a,b,...,g} by adding in 3 edges (in grey). Note that the tree is also a spanning tree for the network.

The T-REX software constructs networks (also called reticulograms) by adding edges into a phylogenetic tree . Using this approach, many different networks can be constructed from starting with the collection of all phylogenetic trees. However, it is not possible to construct every possible network in this manner. Indeed, the networks that can be constructed in this way are of precisely the following type.

- A network is *tree-based (on X)* if there is a spanning tree[1] in N whose leaf set is equal to X.

- Note that in the following we call any spanning tree in N with leaf set X a *support tree (for N)*.

Recently, a great deal of interest has been generated concerning rooted tree-based networks. These are leaf-labelled networks whose underlying graph is a directed acyclic graph with a single root which can be constructed from a rooted phylogenetic tree by adding in extra arcs. In particular, rooted tree-based networks were introduced in and their structural properties have been studied in Francis et al., Hayamizu, Jetten and van Iersel , Semple, Zhang . In addition, various computational properties of these networks have been considered.

Biologically, tree-based networks are a natural object of interest because their presentation of reticulations reflects assumptions about the underlying biological events (such as horizontal gene transfer or hybridization). Such events are regarded as occurring between taxonomic units (such as species) that also undergo vertical evolution; hence they are thought of as arcs between "tree" arcs. Biologists want to detect and understand horizontal evolution through events such as gene transfer and hybridization since this process plays an important role in the evolution of many organisms (e.g. in bacteria and plants). Moreover, detecting horizontal evolution can be useful in applications, e.g. horizontal gene transfer is the primary mechanism for the spread of antibiotic resistance in bacteria.

Decomposing Tree-based Networks

We begin by showing that networks can be decomposed into simpler pieces, which can then be used to deduce properties of the full network. Note that decomposition results have also been proven for rooted tree-based networks, although these are quite different in nature.

We begin by presenting some definitions. A *cut-edge*, or *bridge*, of a network is an edge whose removal disconnects the graph. A cut-edge is *trivial* if one of the connected components induced by deleting the cut-edge is a vertex (which must necessarily be a leaf). A *simple* network is one all of whose cut-edges are trivial (so for instance, note that trees on more than 3 leaves are *not* simple networks). A *blob* in a network is a maximal subgraph that has no cut-edge and that is not a vertex . For example, the network in figure contains one non-trivial cut-edge and two blobs.

Now, given a network N and a blob B in N, we define a simple network B_N by taking the union of B and all cut-edges in N incident with B (the leaf set of B_N is just the set of end vertices of these cut-edges that are not already a vertex in B).

Proposition: Suppose N is a network. Then N is tree-based if and only if B_N is tree-based for every blob B in N.

Proof: If N is tree-based, then it contains a support tree T. Since every cut-edge in N must be contained in a support tree, it follows that if B is a blob in N, then T must induce a spanning tree of BNBN that contains every vertex in B_N. Therefore, B_N is tree-based.

Conversely, if BNBN is tree-based for every blob B in N, then by taking a support tree in B_N for each blob B in N, we can clearly construct a spanning tree for N that contains all vertices in N. Therefore, N is tree-based.

Using the last result, we can immediately classify the tree-based networks having a single leaf.

Observation: Suppose N is a network on $\{x\}$. Then N is tree-based if and only if $N = (\{x\}, 0)$.

We now look in more detail at the cut-edges of a tree-based network. A *split* of X is a bipartition of X into two non-empty sets. If we remove a cut-edge from a network, then in some cases the two resulting graphs will induce a split of X. We now show that if N is tree-based, then this is always the case.

Lemma: If N is a tree-based network, then every cut-edge of N induces a split of X.

Proof: If we have a cut-edge of N that does not induce a split of X, then it follows that there must be some blob B in N such that B_N is a network with one leaf. But then B_N is not tree-based by Observation. This is a contradiction by Proposition.

We call a network N *proper* if every cut-edge induces a split of X. By Lemma, all tree-based networks are proper.

Interestingly, using Proposition 1, we are able to now show that certain low complexity proper networks are always tree-based. We first make a useful observation.

Lemma: Let N be a network on X with $|X| \geq 2$. For any $x \in X$ let $N - x$ denote the network obtained from N by deleting x and its incident edge, and suppressing the resulting degree 2 vertex. If $N - x$ is tree-based, then so is N.

Proof: Suppose $x \in X$ and T is a support tree for $N - x$. Let $v \in V(N)$ denote the vertex adjacent with x that was suppressed in the construction of $N - x$ and let $e \in E(N - x)$ denote the resulting edge in $N - x$. If $e \in E(T)$, then we can obtain a support tree for N by subdividing e with a new vertex w and adding the edge $\{w, x\}$ to T. If $e \notin E(T)$, then, since T is a support tree for $N-xN-x$, T must contain both vertices in e, say $v1v1$ and $v2$. Therefore, we can obtain a support tree for N by adding a new vertex w and the edges $\{v_{1,w}}$ and $\{w, x\}$ (or indeed $\{v_{2,w}}$ and $\{w, x\}$) to T.

Suppose N is a network on X and $k \geq 0$ is an integer. Then N is called a *level-k network* if at most k edges have to be removed from each blob of N to obtain a tree. For example, the network in figure is a level-2 network.

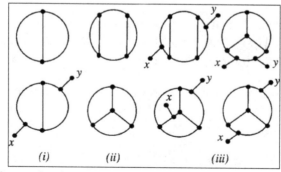

Diagram for proving that simple level-2 and level-3 networks are tree-based
used in the proof of Theorem.

Theorem: All proper level-4 networks are tree-based. Moreover, networks of level greater than 4 need not be tree-based.

Proof: First observe that by definition of level-k network, the main claim applies to level-1, 2, 3, and 4 networks.

Note that since N is a proper network on X, it must contain at least two leaves. Also note that the theorem is straight-forward to check in case N is level-0 or level-1.

In case N has level $2 \le k \le 4$, since N is proper, by Proposition 1 it suffices to prove that every simple, level-4 network with two leaves is tree-based. This is because we can decompose N into a collection of simple networks B_N (one for each blob B of N) each having at least 2 leaves, and if each of these simple networks is tree-based, then so is N. Moreover, for each of these simple networks B_N, if we remove all but 2 leaves from B_N and obtain a tree-based network, then it is straight-forward to see using Lemma 3 that B_N must have been tree-based.

Now, to see that any simple, level-4 network with two leaves x and y is tree-based, we begin with the case k = 2. It is clear that any simple level-2 network on some set Y can be obtained by inserting pendant edges in the multigraph at the top of figure (i) and labelling the leaves by the elements of Y. It is now straight-forward to check that, up to isomorphism, the only possible simple level-2 network on $\{x, y\}$ is isomorphic to the one at the bottom of figure (i). Clearly, this network is tree-based.

We now consider the case k = 3. As before, it is known that any simple level-3 network on some finite set Y can be obtained by inserting a pendant edge into one of the multi-graphs in figure (ii) and labelling the leaves by the elements of Y. It is now straight-forward to check that the only possible simple level-3 networks on $\{x, y\}$ are isomorphic to one of the networks in figure (iii), and that each of these is tree-based.

We conclude with the case k = 4. We use the fact that any simple level-4 network with leaf set Y can be obtained by inserting pendant edges in one of the five multigraphs in the top row of figure and labelling the leaves by the elements of Y. Using this fact, it is now straight-forward to check that, up to isomorphism, any simple level-4 network on $\{x, y\}$ is isomorphic to one of the networks on $\{x, y\}$ that can be generated from the bottom row of figure as described in the figure's caption [note that we can exclude the case (i) in the bottom row as it is not possible for this to be made into a simple network with leaf set $\{x, y\}$It is now straight-forward to check that each of these networks on $\{x, y\}$is tree-based, which concludes the case k = 4.

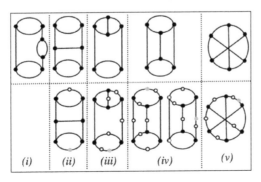

(i)   (ii)   (iii)   (iv)   (v)

Diagram for proving that simple level-4 networks are tree-based used in the proof of Theorem: In the bottom row, each grey vertex corresponds to inserting a pendant edge labelled by x, and each circle vertex corresponds to inserting a pendant edge labelled by y, so that a network on $\{x, y\}$ is produced [so, for example, there are 5 possible networks associated to the diagram in the bottom row of column (iii)].

We now prove the last statement of the theorem. An example of a level-5 network is presented in figure. This network can be seen to be not tree-based as follows.

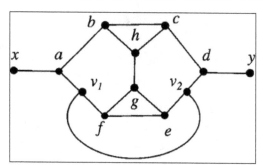

A level-5 network on $\{x, y\}$ that is not tree-based (Steel). The labels of the interior vertices are included for proof purposes.

If it were tree-based, then there would be a path from x to y passing through every vertex exactly once. If the path began x, a, b, or ended c, d, y, then it could not pass through v_1 or v_2 without going through some vertex twice. Therefore, such a path begins x, a, v_1 and ends $v_{2,d,y}$. The edge $\{v_{1,v2}\}$ cannot be included in such a path, because that completes the path without passing through all vertices, so the path actually must begin $x, a, v_{1,f}$ and end $e, v_{2,d,y}$. At this point the path cannot include vertices b, c, h without passing through g twice: a contradiction.

This example demonstrates that not all level-5 networks are tree-based, and since by definition of level, this network is also level-k for any $k \geq 5$, the result follows.

Remark: The level-5 example used in the proof of Theorem 1 can be used to show that it is possible to construct networks that are *strictly* level-k [in that they are level-k and not level-$(k-1)$] and that are not tree-based. Take a network N of level-$k \geq 5$ and choose a pendant edge $\{x, y\}$ in N. Replace this edge by the level-5 network shown in figure. The resulting network has unchanged level and is not tree-based.

Recognizing Tree-based Networks

we consider the complexity of the computational problem of deciding whether or not a given network N is tree-based.

We begin with a useful result. Suppose that C is a cubic graph. Pick some edge e in C. Introduce two pendant edges into e containing the new degree 1 vertices x and y. This new graph Ce (x, y) is a network on $\{x, y\}$. We illustrate this construction in figure. The following observation concerning this construction is straight-forward to check.

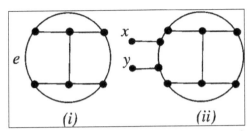

(i) Cubic graph C with edge e indicated. (ii) The network Ce (x, y).

Lemma: Suppose that C is a cubic graph. The following statements are equivalent:

1. C is Hamiltonian.

2. There is some edge e in C such that the network Ce (x, y) is tree-based.

3. There is some edge e in C such that the network Ce (x, y) has a support tree consisting of a path with end vertices x and y.

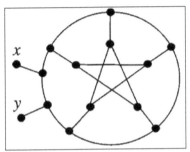

A simple level-6 network that is not tree-based. Removing the two pendant edges labelled with x and y and their vertices results in the Petersen graph.

Note that using Lemma 4, it immediately follows that the network in figure is not tree-based, since if P is the Petersen graph (which is not Hamiltonian), then this network is of the form Pe (x,y) for some edge e of P.

We now use the last lemma to prove two NP-completeness results. In our proofs, we shall use the fact that the following problem is NP-complete:

- *PC3C-Hamiltonian*

- Instance: Planar, cubic, 3-connected graph G.

- Question: Is G Hamiltonian?

- We begin by showing that the following problem is NP-complete.

- *Unrooted tree-based*

- Instance: Network N on X.

- Question: Is N tree-based?

Theorem: The problem Unrooted tree-based is NP-complete.

Proof: First note that Unrooted tree-based is in NP since we can check in polynomial time if a given tree in N is a spanning tree for N with leaf set X.

To complete the proof, we show that there is a polynomial-time reduction from PC3C-Hamiltonian to Unrooted tree-based.

Let C be a planar, cubic, 3-connected graph. By Lemma 4(ii) it follows that C is Hamiltonian if and only if the network Ce (x, y) on the set {x, y} is tree-based for some edge e in C. Since the number of edges in C is equal to $3|V(C)| / 2$, it follows that there is a polynomial-time reduction from PC3C-Hamiltonian to Unrooted tree-based (just check if Ce (x, y) is tree-based for each edge e in C; if the answer is no for every e, then C is not Hamiltonian; otherwise, C is Hamiltonian).

Interestingly, the analogous decision problem to Unrooted tree-based for rooted phylogenetic networks can be decided in polynomial time.

We now prove that a related decision problem is NP-complete. We say that a phylogenetic tree T on X is displayed by a network N on X if T can be obtained from a subtree T' of N by suppressing all degree 2 vertices in T' In addition, we say that T is a base-tree of N or N is based on T if T can be obtained in this way from a support tree T' of N. Note that a phylogenetic tree may be displayed by a network but need not be a support tree for the network. For example, the phylogenetic tree consisting of an edge with leaves x, y is displayed by the network in figure (e.g. consider the path of length 3 in the network between x and y), but it is not a support tree for that network.

We now consider the following decision problem.

Unrooted base-tree containment

Instance: Network N on X and a phylogenetic tree T on X.

Question: Is N based on T?

The analogous version of this decision problem for rooted phylogenetic networks is NP-complete. We now show that this is also the case for networks.

Theorem: The problem Unrooted base-tree containment is NP-complete.

Proof: First note that Unrooted base-tree containment is in NP since we can check in polynomial time if a subtree T' of N is a support tree of N, and that a given phylogenetic tree T can be obtained from T' by suppressing all degree 2 vertices in T'.

To complete the proof, we show that there is a polynomial-time reduction from PC3C-Hamiltonian to Unrooted base-tree containment.

Let C be a planar, cubic, 3-connected graph. By Lemma 4(iii) it follows that C is

Hamiltonian if and only if there is some edge e in C such that the network Ce (x, y) has a support tree consisting of a path with end vertices x and y which, in turn, holds if and only if the phylogenetic tree T consisting of a single edge and leaf set X={x, y} is a base-tree for the network Ce (x, y) for some edge e in C. Since the number of edges in C is equal to $3|V(C)| / 2$, it follows that there is a polynomial-time reduction from *PC3C-Hamiltonian* to *Unrooted base-tree containment* (just check if the single-edged phylogenetic tree T on {x, y} is a base-tree for the network Ce (x, y) for each edge e in C; if the answer is no for every e, then C is not Hamiltonian; otherwise, C is Hamiltonian).

It is also NP-complete to decide whether or not a network N displays a phylogenetic tree T.

Universal Tree-based Networks

In this section, we shall show that there are networks on X which can have *every* phylogenetic tree on X as a base-tree. To prove this, we will relate networks with rooted phylogenetic networks, which we now formally define.

A *rooted* phylogenetic network M (on X) is a directed acyclic graph with a single root (vertex with indegree 0 and outdegree 2), leaf set X (vertices with indegree 1 and outdegree 0), and all vertices except the root having degree 1 or 3. If M is a tree, then it is called a *rooted*phylogenetic tree on X. A rooted phylogenetic network M is called *tree-based* if it contains a directed spanning tree (an "arborescence") T such that the leaf set of T is X. In that case, T is called a *support tree* for M.

In Hayamizu it is shown that for every X there exists a "universal" rooted phylogenetic network M on X, that is, M is a tree-based, rooted phylogenetic network and has every possible rooted phylogenetic tree on X as a base-tree. We shall use this result to show that there are also universal networks. First, we present a relationship between tree-based networks and rooted phylogenetic networks.

Given a network N on X with $|X| \geq 2|$, a leaf $x \in X$, and some orientation o of the edges of N, we let N_o^x denote the directed graph which results by removing x and its pendant edge from N with edges oriented according to o.

Theorem: Suppose that N is a network on X and $x \in X$. Then N is tree-based if and only if there exists some orientation o of the edges of N making N_o^x a tree-based (rooted) network on $X - \{x\}$.

Proof: Suppose o is an orientation of the edges of N such that N_o^x is a tree-based, rooted network on $X - \{x\}$.. Pick some base-tree T in N_o^x Let v_x denote the vertex in N that is adjacent with $x$and let $v_1 \in V(N)$ denote one of the two other vertices in N adjacent with v_x. Then $v_1 \in V(T)$. Let T' be the tree obtained from T by first adding x to its leaf set, v_x to its vertex set, and (v_x, x) and (v_1, v_x) to its edge set and then ignoring the directions of the edges of T. Since T is a spanning tree of N_o^x with leaf set X–{x}, we clearly have that T′ is a spanning tree for N with leaf set X. Thus, N is tree-based.

Conversely, suppose that N is tree-based. Pick some support tree T in N and orient all edges in T away from x. Let $x, v_1, v_2, \ldots, v_m$ be some topological ordering of the vertices in T (i. e. an ordering that is consistent with the partial ordering induced by T). For each vertex v in T that is the end vertex of some edge in N not in T, starting with a vertex that comes earliest in the ordering, direct the edge away from v, and if such an edge is encountered that has already been directed, then ignore this. This choice o of orientations of the edges of N implies that N_o^x is a rooted phylogenetic network on X–{x} (since it has no directed cycles) with support tree T_o^x where o′ is the orientation of the edges induced by o.

Corollary: There exists a tree-based network N on X such that every phylogenetic tree T on X is a base-tree for N.

Proof: The cases X| = 1 and |X|=2 are obvious. Assume |X| ≥ 3. Let x ∈ X and set Y=X–{x}. Let M be a universal rooted network on Y Let ρ denote the root of M. Let N be the network on X obtained by adding x to the leaf set of M, a new vertex r to the vertex set of N, new edges {r, x} and {r, ρ} to M, and ignoring the orientations of all edges of M. Clearly, N is a network on X and M and N_o^x are isomorphic where o is the orientation of the edges of M. By Theorem 4, N is tree-based. Moreover, if T is any rooted phylogenetic tree on Y, then T is a base-tree for M because M is a universal network on Y. Hence, the tree T_x btained by adjoining the element x as a leaf to the root of T is a phylogenetic tree on X and ignoring its edge orientations renders it a base-tree for N. But it is straight-forward to check that the set,

$$\{T_x : x \in X \text{ and } T \text{ a rooted phylogenetic tree on } X - \{x\}\}$$

is equal to the set of phylogenetic trees on X. The corollary follows immediately.

Fully Tree-based Networks

In Semple (2016) a characterization of rooted phylogenetic networks in which every embedded phylogenetic tree with the same leaf set is a base-tree is given (these are precisely the "tree-child" networks). In our last result, we will characterize networks that have an analogous property.

Note that a network N on X always contains a subtree with the same leaf set as N. For example, if we fix some x ∈ X and let p_{xy} be some path in N for all y ∈ X–{x} , then the tree obtained by removing (if necessary) a minimum number of edges from the union of the paths p_{xy} over all y ∈ X–{x} is a subtree of N with leaf set X.

We call a network N on X *fully tree-based* if every subtree of N with leaf set X is a support tree for N. Note that by the previous remark, any fully tree-based network is tree-based.

Lemma: Suppose that N is a simple, tree-based network and that T is a base-tree for N. If $e = \{v1, v\}, e' = \{v, v2\}$ are incident edges in T such that neither e nor e' are pendant edges of T, and Te and Te' are the trees which are obtained by deleting e and e', respectively, that do not contain v, then there must exist some edge e'' in N which has one vertex in Te and the other in Te'.

Proof: Suppose that there is no edge e'' with the stated properties. Then there exists only one path in N between v_1 and v_2. But this contradicts the fact that N is simple, and therefore the graph N with all pendant edges removed is 2-connected.

Lemma: Suppose that N is a simple, level-k network, k≥1 ,on X, |X|≥2 . Then N contains a vertex which is not contained in a pendant edge of N if and only if k≠1 .

Proof: Since N is simple, $|V(N)| = 2\,(|X|-1+k)$. Now, let q be the number of vertices in N which are not contained in any pendant edge of N. Then clearly,

$$|V(N)| = 2\,|X| + q.$$

Therefore, q=2 k−2. The lemma now follows immediately.

We now characterize fully tree-based networks. Note that these are significantly less complex than the tree-child networks mentioned above.

Theorem: Suppose that N is a network on X. Then N is fully tree-based if and only if N is a level-1 network.

Proof: The statement is clearly true if |X|=1. So we assume from now on that |X|≥2.

By Proposition 1, it suffices to assume that N is simple.

If N is a simple, level-1 network, then it is straight-forward to check that it is fully tree-based.

Conversely, suppose for contradiction that N is a simple network on X which is not level-1, and that N is fully tree-based. Let T be a support tree for N.

Suppose that v is a vertex in T that is not contained in some pendant edge of N. Note that such a vertex exists by Lemma 6 since N is not level-1.

If the degree of v in T is 2, then let $e = \{v_1, v\}, e' = \{v, v_2\}$ enote its incident edges neither of which can be a pendant edge in N. Then, by Lemma 5, we can remove edges e,e' from T and add in an edge $e'' \in E(N)$ in between a vertex of Te and a vertex of Te' where Te and Te′ are as in the proof of that lemma. Since the degree of v in T is 2, the resulting tree T′ has leaf set X. Moreover T′ does not contain the vertex v. But this contradicts the fact that N is fully tree-based.

If the degree of v in T is 3, then let $e = \{v_1, v\}, e' = \{v, v_2\}$ be two edges incident with v. Then by Lemma 5, there is an edge e″ between a vertex of Te and a vertex of Te′. Now, if we remove e from T and add in edge e″, we obtain a new tree T′ that is a support tree for N and which contains a vertex (namely v) with degree 2, such that neither of the edges in T′ incident with v is a pendant edge of T′. But this is impossible by the argument presented above.

Advances in Computational Methods for Phylogenetic Networks

Phylogenetic networks extend phylogenetic trees to allow for modeling reticulate evolutionary processes such as hybridization. They take the shape of a rooted, directed, acyclic graph, and when parameterized with evolutionary parameters, such as divergence times and population sizes, they form a generative process of molecular sequence evolution. Early work on computational methods for phylogenetic network inference focused exclusively on reticulations and sought networks with the fewest number of reticulations to fit the data. As processes such as incomplete lineage sorting (ILS) could be at play concurrently with hybridization, work in the last decade has shifted to computational approaches for phylogenetic network inference in the presence of ILS. In such a short period, significant advances have been made on developing and implementing such computational approaches. In particular, parsimony, likelihood, and Bayesian methods have been devised for estimating phylogenetic networks and associated parameters using estimated gene trees as data. Use of those inference methods has been augmented with statistical tests for specific hypotheses of hybridization, like the D-statistic. Most recently, Bayesian approaches for inferring phylogenetic networks directly from sequence data were developed and implemented. In this chapter, we survey such advances and discuss model assumptions as well as methods' strengths and limitations.

References

- Phylogenetics, science: britannica.com, Retrieved 1 August, 2019

- Gu X, Li WH (September 1992). "Higher rates of amino acid substitution in rodents than in humans". Mol. Phylogenet. Evol. 1 (3): 211–4. doi:10.1016/1055-7903(92)90017-B. PMID 1342937, Retrieved 3 February, 2019

- Felsenstein J (1981). "Evolutionary trees from DNA sequences: a maximum likelihood approach". J. Mol. Evol. 17 (6): 368–76. doi:10.1007/BF01734359. PMID 7288891, Retrieved 12 April, 2019

- Mount DM (2004). Bioinformatics: Sequence and Genome Analysis (2nd ed.). Cold Spring Harbor, New York: Cold Spring Harbor Laboratory Press. ISBN 978-0-87969-712-9, Retrieved 19 January, 2019

- Ratner VA, Zharkikh AA, Kolchanov N, Rodin S, Solovyov S, Antonov AS (1995). Molecular Evolution. Biomathematics Series. 24. New York: Springer-Verlag. ISBN 978-3-662-12530-4, Retrieved 9 March, 2019

Chapter 4

Bioinformatics: Algorithms and Analysis

The branch of science which is involved in developing methods and software tools in order to understand biological data is referred to as bioinformatics. It is used in sequence analysis and gene prediction. The topics elaborated in this chapter will help in gaining a better perspective about the different techniques and processes associated with bioinformatics.

Bioinformatics is a hybrid science that links biological data with techniques for information storage, distribution, and analysis to support multiple areas of scientific research, including biomedicine. Bioinformatics is fed by high-throughput data-generating experiments, including genomic sequence determinations and measurements of gene expression patterns. Database projects curate and annotate the data and then distribute it via the World Wide Web. Mining these data leads to scientific discoveries and to the identification of new clinical applications. In the field of medicine in particular, a number of important applications for bioinformatics have been discovered. For example, it is used to identify correlations between gene sequences and diseases, to predict protein structures from amino acid sequences, to aid in the design of novel drugs, and to tailor treatments to individual patients based on their DNA sequences (pharmacogenomics).

The Data of Bioinformatics

The classic data of bioinformatics include DNA sequences of genes or full genomes; amino acid sequences of proteins; and three-dimensional structures of proteins, nucleic acids and protein–nucleic acid complexes. Additional "-omics" data streams include: transcriptomics, the pattern of RNA synthesis from DNA; proteomics, the distribution of proteins in cells; interactomics, the patterns of protein-protein and protein–nucleic acid interactions; and metabolomics, the nature and traffic patterns of transformations of small molecules by the biochemical pathways active in cells. In each case there is interest in obtaining comprehensive, accurate data for particular cell types and in identifying patterns of variation within the data. For example, data may fluctuate depending on cell type, timing of data collection (during the cell cycle, or diurnal, seasonal, or annual variations), developmental stage, and various external conditions. Metagenomics and metaproteomics extend these measurements to a comprehensive description of the organisms in an environmental sample, such as in a bucket of ocean water or in a soil sample.

Bioinformatics has been driven by the great acceleration in data-generation processes in biology. Genome sequencing methods show perhaps the most dramatic effects. In 1999 the nucleic acid sequence archives contained a total of 3.5 billion nucleotides, slightly more than the length of a single human genome; a decade later they contained more than 283 billion nucleotides, the length of about 95 human genomes. The U.S. National Institutes of Health has challenged researchers by setting a goal to reduce the cost of sequencing a human genome to $1,000; this would make DNA sequencing a more affordable and practical tool for U.S. hospitals and clinics, enabling it to become a standard component of diagnosis.

Storage and Retrieval of Data

In bioinformatics, data banks are used to store and organize data. Many of these entities collect DNA and RNA sequences from scientific papers and genome projects. Many databases are in the hands of international consortia. For example, an advisory committee made up of members of the European Molecular Biology Laboratory Nucleotide Sequence Database (EMBL-Bank) in the United Kingdom, the DNA Data Bank of Japan (DDBJ), and GenBank of the National Center for Biotechnology Information (NCBI) in the United States oversees the International Nucleotide Sequence Database Collaboration (INSDC). To ensure that sequence data are freely available, scientific journals require that new nucleotide sequences be deposited in a publicly accessible database as a condition for publication of an article. (Similar conditions apply to nucleic acid and protein structures.) There also exist genome browsers, databases that bring together all the available genomic and molecular information about a particular species.

The major database of biological macromolecular structure is the worldwide Protein Data Bank (wwPDB), a joint effort of the Research Collaboratory for Structural Bioinformatics (RCSB) in the United States, the Protein Data Bank Europe (PDBe) at the European Bioinformatics Institute in the United Kingdom, and the Protein Data Bank Japan at Ōsaka University. The homepages of the wwPDB partners contain links to the data files themselves, to expository and tutorial material (including news items), to facilities for deposition of new entries, and to specialized search software for retrieving structures.

Information retrieval from the data archives utilizes standard tools for identification of data items by keyword; for instance, one can type "aardvark myoglobin" into Google and retrieve the molecule's amino acid sequence. Other algorithms search data banks to detect similarities between data items. For example, a standard problem is to probe a sequence database with a gene or protein sequence of interest in order to detect entities with similar sequences.

Goals of Bioinformatics

The development of efficient algorithms for measuring sequence similarity is an important goal of bioinformatics. The Needleman-Wunsch algorithm, which is based on dynamic programming, guarantees finding the optimal alignment of pairs of sequences.

This algorithm essentially divides a large problem (the full sequence) into a series of smaller problems (short sequence segments) and uses the solutions of the smaller problems to construct a solution to the large problem. Similarities in sequences are scored in a matrix, and the algorithm allows for the detection of gaps in sequence alignment.

Although the Needleman-Wunsch algorithm is effective, it is too slow for probing a large sequence database. Therefore, much attention has been given to finding fast information-retrieval algorithms that can deal with the vast amounts of data in the archives. An example is the program BLAST (Basic Local Alignment Search Tool). A development of BLAST, known as position-specific iterated- (or PSI-) BLAST, makes use of patterns of conservation in related sequences and combines the high speed of BLAST with very high sensitivity to find related sequences.

Another goal of bioinformatics is the extension of experimental data by predictions. A fundamental goal of computational biology is the prediction of protein structure from an amino acid sequence. The spontaneous folding of proteins shows that this should be possible. Progress in the development of methods to predict protein folding is measured by biennial Critical Assessment of Structure Prediction (CASP) programs, which involve blind tests of structure prediction methods.

Bioinformatics is also used to predict interactions between proteins, given individual structures of the partners. This is known as the "docking problem." Protein-protein complexes show good complementarity in surface shape and polarity and are stabilized largely by weak interactions, such as burial of hydrophobic surface, hydrogen bonds, and van der Waals forces. Computer programs simulate these interactions to predict the optimal spatial relationship between binding partners. A particular challenge, one that could have important therapeutic applications, is to design an antibody that binds with high affinity to a target protein.

Initially, much bioinformatics research has had a relatively narrow focus, concentrating on devising algorithms for analyzing particular types of data, such as gene sequences or protein structures. Now, however, the goals of bioinformatics are integrative and are aimed at figuring out how combinations of different types of data can be used to understand natural phenomena, including organisms and disease.

Bioinformatics Algorithms

Algorithmic techniques for solving problems in bioinformatics, including applications that shed new light on molecular biology. This book introduces algorithmic techniques in bioinformatics, emphasizing their application to solving novel problems in post-genomic molecular biology. Beginning with a thought-provoking discussion on the role of algorithms in twenty-first-century bioinformatics education, Bioinformatics

Algorithms covers: General algorithmic techniques, including dynamic programming, graph-theoretical methods, hidden Markov models, the fast Fourier transform, seeding, and approximation algorithms. Algorithms and tools for genome and sequence analysis, including formal and approximate models for gene clusters, advanced algorithms for non-overlapping local alignments and genome tilings, multiplex PCR primer set selection, and sequence/network motif finding. Microarray design and analysis, including algorithms for microarray physical design, missing value imputation, and meta-analysis of gene expression data. Algorithmic issues arising in the analysis of genetic variation across human population, including computational inference of haplotypes from genotype data and disease association search in case/control epidemiologic studies. Algorithmic approaches in structural and systems biology, including topological and structural classification in biochemistry, and prediction of protein-protein and domain-domain interactions.

An algorithm is a computable set of steps to achieve a desired result.

We use algorithms every day. For example, a recipe for baking a cake is an algorithm. Most programs, with the exception of some artificial intelligence applications, consist of algorithms. Inventing elegant algorithms-algorithms that are simple and require the fewest steps possible is one of the principal challenges in programming. An algorithm is a description of a procedure which terminates with a result. In other words an algorithm is a set of instructions, sometimes called a procedure or a function, that is used to perform a certain task. This can be a simple process, such as adding two numbers together, or a complex function, such as adding effects to an image. For example, in order to sharpen a digital photo, the algorithm would need to process each pixel in the image and determine which ones to change and how much to change them in order to make the image look sharper.

In mathematics, computer science, and related subjects, an algorithm is an effective method for solving a problem using a finite sequence of instructions. Algorithms are used for calculation, data processing, and many other fields.

Each algorithm is a list of well-defined instructions for completing a task. Starting from an initial state, the instructions describe a computation that proceeds through a well-defined series of successive states, eventually terminating in a final ending state. The transition from one state to the next is not necessarily deterministic; some algorithms, known as randomized algorithms, incorporate randomness.

Classification

Classification by Purpose

Each algorithm has a goal, for example, the purpose of the Quick Sort algorithm is to sort data in ascending or descending order. But the number of goals is infinite, and we have to group them by kind of purposes.

Classification by Implementation

An algorithm may be implemeted according to different basical principles:

- Recursive or iterative

A recursive algorithm is one that calls itself repeatedly until a certain condition matches. It is a method common to functional programming.

Iterative algorithms use repetitive constructs like loops.

Some problems are better suited for one implementation or the other. For example, the towers of hanoi problem is well understood in recursive implementation. Every recursive version has an iterative equivalent iterative, and vice versa.

- Logical or procedural

An algorithm may be viewed as controlled logical deduction.

A logic component expresses the axioms which may be used in the computation and a control component determines the way in which deduction is applied to the axioms.

This is the basis of the logic programming. In pure logic programming languages the control component is fixed and algorithms are specified by supplying only the logic component.

- Serial or parallel

Algorithms are usually discussed with the assumption that computers execute one instruction of an algorithm at a time. This is a serial algorithm, as opposed to parallel algorithms, which take advantage of computer architectures to process several instructions at once. They divide the problem into sub-problems and pass them to several processors. Iterative algorithms are generally parallelizable. Sorting algorithms can be parallelized efficiently.

- Deterministic or non-deterministic

Deterministic algorithms solve the problem with a predefined process whereas non-deterministic algorithm must perform guesses of best solution at each step through the use of heuristics.

Classification by Design Paradigm

A design paradigm is a domain in research or class of problems that requires a dedicated kind of algorithm:

- Divide and conquer

A divide and conquer algorithm repeatedly reduces an instance of a problem to one or more smaller instances of the same problem (usually recursively), until the instances are small enough to solve easily. One such example of divide and conquer is merge sorting. Sorting can be done on each segment of data after dividing data into segments and sorting of entire data can be obtained in conquer phase by merging them.

The binary search algorithm is an example of a variant of divide and conquer called decrease and conquer algorithm, that solves an identical subproblem and uses the solution of this subproblem to solve the bigger problem.

- Dynamic programming

The shortest path in a weighted graph can be found by using the shortest path to the goal from all adjacent vertices.

When the optimal solution to a problem can be constructed from optimal solutions to subproblems, using dynamic programming avoids recomputing solutions that have already been computed.

The main difference with the "divide and conquer" approach is, subproblems are independent in divide and conquer, where as the overlap of subproblems occur in dynamic programming.

Dynamic programming and memoization go together. The difference with straightforward recursion is in caching or memoization of recursive calls. Where subproblems are independent, this is useless. By using memoization or maintaining a table of subproblems already solved, dynamic programming reduces the exponential nature of many problems to polynomial complexity.

- The greedy method

A greedy algorithm is similar to a dynamic programming algorithm, but the difference is that solutions to the subproblems do not have to be known at each stage. Instead a "greedy" choice can be made of what looks the best solution for the moment. The most popular greedy algorithm is finding the minimal spanning tree as given by Kruskal.

- Linear programming

The problem is expressed as a set of linear inequalities and then an attempt is made to maximize or minimize the inputs. This can solve many problems such as the maximum flow for directed graphs, notably by using the simplex algorithm.

A complex variant of linear programming is called integer programming, where the solution space is restricted to all integers.

- Reduction also called transform and conquer

Solve a problem by transforming it into another problem. A simple example: finding the median in an unsorted list is first translating this problem into sorting problem and finding the middle element in sorted list. The main goal of reduction is finding the simplest transformation possible.

- Using graphs

Many problems, such as playing chess, can be modeled as problems on graphs. A graph exploration algorithms are used.

This category also includes the search algorithms and backtracking.

The Probabilistic and Heuristic Paradigm

- Probabilistic

Those that make some choices randomly.

- Genetic

Attempt to find solutions to problems by mimicking biological evolutionary processes, with a cycle of random mutations yielding successive generations of "solutions". Thus, they emulate reproduction and "survival of the fittest".

- Heuristic

Whose general purpose is not to find an optimal solution, but an approximate solution where the time or resources to find a perfect solution are not practical.

Classification by Complexity

Some algorithms complete in linear time, and some complete in exponential amount of time, and some never complete.

Hirschberg's Algorithm

Hirschberg's a dynamic programming algorithm algorithm developed by Dan Hirschberg has the capability of finding the best sequence alognment of two sequences. The algorithm utilizes Levenshtein edit distance which is distance between two strings is the number of single character deletions, insertions, or substitutions required to transform one string into the other. It can also be defined as an modified version of Needleman-Wunsh algorithm, it is more space efficient and uses the divide and conquer strategy.

Time and Space Calculations

The major application of this algorithm is to search optimal sequence alignment between two nucleotide or amino acid sequences. There are also suboptimal heuristics approaches of sequence alignment e.g BLAST and FASTA. Finding optimal sequence alignment requires computational resources in terms of time and space. For example, Needle-man-Wunsh algorithm will take O(nm) time and O(nm) space for finding an optimal sequence alignment of two strings of x and y, where length(x) = n and length(y) = m. On the other hand Hirschberg's algorithm still takes O(nm) time, but needs only O(min{n,m}) space. Hirschberg's algorithm is also a space-efficient way to calculate the longest common subsequence between two sets of data such as with the common diff tool.

How we Compute Levenshtein Edit Distance

For calculating the least score (Edit(x,y)) required for change x into y by using insertions, substitutions and deletions, we give a score to each of the event. For example, we give a score for inserting a character "A" into substring, a score for substituting character "B" with "A" in the string and similarly a score for deleting a character "A" from the string. The standard score can be Ins(a) = Del(a) = 1 for each character a, Sub(a,a) = 0, and Sub(a,b) = 1 if a is not equal to b.

Differences with Needleman-wunsch Algorithm

Levenshtein edit distances can be computed using linear space. What we call the "forward subprogram" computes the values of Edit(Prefix[x,i],Prefix[y,j]) for all i and j, just as the Needleman-Wunsch and returns the array {Edit(x,Prefix[y,j])}0 = j = m. The "backward subprogram" is similar, except that the dynamic program is done in the opposite direction, i.e., starting from the right ends of the strings. It returns the array {Edit(x,Suffix[y,j])}0 = j = m, where Suffix[y,j] is the suffix of y of length j.

The Algorithm

Compute V(A, B) while saving the values of the -th row. Denote D(A,B) as the Forward Matrix F.

Compute V(Ar, Br) while saving the -th row. Denote D(Ar, Br) as the Backward Matrix B.

Find the column k* so that the crossing point (, k*) satisfies:

Now that k* is found, recursively partition the problem to two sub problems:

Find the path from (0,0) to (, k*).

Find the path from (n, m) to (, m - k*).

High-level Description of the Forwards Subprogram

Forwards[x,y] is:

```
1.  n = length(x); m = length(y)

2.  Edit[Prefix[0,0]] = 0;
```

```
3. For all i from 1 to n:

   Edit[Prefix[x,i],Prefix[y,0]] = Edit[Prefix[x,i-1],Prefix[y,0]]

   + Del(x_i)

4. For all j from 1 to m:

   A. Edit[Prefix[x,0],Prefix[y,j]] = Edit[Prefix[x,0],Prefix[y,j-1]]

      + Ins(y_j)

   B. For all i from 1 to n, execute the following steps:

      i. Edit[Prefix[x,i],Prefix[y,j]] =

         min{Edit[Prefix[x,i-1],Prefix[y,j]] + Del(x_i),

         Edit[Prefix[x,i-1],Prefix[y,j-1]] + Sub(x_i,y_j),

         Edit[Prefix[x,i],Prefix[y,j-1]] + Ins(y_j)}

      ii. Erase Edit[Prefix[x,i-1],Prefix[y,j-1]]

   C. Erase Edit[Prefix[x,i-1],Prefix[y,j]]

5. RETURN Edit[x] %% an array of length m+1
```

High-level Description of the Backwards Subprogram

Backwards[x,y] is:

```
1. n = length(x); m = length(y)

2. For all i from 1 to n:

   Edit[Suffix[x,i],Suffix[y,0]] = 0

3. For all j from 1 to m:

   A. Edit[Suffix[x,0],Suffix[y,j]] = Edit[Suffix[x,n],Suffix[y,j-1]] +

      Ins(y_{m-j+1})

   B. For all i from 1 to n:

      i. Edit[Suffix[x,i],Suffix[y,j]] =

         min{Edit[Suffix[x,i-1],Suffix[y,j]] + Del(x_{n-i-1}),

         Edit[Suffix[x,i-1],Suffix[y,j-1]] +

         Sub(x_{n-i-1},y_{m-j+1}),

         Edit[Suffix[x,i],Suffix[y,j-1]] + Ins(y_{m-j+1})}

      ii. Erase Edit[Suffix[x,i-1],Suffix[y,j-1]]

   C. Erase Edit[Suffix[x,i-1],Suffix[y,j]]

4. RETURN Edit[x] %% an array of length m+1
```

High level description of Hirschberg's algorithm

Hirschberg(x,y) is:

```
1. n = length(x); m = length(y)

2. If n <= 1 or m <= 1:

   OUTPUT Alignment(x,y) using Needleman-Wunsch.

   Else:

   A. mid = floor(n/2)

   B   x_left = Prefix[x,mid]

   C. x_right = Suffix[x,n-mid]

   D. Edit[x_left] = Forwards(x_left,y)

      %% an array of length m+1

   E. Edit[x_right] = Backwards(x_right,y)

      %% an array of length m+1

   F. cut = ArgMin{Edit[x_left,Prefix[y,j]] +

      Edit[x_right,Suffix[y,m-j]]} %% j ranges from 1 to m-1

   G. Hirschberg(x_left,Prefix[y,cut])

   H. Hirschberg(x_right,Suffix[y,m-cut])
```

Smith-waterman Algorithm

The Smith–Waterman algorithm is a well-known algorithm for performing local sequence alignment; that is, for determining similar regions between two nucleotide or protein sequences. Instead of looking at the total sequence, the Smith–Waterman algorithm compares segments of all possible lengths and optimizes the similarity measure. This algorithm is a variation of Needleman-Wunsch Algorithm developed by Temple F. Smith and Michael S. Waterman in 1981, it is also a dynamic programming algorithm to find the optimal local alignment with respect to the scoring system being used. The major difference from Needleman-Wunsch algorithm includes:

1. In order to highlight the best local alignments; negative scoring matrix cells are set to zero.

2. Traceback procedure starts at the highest scoring matrix cell and proceeds until a cell with score zero is encountered.

This algorithm was designed to sensitively detect similarities in highly diverged sequences. For the purpose of explanation, first summarizing the algorithm in to simple steps and then I will move forwards with examples and explanations.

Algorithm is similar to global alignment with modified boundary conditions and recurrence rules:

1. The top row and left column are now filled with 0.

2. If the (sub-)alignment score becomes negative, restart the search:

$$F(i, j) = \max \begin{cases} 0, \\ F(i-1, j-1) + s(x_i, y_i), \\ F(i-1, j) - d, \\ F(i, j-1) - d. \end{cases}$$

3. Traceback is from the maximum of F (i, j) in the whole matrix to the first 0.

4. Example: the optimal local alignment between HEAGAWGHEE and PAWHEAE is AWGHE::AW-HE.

5. Issue: In gapped alignments, the expected score for a random match may be positive.

Example of Smith–Waterman Algorithm

1. Start with a N x N integer matrix where N is sequence length (both s and t). Compute M[i][j] based on Score Matrix and optimum score compute so far (DP).

	0	C	G	G	G	T	A	T	C	C	A	A
0												
C												
C												
C												
T												
A												
G												
G												
T												
C												
C												
C												
C												

2. Understanding the Matrix

- Alignment

  t : - - - - - - - -
  s : c c c t a g g t

	0	C	G	G	G	T	A	T	C	C	A	A
0	0											
C	0											
C	0											
C	0											
T	0											
A	0											
G	0											
G	0											
T	0											
C	0											
C	0											
C	0											
C	0											

- Alignment

  t : c g g g t a t ...
  s : - - - - - - - ...

	0	C	G	G	G	T	A	T	C	C	A	A
0	0	0	0	0	0	0	0	0	0	0	0	0
C	0											
C	0											
C	0											
T	0											
A	0											
G	0											
G	0											
T	0											
C	0											
C	0											
C	0											
C	0											

3. Computing cell scores: Finding m[i][j]: There are three ways to finish the alignment of so..i and to..j

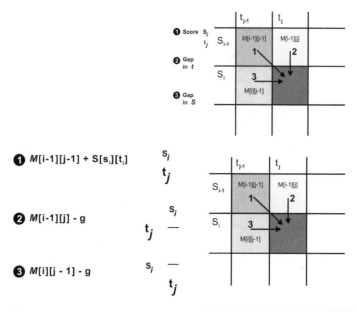

① $M[i-1][j-1] + S[s_i][t_j]$

② $M[i-1][j] - g$

③ $M[i][j-1] - g$

4. Scoring process: Element Computation M[i][j]:

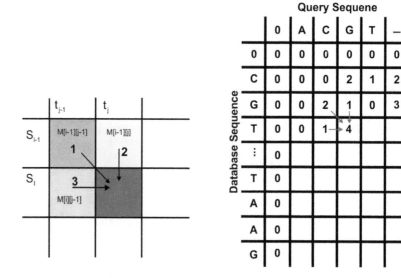

$$M[i][0] = 0 \; M[0][j] = 0$$

$$M[i][j] = \max \begin{cases} M[i-1][j-1] + S[s_i][t_j] & \text{if } s_i t_j \\ M[i-1][j] - d & \text{if } s_i - \\ M[i][j-1] - d & \text{if} - t_j \end{cases}$$

5. Backtracking Process: For finding the BEST local alignment, find the highest score and then traceback to first 0.

Scoring used in this example:

	A	R	N	D	C	Q	E	G	H	I	L	K	M	F	P	S	T	W	Y	V
A	2																			
R	-2	6																		
N	0	0	2																	
D	0	-1	2	4																
C	-2	-4	-4	-5	4															
Q	0	1	1	2	-5	4														
E	0	-1	1	3	-5	2	4													
G	1	-3	0	1	-3	-1	0	5												
H	-1	2	2	1	-3	3	1	-2	6											
I	-1	-2	-2	-2	-2	-2	-2	-3	-2	5										
L	-2	-3	-3	-4	-6	-2	-3	-4	-2	2	6									
K	-1	3	1	0	-5	1	0	-2	0	-2	-3	5								
M	-1	0	-2	-3	-5	-1	-2	-3	-2	2	4	0	6							
F	-4	-4	-4	-6	-4	-5	-5	-5	-2	1	2	-5	0	9						
P	1	0	-1	-1	-3	0	-1	-1	0	-2	-3	-1	-2	-5	6					
S	1	0	1	0	0	-1	0	1	-1	-1	-3	0	-2	-3	1	3				
T	1	-1	0	0	-2	-1	0	0	-1	0	-2	0	-1	-2	0	1	3			
W	-6	2	-4	-7	-8	-5	-7	-7	-3	-5	-2	-3	-4	0	-6	-2	-5	17		
Y	-3	-4	-2	-4	0	-4	-4	-5	0	-1	-1	-4	-2	7	-5	-3	-3	0	10	
V	0	-2	-2	-2	-2	-2	-2	-1	-2	4	2	-2	2	-1	-1	-1	0	-6	2	4

- Diag - the letters from two sequences are aligned

- Left - a gap is introduced in the left sequence

- Up - a gap is introduced in the top sequence

$$Score_{opt} = \max_{i,j=1}^{N} M[i][j]$$

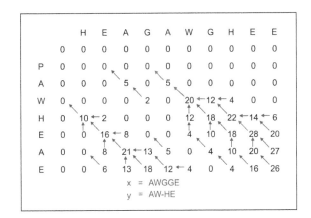

Structural Bioinformatics

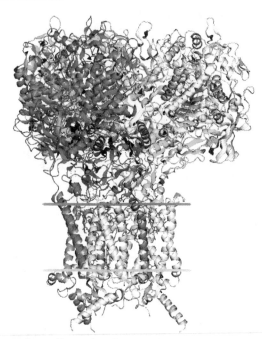

Three-dimensional structure of a protein.

Structural bioinformatics is the branch of bioinformatics which is related to the analysis and prediction of the three-dimensional structure of biological macromolecules such as proteins, RNA, and DNA. It deals with generalizations about macromolecular 3D structure such as comparisons of overall folds and local motifs, principles of molecular folding, evolution, and binding interactions, and structure/function relationships, working both from experimentally solved structures and from computational models. The term *structural* has the same meaning as in structural biology, and structural bioinformatics can be seen as a part of computational structural biology.

Informatics approaches used in structural bioinformatics are:

- Selection of Target - Potential targets are identified by comparing them with databases of known structures and sequence. The importance of a target can be decided on the basis of published literature. Target can also be selected on the basis of its protein domain. Protein domain are building blocks that can be rearranged to form new proteins. They can be studied in isolation initially.

- Tracking X-ray crystallography trials - X-Ray crystallography can be used to reveal three-dimensional structure of a protein. But, in order to use X-ray for studying protein crystals, pure proteins crystals must be formed, which can take a lot of trials. This leads to a need for tracking the conditions and results of trials. Furthermore, supervised machine learning algorithms can be used on the stored data to identify conditions that might increase the yield of pure crystals.

- Analysis of X-Ray crystallographic data - The diffraction pattern obtained as a result of bombarding X-rays on electrons is Fourier transform of electron density distribution. There is a need for algorithms that can deconvolve Fourier transform with partial information (due to missing phase information, as the detectors can only measure amplitude of diffracted X-rays, and not the phase shifts). Extrapolation technique such as Multiwavelength anomalous dispersion can be used to generate electron density map, which uses the location of selenium atoms as a reference to determine rest of the structure. Standard Ball-and-stick model is generated from the electron density map.

- Analysis of NMR spectroscopy data - Nuclear magnetic resonance spectroscopy experiments produce two (or higher) dimensional data, with each peak corresponding to a chemical group within the sample. Optimization methods are used to convert spectra into three dimensional structures.

- Correlating Structural information with functional information - Structural studies can be used as probe for structural-functional relationship.

Sequence Analysis

Since the Phage Φ-X174 was sequenced in 1977, the DNA sequences of thousands of organisms have been decoded and stored in databases. This sequence information is analyzed to determine genes that encode proteins, RNA genes, regulatory sequences, structural motifs, and repetitive sequences. A comparison of genes within a species or between different species can show similarities between protein functions, or relations between species (the use of molecular systematics to construct phylogenetic trees). With the growing amount of data, it long ago became impractical to analyze DNA sequences manually. Today, computer programs such as BLAST are used daily to search sequences from more than 260 000 organisms, containing over 190 billion nucleotides. These programs can compensate for mutations (exchanged, deleted or inserted bases) in the DNA sequence, to identify sequences that are related, but not identical. A variant of this sequence alignment is used in the sequencing process itself. For the special task of taxonomic classification of sequence snippets, modern k-mer based software like Kraken achieves throughput unreachable by alignment methods.

DNA Sequencing

Before sequences can be analyzed they have to be obtained. DNA sequencing is still a non-trivial problem as the raw data may be noisy or afflicted by weak signals. Algorithms have been developed for base calling for the various experimental approaches to DNA sequencing.

Sequence Assembly

Most DNA sequencing techniques produce short fragments of sequence that need to be assembled to obtain complete gene or genome sequences. The so-called shotgun sequencing technique (which was used, for example, by The Institute for Genomic Research (TIGR) to sequence the first bacterial genome, *Haemophilus influenzae*) generates the sequences of many thousands of small DNA fragments (ranging from 35 to 900 nucleotides long, depending on the sequencing technology). The ends of these fragments overlap and, when aligned properly by a genome assembly program, can be used to reconstruct the complete genome. Shotgun sequencing yields sequence data quickly, but the task of assembling the fragments can be quite complicated for larger genomes. For a genome as large as the human genome, it may take many days of CPU time on large-memory, multiprocessor computers to assemble the fragments, and the resulting assembly usually contains numerous gaps that must be filled in later. Shotgun sequencing is the method of choice for virtually all genomes sequenced today, and genome assembly algorithms are a critical area of bioinformatics research.

Genome Annotation

In the context of genomics, annotation is the process of marking the genes and other biological features in a DNA sequence. This process needs to be automated because most genomes are too large to annotate by hand, not to mention the desire to annotate as many genomes as possible, as the rate of sequencing has ceased to pose a bottleneck. Annotation is made possible by the fact that genes have recognisable start and stop regions, although the exact sequence found in these regions can vary between genes.

The first description of a comprehensive genome annotation system was published in 1995 by the team at The Institute for Genomic Research that performed the first complete sequencing and analysis of the genome of a free-living organism, the bacterium *Haemophilus influenzae*. Owen White designed and built a software system to identify the genes encoding all proteins, transfer RNAs, ribosomal RNAs (and other sites) and to make initial functional assignments. Most current genome annotation systems work similarly, but the programs available for analysis of genomic DNA, such as the GeneMark program trained and used to find protein-coding genes in *Haemophilus influenzae*, are constantly changing and improving.

Following the goals that the Human Genome Project left to achieve after its closure in 2003, a new project developed by the National Human Genome Research Institute in the U.S appeared. The so-called ENCODE project is a collaborative data collection of the functional elements of the human genome that uses next-generation DNA-sequencing technologies and genomic tiling arrays, technologies able to automatically generate large amounts of data at a dramatically reduced per-base cost but with the same accuracy (base call error) and fidelity (assembly error).

Computational Evolutionary Biology

Evolutionary biology is the study of the origin and descent of species, as well as their change over time. Informatics has assisted evolutionary biologists by enabling researchers to:

- Trace the evolution of a large number of organisms by measuring changes in their DNA, rather than through physical taxonomy or physiological observations alone,

- Compare entire genomes, which permits the study of more complex evolutionary events, such as gene duplication, horizontal gene transfer, and the prediction of factors important in bacterial speciation,

- Build Complex computational population genetics models to predict the outcome of the system over time,

- Track and share information on an increasingly large number of species and organisms.

Future work endeavours to reconstruct the now more complex tree of life.

The area of research within computer science that uses genetic algorithms is sometimes confused with computational evolutionary biology, but the two areas are not necessarily related.

Comparative Genomics

The core of comparative genome analysis is the establishment of the correspondence between genes (orthology analysis) or other genomic features in different organisms. It is these intergenomic maps that make it possible to trace the evolutionary processes responsible for the divergence of two genomes. A multitude of evolutionary events acting at various organizational levels shape genome evolution. At the lowest level, point mutations affect individual nucleotides. At a higher level, large chromosomal segments undergo duplication, lateral transfer, inversion, transposition, deletion and insertion. Ultimately, whole genomes are involved in processes of hybridization, polyploidization and endosymbiosis, often leading to rapid speciation. The complexity of genome evolution poses many exciting challenges to developers of mathematical models and algorithms, who have recourse to a spectrum of algorithmic, statistical and mathematical techniques, ranging from exact, heuristics, fixed parameter and approximation algorithms for problems based on parsimony models to Markov chain Monte Carlo algorithms for Bayesian analysis of problems based on probabilistic models.

Many of these studies are based on the detection of sequence homology to assign sequences to protein families.

Pan Genomics

Pan genomics is a concept introduced in 2005 by Tettelin and Medini which eventually took root in bioinformatics. Pan genome is the complete gene repertoire of a particular taxonomic group: although initially applied to closely related strains of a species, it can be applied to a larger context like genus, phylum etc. It is divided in two parts- The Core genome: Set of genes common to all the genomes under study (These are often house-keeping genes vital for survival) and The Dispensable/Flexible Genome: Set of genes not present in all but one or some genomes under study. A bioinformatics tool BPGA can be used to characterize the Pan Genome of bacterial species.

Genetics of Disease

With the advent of next-generation sequencing we are obtaining enough sequence data to map the genes of complex diseases infertility, breast cancer or Alzheimer's disease. Genome-wide association studies are a useful approach to pinpoint the mutations responsible for such complex diseases. Through these studies, thousands of DNA variants have been identified that are associated with similar diseases and traits. Furthermore, the possibility for genes to be used at prognosis, diagnosis or treatment is one of the most essential applications. Many studies are discussing both the promising ways to choose the genes to be used and the problems and pitfalls of using genes to predict disease presence or prognosis.

Analysis of Mutations in Cancer

In cancer, the genomes of affected cells are rearranged in complex or even unpredictable ways. Massive sequencing efforts are used to identify previously unknown point mutations in a variety of genes in cancer. Bioinformaticians continue to produce specialized automated systems to manage the sheer volume of sequence data produced, and they create new algorithms and software to compare the sequencing results to the growing collection of human genome sequences and germline polymorphisms. New physical detection technologies are employed, such as oligonucleotide microarrays to identify chromosomal gains and losses (called comparative genomic hybridization), and single-nucleotide polymorphism arrays to detect known *point mutations*. These detection methods simultaneously measure several hundred thousand sites throughout the genome, and when used in high-throughput to measure thousands of samples, generate terabytes of data per experiment. Again the massive amounts and new types of data generate new opportunities for bioinformaticians. The data is often found to contain considerable variability, or noise, and thus Hidden Markov model and change-point analysis methods are being developed to infer real copy number changes.

Two important principles can be used in the analysis of cancer genomes bioinformatically pertaining to the identification of mutations in the exome. First, cancer is a disease of accumulated somatic mutations in genes. Second cancer contains driver mutations which need to be distinguished from passengers.

With the breakthroughs that this next-generation sequencing technology is providing to the field of Bioinformatics, cancer genomics could drastically change. These new methods and software allow bioinformaticians to sequence many cancer genomes quickly and affordably. This could create a more flexible process for classifying types of cancer by analysis of cancer driven mutations in the genome. Furthermore, tracking of patients while the disease progresses may be possible in the future with the sequence of cancer samples.

Another type of data that requires novel informatics development is the analysis of lesions found to be recurrent among many tumors.

Gene and Protein Expression

Analysis of Gene Expression

The expression of many genes can be determined by measuring mRNA levels with multiple techniques including microarrays, expressed cDNA sequence tag (EST) sequencing, serial analysis of gene expression (SAGE) tag sequencing, massively parallel signature sequencing (MPSS), RNA-Seq, also known as "Whole Transcriptome Shotgun Sequencing" (WTSS), or various applications of multiplexed in-situ hybridization. All of these techniques are extremely noise-prone and/or subject to bias in the biological measurement, and a major research area in computational biology involves developing statistical tools to separate signal from noise in high-throughput gene expression studies. Such studies are often used to determine the genes implicated in a disorder: one might compare microarray data from cancerous epithelial cells to data from non-cancerous cells to determine the transcripts that are up-regulated and down-regulated in a particular population of cancer cells.

Analysis of Protein Expression

Protein microarrays and high throughput (HT) mass spectrometry (MS) can provide a snapshot of the proteins present in a biological sample. Bioinformatics is very much involved in making sense of protein microarray and HT MS data; the former approach faces similar problems as with microarrays targeted at mRNA, the latter involves the problem of matching large amounts of mass data against predicted masses from protein sequence databases, and the complicated statistical analysis of samples where multiple, but incomplete peptides from each protein are detected. Cellular protein localization in a tissue context can be achieved through affinity proteomics displayed as spatial data based on immunohistochemistry and tissue microarrays.

Analysis of Regulation

Gene regulation is the complex orchestration of events by which a signal, potentially an extracellular signal such as a hormone, eventually leads to an increase or decrease in the activity of one or more proteins. Bioinformatics techniques have been applied to explore various steps in this process.

For example, gene expression can be regulated by nearby elements in the genome. Promoter analysis involves the identification and study of sequence motifs in the DNA surrounding the coding region of a gene. These motifs influence the extent to which that region is transcribed into mRNA. Enhancer elements far away from the promoter can also regulate gene expression, through three-dimensional looping interactions. These interactions can be determined by bioinformatic analysis of chromosome conformation capture experiments.

Expression data can be used to infer gene regulation: one might compare microarray data from a wide variety of states of an organism to form hypotheses about the genes involved in each state. In a single-cell organism, one might compare stages of the cell cycle, along with various stress conditions (heat shock, starvation, etc.). One can then apply clustering algorithms to that expression data to determine which genes are co-expressed. For example, the upstream regions (promoters) of co-expressed genes can be searched for over-represented regulatory elements. Examples of clustering algorithms applied in gene clustering are k-means clustering, self-organizing maps (SOMs), hierarchical clustering, and consensus clustering methods.

Analysis of Cellular Organization

Several approaches have been developed to analyze the location of organelles, genes, proteins, and other components within cells. This is relevant as the location of these components affects the events within a cell and thus helps us to predict the behavior of biological systems. A gene ontology category, cellular compartment, has been devised to capture subcellular localization in many biological databases.

Microscopy and Image Analysis

Microscopic pictures allow us to locate both organelles as well as molecules. It may also help us to distinguish between normal and abnormal cells, e.g. in cancer.

Protein Localization

The localization of proteins helps us to evaluate the role of a protein. For instance, if a protein is found in the nucleus it may be involved in gene regulation or splicing. By contrast, if a protein is found in mitochondria, it may be involved in respiration or other metabolic processes. Protein localization is thus an important component of protein function prediction. There are well developed protein subcellular localization prediction resources available, including protein subcellular location databases, and prediction tools.

Nuclear Organization of Chromatin

Data from high-throughput chromosome conformation capture experiments, such as Hi-C (experiment) and ChIA-PET, can provide information on the spatial proximity of DNA loci. Analysis of these experiments can determine the three-dimensional structure and nuclear organization of chromatin. Bioinformatic challenges in this field include partitioning the genome into domains, such as Topologically Associating Domains (TADs), that are organised together in three-dimensional space.

Protein structure prediction is another important application of bioinformatics. The amino acid sequence of a protein, the so-called primary structure, can be easily determined from the sequence on the gene that codes for it. In the vast majority of cases, this primary structure uniquely determines a structure in its native environment. (Of course, there are exceptions, such as the bovine spongiform encephalopathy – a.k.a. Mad Cow Disease – prion.) Knowledge of this structure is vital in understanding the function of the protein. Structural information is usually classified as one of *secondary*, *tertiary* and *quaternary* structure. A viable general solution to such predictions remains an open problem. Most efforts have so far been directed towards heuristics that work most of the time.

One of the key ideas in bioinformatics is the notion of homology. In the genomic branch of bioinformatics, homology is used to predict the function of a gene: if the sequence of gene *A*, whose function is known, is homologous to the sequence of gene *B*, whose function is unknown, one could infer that B may share A's function. In the structural branch of bioinformatics, homology is used to determine which parts of a protein are important in structure formation and interaction with other proteins. In a technique called homology modeling, this information is used to predict the structure of a protein once the structure of a homologous protein is known. This currently remains the only way to predict protein structures reliably.

One example of this is hemoglobin in humans and the hemoglobin in legumes (leghemoglobin), which are distant relatives from the same protein superfamily. Both serve the same purpose of transporting oxygen in the organism. Although both of these proteins have completely different amino acid sequences, their protein structures are virtually identical, which reflects their near identical purposes and shared ancestor.

Other techniques for predicting protein structure include protein threading and *de novo* (from scratch) physics-based modeling.

Another aspect of structural bioinformatics include the use of protein structures for Virtual Screening models such as Quantitative Structure-Activity Relationship models and proteochemometric models (PCM). Furthermore, a protein's crystal structure can be used in simulation of for example ligand-binding studies and *in silico* mutagenesis studies.

Alignment-free Sequence Analysis

In bioinformatics, alignment-free sequence analysis approaches to molecular sequence and structure data provide alternatives over alignment-based approaches.

The emergence and need for the analysis of different types of data generated through biological research has given rise to the field of bioinformatics. Molecular sequence and structure data of DNA, RNA, and proteins, gene expression profiles or microarray data, metabolic pathway data are some of the major types of data being analysed in bioinformatics. Among them sequence data is increasing at the exponential rate due to advent of next-generation sequencing technologies. Since the origin of bioinformatics, sequence analysis has remained the major area of research with wide range of applications in database searching, genome annotation, comparative genomics, molecular phylogeny and gene prediction. The pioneering approaches for sequence analysis were based on sequence alignment either global or local, pairwise or multiple sequence alignment. Alignment-based approaches generally give excellent results when the sequences under study are closely related and can be reliably aligned, but when the sequences are divergent, a reliable alignment cannot be obtained and hence the applications of sequence alignment are limited. Another limitation of alignment-based approaches is their computational complexity and are time-consuming and thus, are limited when dealing with large-scale sequence data. The advent of next-generation sequencing technologies has resulted in generation of voluminous sequencing data. The size of this sequence data poses challenges on alignment-based algorithms in their assembly, annotation and comparative studies.

Alignment-free Methods

Alignment-free methods can broadly be classified into five categories: a) methods based on k-mer/word frequency, b) methods based on the length of common substrings, c) methods based on the number of (spaced) word matches, d) methods based on *micro-alignments*, e) methods based on information theory and f) methods based on graphical representation. Alignment-free approaches have been used in sequence similarity searches, clustering and classification of sequences, and more recently in phylogenetics.

Such molecular phylogeny analyses employing alignment-free approaches are said to be part of next-generation phylogenomics. A number of review articles provide in-depth review of alignment-free methods in sequence analysis.

The AFproject is an international collaboration to benchmark and compare software tools for alignment-free sequence comparison.

Methods Based on k-mer/Word Frequency

The popular methods based on k-mer/word frequencies include feature frequency profile (FFP), Composition vector (CV), Return time distribution (RTD), frequency chaos game representation (FCGR) and Spaced Words.

Feature Frequency Profile (FFP)

The methodology involved in FFP based method starts by calculating the count of each possible k-mer (possible number of k-mers for nucleotide sequence: 4^k, while that for protein sequence: 20^k) in sequences. Each k-mer count in each sequence is then normalized by dividing it by total of all k-mers' count in that sequence. This leads to conversion of each sequence into its feature frequency profile. The pair wise distance between two sequences is then calculated Jensen–Shannon (JS) divergence between their respective FFPs. The distance matrix thus obtained can be used to construct phylogenetic tree using clustering algorithms like neighbor-joining, UPGMA etc.

Composition Vector (CV)

In this method frequency of appearance of each possible k-mer in a given sequence is calculated. The next characteristic step of this method is the subtraction of random background of these frequencies using Markov model to reduce the influence of random neutral mutations to highlight the role of selective evolution. The normalized frequencies are put a fixed order to form the composition vector (CV) of a given sequence. Cosine distance function is then used to compute pairwise distance between CVs of sequences. The distance matrix thus obtained can be used to construct phylogenetic tree using clustering algorithms like neighbor-joining, UPGMA etc. This method can be extended through resort to efficient pattern matching algorithms to include in the computation of the composition vectors: (i) all k-mers for any value of k, (ii) all substrings of any length up to an arbitrarily set maximum k value, (iii) all maximal substrings, where a substring is maximal if extending it by any character would cause a decrease in its occurrence count.

Return Time Distribution (RTD)

The RTD based method does not calculate the count of k-mers in sequences, instead it computes the time required for the reappearance of k-mers. The time refers to the number of residues in successive appearance of particular k-mer. Thus the occurrence of each k-mer in a sequence is calculated in the form of RTD, which is then summarised using two statistical parameters mean (μ) and standard deviation (σ). Thus each sequence is represented in the form of numeric vector of size $2 \cdot 4^k$ containing μ and σ of 4^k RTDs. The pair wise distance between sequences is calculated using Euclidean distance measure. The distance matrix thus obtained can be used to construct phylogenetic tree using clustering algorithms like neighbor-joining, UPGMA etc.

Frequency Chaos Game Representation (FCGR)

The FCGR methods have evolved from chaos game representation (CGR) technique, which provides scale independent representation for genomic sequences. The CGRs can be divided by grid lines where each grid square denotes the occurrence of oligonucleotides of a specific length in the sequence. Such representation of CGRs is termed as Frequency Chaos Game Representation (FCGR). This leads to representation of each sequence into FCGR. The pair wise distance between FCGRs of sequences can be calculated using the Pearson distance, the Hamming distance or the Euclidean distance.

Spaced-word Frequencies

While most alignment-free algorithms compare the word-composition of sequences, Spaced Words uses a pattern of care and don't care positions. The occurrence of a spaced word in a sequence is then defined by the characters at the match positions only, while the characters at the don't care positions are ignored. Instead of comparing the frequencies of contiguous words in the input sequences, this approach compares the frequencies of the spaced words according to the pre-defined pattern. Note that the pre-defined pattern can be selected by analysis of the Variance of the number of matches, the probability of the first occurrence on several models, or the Pearson correlation coefficient between the expected word frequency and the true alignment distance.

Methods based on Length of Common Substrings

The methods in this category employ the similarity and differences of substrings in a pair of sequences. These algorithms were mostly used for string processing in computer science.

Average Common Substring (ACS)

In this approach, for a chosen pair of sequences (A and B of lengths n and m respectively), longest substring starting at some position is identified in one sequence (A) which exactly matches in the other sequence (B) at any position. In this way, lengths of longest substrings starting at different positions in sequence A and having exact matches at some positions in sequence B are calculated. All these lengths are averaged to derive a measure $L(A, B)$. Intuitively, larger the $L(A, B)$, the more similar the two sequences are. To account for the differences in the length of sequences, $L(A, B)$ is normalized [i.e. $L(A, B) / \log(m)$]. This gives the similarity measure between the sequences.

In order to derive a distance measure, the inverse of similarity measure is taken and a correction term is subtracted from it to assure that $d(A, A)$ will be zero. Thus,

$$d(A, B) = \left[\frac{\log m}{L(A, B)} \right] - \left[\frac{\log n}{L(A, A)} \right].$$

This measure $d(A, B)$ is not symmetric, so one has to compute,

$$d_s(A, B) = d_s(B, A) = (d(A, B) + d(B, A))/2,$$

which gives final ACS measure between the two strings (A and B). The subsequence/substring search can be efficiently performed by using suffix trees.

k-mismatch Average Common Substring Approach (kmacs)

This approach is a generalization of the ACS approach. To define the distance between two DNA or protein sequences, kmacs estimates for each position i of the first sequence the longest substring starting at i and matching a substring of the second sequence with up to k mismatches. It defines the average of these values as a measure of similarity between the sequences and turns this into a symmetric distance measure. Kmacs does not compute exact k-mismatch substrings, since this would be computational too costly, but approximates such substrings.

Mutation Distances (Kr)

This approach is closely related to the ACS, which calculates the number of substitutions per site between two DNA sequences using the shortest absent substring (termed as shustring).

Length Distribution of k-mismatch Common Substrings

This approach uses the program kmacs to calculate longest common substrings with up to k mismatches for a pair of DNA sequences. The phylogenetic distance between the sequences can then be estimated from a local maximum in the length distribution of the k-mismatch common substrings.

Methods based on the Number of (Spaced) Word Matches

D_2^S and D_2^*

These approachese are variants of the D_2 statistics that counts the number of k-mer matches between two sequences. They improve the simple D_2 statistics by taking the background distribution of the compared sequences into account.

MASH

This is an extremely fast method that uses the MinHash bottom sketch strategy for estimating the Jaccard index of the multi-sets of k-mers of two input sequences. That is, it estimates the ratio of k-mer matches to the total number of k-mers of the sequences. This can be used, in turn, to estimate the evolutionary distances between the compared sequences, measured as the number of substitutions per sequence position since the sequences evolved from their last common anchestor.

Slope-Tree

This approach calculates a disatance value between two protein sequences based on the decay of the number of k-mer matches if k increases.

Slope-SpaM

This method calculates the number N_k of k-mer or spaced-word matches (*SpaM*) for different values for the word length or number of match positions k in the underlying pattern, respectively. The slope of an affine-linear function F that depends on N_k is calculated to estimate the Jukes-Cantor distance between the input sequences.

Skmer

Skmer calculates distances between species from unassembled sequencing reads. Similar to *MASH*, it uses the Jaccard index on the sets of k-mers from the input sequences. In contrast to *MASH*, the program is still accurate for low sequencing coverage, so it can be used for *genome skimming*.

Methods based on Micro-alignments

Strictly spoken, these methods are not *alignment-free*. They are using simple gap-free *micro-alignments* where sequences are required to match at certain pre-defined positions. The positions aligned at the remaining positions of the *micro-alignments* where mismatches are allowed, are then used for phylogeny inference.

Co-phylog

This method searches for so-called structures that are defined as pairs of k-mer matches between two DNA sequences that are one position apart in both sequences. The two k-mer matches are called the context, the position between them is called the object. Co-phylog then defines the distance between two sequences the fraction of such structures for which the two nucleotides in the object are different. The approach can be applied to unassembled sequencing reads.

andi

andi estimates phylogenetic distances between genomic sequences based on ungapped local alignments that are flanked by maximal exact word matches. Such word matches can be efficiently found using suffix arrays. The gapfree alignments between the exact word matches are then used to estimate phylogenetic distances between genome sequences. The resulting distance estimates are accurate for up to around 0.6 substitutions per position.

Filtered Spaced-word Matches (FSWM)

FSWM uses a pre-defined binary pattern P representing so-called *match positions* and *don't-care positions*. For a pair of input DNA sequences, it then searches for *spaced-word matches* w.r.t. P, i.e. for local gap-free alignments with matching nucleotides at the *match positions* of P and possible mismatches at the *don't-care positions*. Spurious low-scoring spaced-word matches are discarded, evolutionary distances between the input sequences are estimated based on the nucleotides aligned to each other at the *don't-care positions* of the remaining, homologous spaced-word matches. FSWM has been adapted to estimate distances based on unassembled NGS reads, this version of the program is called *Read-SpaM*.

Prot-SpaM

Prot-SpaM (Proteome-based Spaced-word Matches) is an implementation of the FSWM algorithm for partial or whole proteome sequences.

Multi-SpaM

Multi-SpaM (MultipleSpaced-word Matches) is an approach to genome-based phylogeny reconstruction that extends the FSWM idea to multiple sequence comparison. Given a binary pattern P of *match positions* and *don't-care positions*, the program searches for P-blocks, i.e. local gap-free four-way alignments with matching nucleotides at the *match positions* of P and possible mismatches at the *don't-care positions*. Such four-way alignments are randomly sampled from a set of input genome sequences. For each P-block, an unrooted tree topology is calculated using *RAxML*. The program *Quartet MaxCut* is then used to calculate a supertree from these trees.

Methods based on Information Theory

Information Theory has provided successful methods for alignment-free sequence analysis and comparison. The existing applications of information theory include global and local characterization of DNA, RNA and proteins, estimating genome entropy to motif and region classification. It also holds promise in gene mapping, next-generation sequencing analysis and metagenomics.

Base–Base Correlation (BBC)

Base–base correlation (BBC) converts the genome sequence into a unique 16-dimensional numeric vector using the following equation,

$$T_{ij}(K) = \sum_{\ell=1}^{K} P_{ij}(\ell) \cdot \log_2 \left(\frac{P_{ij}(\ell)}{P_i P_j} \right)$$

The P_i and P_j denotes the probabilities of bases i and j in the genome. The $P_{ij}(\ell)$ indicates the probability of bases i and j at distance ℓ in the genome. The parameter K indicates the maximum distance between the bases i and j. The variation in the values of 16 parameters reflect variation in the genome content and length.

Information Correlation and Partial Information Correlation (IC-PIC)

IC-PIC (information correlation and partial information correlation) based method employs the base correlation property of DNA sequence. IC and PIC were calculated using following formulas,

$$IC_\ell = -2\sum_i P_i \log_2 P_i + \sum_{ij} P_{ij}(\ell) \log_2 P_{ij}(\ell)$$

$$PIC_{ij}(\ell) = (P_{ij}(\ell) - P_i P_j(\ell))^2$$

The final vector is obtained as follows:

$$V = \frac{IC_\ell}{PIC_{ij}(\ell)} \text{ where } \ell \in \{\ell_0, \ell_0 + 1, \ldots, \ell_0 + n\},$$

which defines the range of distance between bases.

The pairwise distance between sequences is calculated using Euclidean distance measure. The distance matrix thus obtained can be used to construct phylogenetic tree using clustering algorithms like neighbor-joining, UPGMA, etc.

Lempel–Ziv Compression

Lempel-Ziv complexity uses the relative information between the sequences. This complexity is measured by the number of steps required to generate a string given the prior knowledge of another string and a self-delimiting production process. This measure has a relation to measuring k-words in a sequence, as they can be easily used to generate the sequence. It is computational intensive method. Otu and Sayood (2003) used this method to construct five different distance measures for phylogenetic tree construction.

Context Modeling Compression

In the context modeling complexity the next-symbol predictions, of one or more statistical models, are combined or competing to yield a prediction that is based on events recorded in the past. The algorithmic information content derived from each symbol prediction can be used to compute algorithmic information profiles with a time proportional to the length of the sequence. The process has been applied to DNA sequence analysis.

Methods based on Graphical Representation

Iterated Maps

The use of iterated maps for sequence analysis was first introduced by HJ Jefferey in 1990 when he proposed to apply the Chaos Game to map genomic sequences into a unit square. That report coined the procedure as Chaos Game Representation (CGR). However, only 3 years later this approach was first dismissed as a projection of a Markov transition table by N Goldman. This objection was overruled by the end of that decade when the opposite was found to be the case – that CGR bijectively maps Markov transition is into a fractal, order-free (degree-free) representation. The realization that iterated maps provide a bijective map between the symbolic space and numeric space led to the identification of a variety of alignment-free approaches to sequence comparison and characterization. These developments were reviewed in late 2013 by JS Almeida in. A number of web apps such as https://usm. github.com, are available to demonstrate how to encode and compare arbitrary symbolic sequences in a manner that takes full advantage of modern MapReduce distribution developed for cloud computing.

Comparison of Alignment based and Alignment-free Methods

Alignment-based methods	Alignment-free methods
These methods assume that homologous regions are contiguous (with gaps).	Does not assume such contiguity of homologous regions.
Computes all possible pairwise comparisons of sequences; hence computationally expensive.	Based on occurrences of sub-sequences; composition; computationally inexpensive, can be memory-intensive.
Well-established approach in phylogenomics.	Relatively recent and application in phylogenomics is limited; needs further testing for robustness and scalability.
Requires substitution/evolutionary models.	Less dependent on substitution/evolutionary models.
Sensitive to stochastic sequence variation, recombination, horizontal (or lateral) genetic transfer, rate heterogeneity and sequences of varied lengths, especially when similarity lies in the "twilight zone."	Less sensitive to stochastic sequence variation, recombination, horizontal (or lateral) genetic transfer, rate heterogeneity and sequences of varied lengths.
Best practice uses inference algorithms with complexity at least $O(n^2)$; less time-efficient.	Inference algorithms typically $O(n^2)$ or less; more time-efficient.
Heuristic in nature; statistical significance of how alignment scores relate to homology is difficult to assess.	Exact solutions; statistical significance of the sequence distances (and degree of similarity) can be readily assessed.
Relies on dynamic programming (computationally expensive) to find alignment that has optimal score.	side-steps computational expensive dynamic programming by indexing word counts or positions in fractal space.

Applications of Alignment-free Methods

- Genomic rearrangements
- Molecular phylogenetics
- Metagenomics
- Next generation sequence data analysis
- Epigenomics
- Barcoding of species

- Population genetics
- Horizontal gene transfer
- Sero/genotyping of viruses
- Allergenicity prediction
- SNP discovery
- Recombination detection

Sequence Alignment

The more similar two sequences are, the more similar should their functions be and more phylogenetically close they should be. The sequences for the same gene in a group of species will be more different the more distant phylogenetically they are. Sequences will get mutations over time, so the more time has passed since two species split, the more mutations will have their sequences and the more different their sequences will be. Mutations can be residue (nucleotide or aminoacid) substitutions, insertions or deletions.

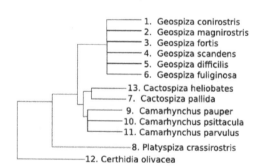

1. Geospiza conirostris
2. Geospiza magnirostris
3. Geospiza fortis
4. Geospiza scandens
5. Geospiza difficilis
6. Geospiza fuliginosa
13. Cactospiza heliobates
7. Cactospiza pallida
9. Camarhynchus pauper
10. Camarhynchus psittacula
11. Camarhynchus parvulus
8. Platyspiza crassirostris
12. Certhidia olivacea

Biological sequences are similar, usually, because they are homologous, because they share a common ancestor. Homology is not a quantitative concept, two sequences can be homologous or not, but they cannot be 50% homologous. They either share a common ancestor or they don't.

How do we know that two sequences are homologous? Usually we infer it from their similarity. If two biological sequences are similar we tend to infer that they are similar because they are homologous.

Alignments could be used to:

- Quantify the phylogenetic distance between two sequences

- Look for functional domains

- Compare a mRNA with its genomic region

- Identify polymorphisms and mutations between sequences

Sequence Alignment

The first step to compare two sequences is, usually, to align them.

```
No alignment

    CGATGCTAGCGTATCGTAGTCTATCGTAC

                 |        ||

    ACGATGCTAGCGTTTCGTATCATCGTA

Alignned

    -CGATGCTAGCGTATCGTAGTCTATCGTAC

     |||||||||||| ||||||||||||||

    ACGATGCTAGCGTTTCGTA-TC-ATCGTA-
```

There could be substitutions, changes of one residue with another, or gaps. Gaps are missing residues and could be due to a deletion in one sequence or an insertion in the other sequence.

Gaps complicate the alignments. Algorithms should take into account the possibility of introducing gaps and once we allow them to create gaps several alignments can be constructed between two sequences.

```
No gaps (10 matches)

    a: ATATTGCTACGTATATCAT

           ||||||||||

    b: ATATATGCTACGTATCAT

With one gap (14 matches)

    a: ATAT-TGCTACGTATATCAT

       ||||  ||||||||||

    b: ATATATGCTACGTATCAT

With two gaps (16 matches)
```

```
a: ATAT-TGCTACGTATATCAT

   ||||  ||||||||  ||||||

b: ATATATGCTACG--TATCAT
```

The objective of a sequence alignment is, usually, to align the homologous positions of the two sequences. The homologous positions are the ones that come from the same position in the ancestral sequence. We don't know the ancestral sequence, so we won't be completely sure that we have succeeded. Another complementary objective could be to align protein regions that have the same structure or function.

Aligning similar sequences by any algorithm usually creates alignments that are usually correct, but when sequences are very different aligning them could be a challenge. Once a long time has passed since the split of the species the sequences can be so changed by the mutations that any meaningful similarities could have been lost an creating a meaningful alignment could be very difficult.

Evaluating the Alignments

To be able to compare the different possible alignments we can score them. We can create a scoring system that gives more points to alignments that are biologically more reasonable. Ideally we would create a scoring system that gives more points to the alignments that align the homologous positions.

A naive scoring system could be to count the number of matching positions, or the number of matching positions along 100 residues. Usually the scoring systems also take into account the number of gaps. They penalize the alignments depending on the number and the length of the gaps present. So the main features taken into account to create an scoring system are usually:

- Number of matching residues (taking into account the similarity if they are aminoacids)

- Number of missmatches

- Number of gaps

- Length of the gaps

We can devise different scoring schemes with those measures. For instances:

- Scoring schema 1: match +1, mismatch: 0, gap creation: -1 gap extension: -1
- Scoring schema 1: match +1, mismatch: -1, gap creation: -1 gap extension: 0

Of course, one alignment will have a different score under different scoring schemes. Speaking of the score of an alignment it is meaningless if we do not take into account the scoring schema used. It also has no sense to compare the scores of different alignments done under different schemes.

Once we have decided which scoring schema to use, the alignment algorithm should try to create the alignment that obtains the maximum score under that particular scoring schema.

Every software implementation of an algorithm will usually have some default values for its parameters. These default values have been calibrated by the software creator to work well in a particular problem. The bioinformatician should be aware of how well those values apply to the particular problem at hand. Usually, if the problem is similar to the one that motivated the creation of the software the default value will work OK because the original creator of the software usually knows how to optimize his software for that task. When our problem is different from the original one we have to be aware of the changes to adapt the software to our needs.

Global and Local Alignments

We could divide the alignment algorithms in two types: global and local. The global algorithms try to create an alignment that covers completely both sequences adding whatever gaps necessary. The local algorithms try to align only the most similar regions. If removing a region from one end of a sequence improves the alignment score they will do it.

Local alignments are usually the best option unless we are sure that the sequences are similar in all its extension. Besides, the local alignment algorithms will create a global alignment with both sequences covered if they are similar enough.

```
Global

  TACGGGGCTAGCTA-TCGTAG

  ||||  |||  ||||||

  TAGC----TAG----TCGTAG

Local

  TAGCTA-TCGTAG

  |||||| ||||||

  TAGCTAGTCGTAG
```

The main practical problem with local alignment algorithms is that they are computationally more demanding that its global equivalents. Global alignments are usually only used within the multiple alignment algorithms (alignments with more than two sequences).

Alignment Methods

Dot Plot (or Dot Matrix)

This alignment method creates a graphical representation of the alignment. It creates intuitive representations and it has the advantage that it will show different alternative alignments between two sequences. Other, more standard, alignment methods usually give back only one alignment, the best one, unless instructed otherwise.

Dot plot methods are quite good to study the structure of the sequences involved. They can show repetitions, insertions and deletions clearly.

Once we have identified the regions that match between two sequences we could use another method to create a more conventional text based alignment.

To create a dot plot alignment one sequence is put in the horizontal axis and the other in vertical one. The matches between both sequences are shown as marks in the corresponding position.

```
        CATGCT

   A   x

   T    x    x

   G      x

   C  x     x
```

The alignment is shown as a diagonal in the plot.

```
        A  C  A  G  T  A  G  G  G
   A    ●        ·        ·
   C       ●
   C       ·        SUSTITUCIÓN
   G          ●              ·  ·  ·
   T             ●
   C       ·           DELECCIÓN
   A    ·     ·        ●
   G             ·        ●  ·  ·
   G             ·           ·  ●
   G             ·              ·  ·  ●
```

There are different programs to create dot plots. An example is dotmatcher from the emboss suite.

It is easy to detect big insertions, deletions and forward and reverse repeats.

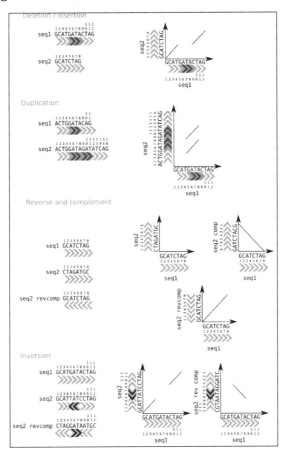

Tandem duplication.

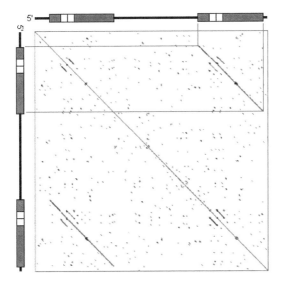

And we can do a genome wide analysis.

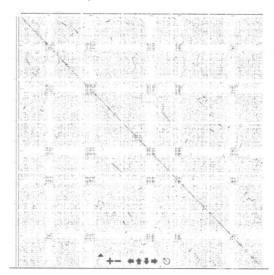

One limitation of the dotplot method is that although we detect similar regions we do not obtain the alignment.

Sensitivity and Specificity

A variation of the dot plot algorithm can compare windows of several residues instead of individual residues. In that case a similarity threshold is set to mark a position as similar. These parameters will influence the sensitivity and specificity of the analysis. If we increase the threshold for a given window size or we decrease the window size for a given threshold we will obtain less spurious signals.

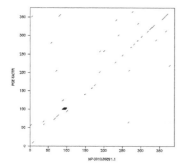
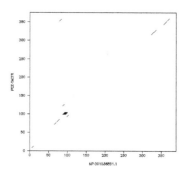

The more stringent the parameters the less noise we will detect, but the more real alignments we will loose. This is related with two very important concepts that can be applied to many bioinformatic and statistical analyses: sensitivity and specificity.

In a dotplot analysis we can draw a dot when two homologous positions match. That would be a true positive. But, if we draw a dot when the two positions are similar but they are not homologous we have a false negative.

With the negatives we have a similar problem. In the dotplot case a negative is a position with no dot. We can have true negatives, positions that does not have a dot and that are not homologous and false negatives, positions that do not have a dot, but that are in fact homologous.

The sentitivity, also called recall, is the proportion of positives that are called positives by the analysis. It is the true positive rate. Ideally we would like to have a 100% percent sensitivity, we would like to mark as positives in the analysis all the true positives.

The specificity is the proportion of true negatives that are called negative by our analysis. It is also know as true negative rate. Ideally we would like to call all true negatives as negatives.

	Truth	
	has the disease	does not has the disease
positive	True Positives (TP)	False Positives (FP)
negative	False Negatives (FN)	True Negatives (TN)
	senstitivity $\frac{TP}{TP + FN}$	**specificity** $\frac{TN}{TN + FP}$

In practice most of the time we will miss some positives, so the sensitivity will be lower than 100% and we will detect signals for some negatives. In the dotplot case a false positive would be a region that is marked as similar, but that it is not homologous and a false negative it is a region that is not marked as similar, but that it really is.

Different analysis or different parameter sets will have different sensitivities and specificities. These are very important characteristics of the analyses.

Smith and Waterman Algorithm

There are plenty of algorithms to create text based pairwise sequence alignments.

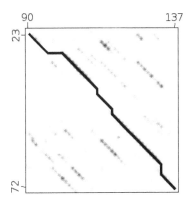

These algorithms are based on creating a matrix equivalent to the 2D representation created by the dot plot. In those matrices the fragments that will constitute the alignments can be seen as diagonals.

Dotplot diagonals suggest paths in the space of possible alignments. Each of these paths are a possible fragment of the final alignment.

A general approach to detect the path through these diagonals is call dinamic programing. One of the first algorithms implemented following these philosophy was the Needleman-Wunsch algorithm. This algorithm creates global alignments of two sequences given a scoring schema. It is implemented in several programs, one of them is needle from the EMBOSS suite.

```
#######################################

# Program:  needle

# Rundate:  Tue Oct 02 10:58:05 2007

# Align_format: srspair

# Report_file: /ebi/extserv/old-work/needle-20071002-10580428983041.output

#######################################


#=========================================
#
# Aligned_sequences: 2

# 1: SNAK_DROME

# 2: PCE_TACTR

# Matrix: EBLOSUM62

# Gap_penalty: 10.0

# Extend_penalty: 0.5
#
# Length: 462

# Identity:     126/462 (27.3%)

# Similarity:   184/462 (39.8%)

# Gaps:         114/462 (24.7%)

# Score: 440.5
#
```

```
#

#=======================================


SNAK_DROME      1 MIILWSLIVH--LQLTCLHLILQTPNLEALDALEIINYQTTKYTIPEVWK     48
                    ::|:   ..|.|..|::.......|        :.|..::..|

PCE_TACTR       1    MLVNNVFSLLCFPLLMSVVRCSTL------SRQRRQFVFP----       34


SNAK_DROME     49 EQPVATIGEDVDDQDTEDEESYLKFGDDAEVRTSVSEGLHEGAFCRRSFD     98
                    |||.                              .|...|.

PCE_TACTR      35 ----------------DEEE---------------------LCSNRFT     45


SNAK_DROME     99 GRSGYCILAYQCLHVIREYRVHGTRIDICTHRNNVPVICCPLADKHVLAQ    148
                    ..|.|.....|..:::.:..:..:..||......|.:|||  ...||

PCE_TACTR      46 -EEGTCKNVLDCRILLQKNDYNLLKESICGFEGITPKVCCP-KSSHV---     90


SNAK_DROME    149 RISATKCQEYNAAARRLHLTDTGRTFSGKQCVPSVP-----------LIV    187
                    ||:|:.........|          ..||..|::|          .|:

PCE_TACTR      91 -ISSTQAPPETTTTER----------PPKQIPPNLPEVCGIHNTTTTRII    129


SNAK_DROME    188 GGTPTRHGLFPHMAALGWTQGSGSKDQDIKWGCGGALVSELYVLTAAHCA    237
                    ||.....|.:|.|.|.|:...||.....|   ||||||:..:|:||:||.

PCE_TACTR     130 GGREAPIGAWPWMTAVYIKQGGIRSVQ-----CGGALVTNRHVITASHCV    174


SNAK_DROME    238 TSGS----KPPDM--VRLGARQLNET--SATQQDIKILIIVLHPKYRSSA    279
                    .:.:    .|.|:  ||||...|..|  .:...|.:.:.:.|..:..:.

PCE_TACTR     175 VNSAGTDVMPADVFSVRLGEHNLYSTDDDSNPIDFAVTSVKHHEHFVLAT    224


SNAK_DROME    280 YYHDIALLKLTRRVKFSEQVRPACL----WQLPELQIPTVVAAGWGRTEF    325
                    |.:|||:|.|...|.|::::||.||    .:..:|.:.....|||.|.|

PCE_TACTR     225 YLNDIAILTLNDTVTFTDRIRPICLPYRKLRYDDLAMRKPFITGWGTTAF    274
```

```
SNAK_DROME      326 LGAKSNALRQVDLDVVPQMTCKQIYRKERRLPRGIIEGQFCAGYLPGGRD      375

                    .|..|..||:|.|.:.....|:|.|.|:    ..|.....|||:..||:|

PCE_TACTR       275 NGPSSAVLREVQLPIWEHEACRQAYEKD----LNITNVYMCAGFADGGKD      320


SNAK_DROME      376 TCQGDSGGPIHALLPEYNCVAFVVGITSFGKFCAAPNAPGVYTRLYSYLD      425

                    .|||||||:  :||.....::|.||||.||.|..|||||::..:||

PCE_TACTR       321 ACQGDSGGPM--MLPVKTGEFYLIGIVSFGKKCALPGFPGVYTKVTEFLD      368


SNAK_DROME      426 WIEKIAFKQH      435

                    ||     .:|

PCE_TACTR       369 WI-----AEHMV      375
```

The main limitation of the Needleman–Wunsch algorithm is that it is global, so we should only use it if we know beforehand that both sequences are similar in all its extension.

Smith and Waterman proposed a variation of the algorithm that is capable of generating local alignments. This approach gives better results because it does not force the sequences to be similar in all its extension. If the best, higher scoring alignment, is a global one that aligns completely both sequences the Smith-Waterman algorithm will create it, otherwise it will generate a local alignment.

This algorithm has multiple implementations, one of them is the water program in the EMBOSS suite.

```
########################################

  # Program:  water

  # Rundate:  Tue Oct 02 11:00:39 2007

  # Align_format: srspair

  # Report_file: /ebi/extserv/old-work/water-20071002-11003873398600.output

########################################


  #=======================================

  #

  # Aligned_sequences: 2

  # 1: SNAK_DROME
```

```
# 2: PCE_TACTR

# Matrix: EBLOSUM62

# Gap_penalty: 10.0

# Extend_penalty: 0.5

#

# Length: 362

# Identity:      116/362 (32.0%)

# Similarity:    165/362 (45.6%)

# Gaps:           50/362 (13.8%)

# Score: 452.0

#

#

#========================================
```

```
SNAK_DROME     89 EGAFCRRSFDGRSGYCILAYQCLHVIREYRVHGTRIDICTHRNNVPVICC   138
                  |...|...|. ..|.|.....|..:::..:.:..||......|.:||
PCE_TACTR      36 EEELCSNRFT-EEGTCKNVLDCRILLQKNDYNLLKESICGFEGITPKVCC    84


SNAK_DROME    139 PLADKHVLAQRISATKCQEYNAAARRLHLTDTGRTFSGKQCVPSVP----   184
                  |  ...||      ||:|:.........|          ..||..|::|
PCE_TACTR      85 P-KSSHV----ISSTQAPPETTTTER---------PPKQIPPNLPEVCG   119


SNAK_DROME    185 -------LIVGGTPTRHGLFPHMAALGWTQGSGSKDQDIKWGCGGALVSE   227
                      .|:||.....|.:|.|.|:...||.....|    ||||||:.
PCE_TACTR     120 IHNTTTTRIIGGREAPIGAWPWMTAVYIKQGGIRSVQ-----CGGALVTN   164


SNAK_DROME    228 LYVLTAAHCATSGS----KPPDM--VRLGARQLNET--SATQQDIKILII   269
                  .:|:||:||..:.:     .|.|: |||...|..| .:...|..:.:
PCE_TACTR     165 RHVITASHCVVNSAGTDVMPADVFSVRLGEHNLYSTDDDSNPIDFAVTSV   214
```

```
SNAK_DROME      270 VLHPKYRSSAYYHDIALLKLTRRVKFSEQVRPACL----WQLPELQIPTV   315

                    ..|..:..:.|.:|||:|.|...|.|::::||.||   .:..:|.:...

PCE_TACTR       215 KHHEHFVLATYLNDIAILTLNDTVTFTDRIRPICLPYRKLRYDDLAMRKP   264


SNAK_DROME      316 VAAGWGRTEFLGAKSNALRQVDLDVVPQMTCKQIYRKERRLPRGIIEGQF   365

                    ...|||.|.|.|..|..||:|.|.:.....|:|.|.|:   ..|.....

PCE_TACTR       265 FITGWGTTAFNGPSSAVLREVQLPIWEHEACRQAYEKD----LNITNVYM   310


SNAK_DROME      366 CAGYLPGGRDTCQGDSGGPIHALLPEYNCVAFVVGITSFGKFCAAPNAPG   415

                    |||:..||:|.|||||||:  :||.....::::||.||||.||.|..||

PCE_TACTR       311 CAGFADGGKDACQGDSGGPM--MLPVKTGEFYLIGIVSFGKKCALPGFPG   358


SNAK_DROME      416 VYTRLYSYLDWI    427

                    |||::..:||||

PCE_TACTR       359 VYTKVTEFLDWI    370
```

Of course, the result will depend not only on the sequences, but on the scoring schema. For instance, if we use a higher penalty for creating gaps we will obtain alignments with fewer gaps.

The nicest property of the Smith-Waterman alignment is that it has been demonstrated that it will generate the optimal alignment, the one with the highest score, given two sequences and a scoring schema. So, if we could, it would be advisable to use always this algorithm. Take into account that several alignments could have the same score, so we can have several alignments with the highest score.

The main problem with the Smith-Waterman algorithm is its slowness. It works very well with small sequences, but it is not practical when the sequences are large. The time it takes to create the scoring matrix for a naive Smith-Waterman implementation depends of m x n (being m and n the length of the sequences).

More than One Alignment

In the dotplot graphical results we saw that some time there could be no just one but several valid alignments. Usually the alignment software that implements the Smith-Waterman algorithm will only print just one alignment by default, the higher scoring one. If there a multiple alignments we will miss them unless we instruct the software otherwise.

Aminoacid Substitution Matrices

When scoring a position of an alignment between two nucleotide sequences we can consider a match if the nucleotide match and a mismatch if the nucleotides are different.

```
ACGT          ACGT
 |
ACGT          ACAT
 ^             ^

  match       mismatch
```

With the aminoacids we can be more subtle because there are aminoacids that are chemically or functionally similar. For instance, we could score higher a substitution of a hydrophobic aminoacid (like Alanine) with another hydrophic aminoacid (like Valine) than with a polar one (like Glutamine).

But if we decide to use such an scoring schema, how should we decided which are the scores to use for each possible aminoacid substitution? A possible way of creating such an aminoacid subtitution scoring matrix would be to count how many times each pair the possible aminoacid substitutions are found at homologous positions in alignments of homologous proteins. The pairs that tend to appear at the same positions could be considered functionally equivalent and scored higher than the ones that in few instances are found at the same positions. Following this method we could create a substitution matrix for all possible aminoacid substitutions.

A series of matrices built in such a way are the PAM matrices. There are several PAM matrices and not just one because they are built from comparison of sequences that are closer or further appart in evolutionary time. They are named by the number of aminoacid mutations for every 100 aminoacids that differentiate the sequences compared to create the matrices. There are, for instance PAM100, PAM160 and PAM200 matrices. Take into account that a substitution can underlie several mutations, hence there could be more than 100 mutations in 100 aminoacids. A higher number is related with a longer evolutionary time.

Another commonly used set of matrices are the BLOSUM matrices. They are based on the same idea, but instead of being built with complete alignments they are built by using highly conserved blocks. This allows the BLOSUM matrices to cover longer evolutionary times than the PAM matrices because aligning very distant sequences in all their extension can be challenging, but aligning the most conserved blocks of those sequences could be easier. In the BLOSUM matrices the number reflects the minimum percentage of identity allowed between the sequences so BLOSUM 70 used sequences that were more similar than BLOSUM 50.

Statistical Significance of the Alignments

One general problem with the bioinformatic algorithms is that they usually generate a result, but some times that result could be meaningless. For instance, we could generate two random sequences and align them. The Smith-Waterman algorithm would generate an alignment, but despite being its optimal alignment it would be meaningless.

In the DNA alignments is quite easy to decide with alignments are meaningful because the spurious ones tend to be very short. In the protein alignments it is usually not that clear because we are allowing to aminoacid to be similar and not just identical and that tends to produce longer alignments even when they are meaningless.

The solution to this problem is to calculate some statistic that reflect the significance of the solution obtained. As we will see there is software that calculate these kind of statistical significance measures, like BLAST.

Multiple Sequence Alignment

A Multiple Sequence Alignment is an alignment of more than two sequences. We could align several DNA or protein sequences.

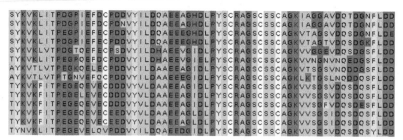

Some of the most usual uses of the multiple alignments are:

- Phylogenetic analysis

- Conserved domains

- Protein structure comparison and prediction

- Conserved regions in promoteres

The multiple sequence alignment asumes that the sequences are homologous, they descend from a common ancestor. The algorithms will try to align homologous positions or regions with the same structure or function.

Multiple Alignment Algorithm

Multiple alignments are computationally much more difficult than pair-wise alignments. It would be ideal to use an analog of the Smith & Waterman algorithm capable of looking for optimal alignments in the diagonals of a multidimensional matrix given a scoring schema. This algorithm would had to create a multidimensional matrix with one dimension for each sequence. The memory and time required for solving the problem would increase geometrically with the lenght of every sequence. Given the number of sequences usually involved no algorithm is capable of doing that. Every algorithm available reverts to a heuristic capable of solving the problem in a much faster time. The drawback is that the result might not be optimal.

Usually the multiple sequence algorithms assume that the sequences are similar in all its length and they behave like global alignment algorithms. They also assume that thre are not many long insertions and delections. Thus the algorithms will work for some sequences, but not for others.

These algorithms can deal with sequences that are quite different, but, as in the pair-wise case, when the sequences are very different they might have problems creating good algorithm. A good algorithm should align the homologous positions or the positions with the same structure or function.

It we are trying to align two homologous proteins from two species that are phylogenetically very distant we might align quite easily the more conserved regions, like the conserved domains, but we will have problems aligning the more different regions. This was also the case in the pair-wise case, but remember that the multiple alignment algorithms are not guaranteed to give back the best possible alignment.

These algorithms are not design to align sequences that do not cover the whole region, like the reads from a sequencing project. There are other algorithms to assemble sequencing projects.

Progressive Contruction Algorithms

In Multiple Sequence Alignment it is quite common that the algorithms use a progressive alignment strategy. These methods are fast and allow to align thousands of sequences.

Before starting the alignemnt, as in the pair-wise case, we have to decide which is the scoring schema that we are going to use for the matches, gaps and gap extensions. The aim of the alignment would be to get the multiple sequence alignment with the highest score possible. In the multiple alignment case we do not have any practical algorithm that guarantees that it going to get the optimal solution, but we hope that the solution will be close enough if the sequences comply with the restrictions assumed by the algorithm.

The idea behind the progressive construction algorithm is to build the pair-wise alignments of the more closely related sequences, that should be easier to build, and to align progressively these alignments once we have them. To do it we need first to determine which are the closest sequence pairs. One rough and fast way of determining which are the closest sequence pairs is to align all the possible pairs and look at the scores of those alignments. The pair-wise alignments with the highest scores should be the ones between the more similar sequences. So the first step in the algorithm is to create all the pair-wise alignments and to create a matrix with the scores between the pairs. These matrix will include the similarity relations between all sequences.

Once we have this matrix we can determine the hierarchical relation between the sequences, which are the closest pairs and how those pairs are related and so on, by creating a hierarchical clustering, a tree. We can create these threes by using different fast algorithms like UPGMA or Neighbor joining. These trees are usually known as guide trees.

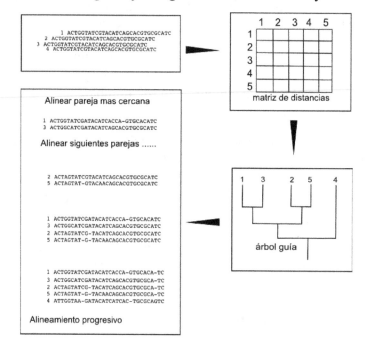

An example:

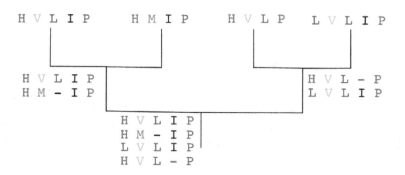

Another example:

```
Secuences:
 IMPRESIONANTE
 INCUESTIONABLE
 IMPRESO


Scores:

   IMPRESIONANTE X IMPRESO 7/13

   IMPRESIONANTE X INCUESTIONABLE 10/14

   INCUESTIONABLE X IMPRESO 4/14


Scoring pair-wise matrix:

                 IMPRESIONANTE   INCUESTIONABLE   IMPRESO
IMPRESIONANTE          1             10/14          7/13
INCUESTIONABLE       10/14             1            4/14
IMPRESO               7/13           4/14             1


Guide Tree:

      |--- IMPRESIONANTE
  |---|--- INCUESTIONABLE
  |
  |----- IMPRESO
```

The first alignment would be: IMPRESIONANTE x INCUESTIONABLE

```
   IMPRES-IONABLE
   INCUESTIANABLE
```

Now we align IMPRESO to the previous alignment.

```
   IMPRES-IONANTE
   INCUESTIONABLE
   IMPRES--O-----
```

We have no guarantee that the final is the one with the highest score.

The main problem of these progressive alignment algorithms is that the errors intro-duced at any point in the process are not revised in the following phases to speed up the process. For instance, if we introduce one gap in the first pair-wise alignment this gap will be propagated to all the following alingments. If the gap was correct that is fine, but if it was not optimal it won't be fixed. These methods are specially prone to fail when the sequences are very different or phylogenetically distant.

Sequences to align already in the order given by a guide tree:

```
Seq A   GARFIELD THE LAST FAT CAT

Seq B   GARFIELD THE FAST CAT

Seq C   GARFIELD THE VERY FAST CAT

Seq D   THE FAT CAT


Step 1

Seq A   GARFIELD THE LAST FAT CAT

Seq B   GARFIELD THE FAST CAT


Step 2

Seq A   GARFIELD THE LAST FA-T CAT

Seq B   GARFIELD THE FAST CA-T

Seq C   GARFIELD THE VERY FAST CAT


Step 3

Seq A   GARFIELD THE LAST FA-T CAT

Seq B   GARFIELD THE FAST CA-T

Seq C   GARFIELD THE VERY FAST CAT

Seq D   -------- THE ---- FA-T CAT
```

Historically the most used of the progressive multiple alignment algorithms was CLUSTALW. Nowadays CLUSTALW is not one of the recommended algorithms any-more because there are other algorithms that create better alignments like Clustal Omega or MAFFT. MAFFT was one of the best contenders in a multiple alignment software comparison.

T-Coffee is another progressive algorithm. T-Coffee tries to solve the errors introduced by the progressive methods by taking into account the pair-wise alignments. First it creates a library of all the possible pair-wise alignments plus a multiple alignment using an algorithm similar to the CLUSTALW one. To this library we can add more alignments based on extra information like the protein structure or the protein domain composition. Then it creates a progressive alignment, but it takes into accounts all the alignments in the library that relate to the sequences aligned at that step to avoid errors. The T-Coffe algorithm follows the steps:

1. Create the pair-wise alignments

2. Calculate the similirity matrix

3. Create the guide tree

4. Build the multiple progressive alignment following the tree, but taking into account the information from the pair-wise alignments.

T-Coffee is usually better than CLUSTALW and performs well even with very different sequences, specially if we feed it more information, like: domains, structures or secondary structure. T-Coffee is slower than CLUSTALW and that is one of its main limitations, it can not work with more than few hundred sequences.

Iterative Algorithms

These methods are similar to the progressive ones, but in each step the previous alignments are reevaluated. Some of the most popular iterative methods are: Muscle and MAFFT are two popular examples of these algorithms.

Hidden Markov Models

The most advanced algorithms to date are based on Hidden Markov Models and they have improvements in the guide tree construction, like the sequence embedding, that reduce the computation time.

Clustal Omega is one of these algorithms and can create alignments as accurate of the T-Coffee, but with many thousands of sequences.

Alignment Evaluation

Once we have created our Multiple Sequence Alignment we should check that the result is OK. We could open the multiple alignment in a viewer to assess the quality of the different regions of the aligment or we could automate this assesment. Usually not all the regions have an alignment of the same quality. The more conserved regions will be more easily aligned than the more variable ones.

It is quite usual to remove the regions that are not well aligned before doing any further analysis, like a phylogenetic reconstruction. We can remove those regions manually or we can use an especialized algorithm like trimAl.

Software for Multiple Alignments

There are different software packages that implement the described algorithms. These softwares include CLI and GUI programs as well as web services.

One package usually employed is MEGA. MEGA is a multiplatform software focused on phylogenetic analyses.

Jalview and STRAP a multiple alignment editor and viewer. Another old software, that has been abandoned by its developer is BioEdit.

Dynamic Programming for Gene Finders

Dynamic programming (DP) is a technique commonly used in bioinformatics algorithms to reduce the evaluation time for recurrence relations, is especially prevalent in the implementation of gene-finding software. The task of gene finding has traditionally been formulated as that of choosing a single parse, or collection of zero or more non-overlapping gene models, of a sequence such that the chosen parse maximizes some objective function. In general, the number of such parses can grow exponentially with the length of the sequence, owing to the combinatorial nature of the parses – that is, n non-overlapping and frame-consistent exons can, in theory, be combined independently to produce 2n different gene models. Thus, the explicit enumeration and evaluation of all possible parses of a sequence is generally too computationally expensive to be undertaken in practice. However, many of the objective functions favored by practitioners, particularly those that are probabilistic, can be expressed as a recurrence relation in which the value of a parse is defined recursively in terms of the values of subparses. It is this class of formulations that are amenable to dynamic programming, or DP.

There are two main approaches to DP: bottom-up and top-down. The latter, also called memoization, simply caches the value returned by a recursive call the first time it is made, so that subsequent calls with the same parameters can retrieve the value from the cache rather than recomputing it from scratch. By contrast, the bottom-up approach, which is more commonly used in gene finding and is slightly more efficient, involves the proactive computation of simpler subproblems before they are explicitly needed for the evaluation of more complex subproblems. The values of these subproblems are stored in an array or matrix, with the evaluation order of the cells in the matrix being determined by the recursive structure of the recurrence relation. Once the matrix has been evaluated, the optimal value can be extracted from the appropriate cell in the matrix, and the corresponding optimal solution can be obtained by tracing back through the recurrence links that were used to compute the value of each cell (assuming such links were explicitly stored or can be reconstructed during trace-back).

Thus, the main tasks in devising a DP implementation of a new gene-finding strategy are (1) to formulate the objective function as a recurrence relation, (2) to map the recursive structure of that recurrence relation to the elements of a multidimensional matrix, and (3) to determine the evaluation order of the cells in that matrix. Optimization of the objective function is then achieved by evaluating all the cells of the DP matrix and then identifying the optimal cell.

Example Uses

Examples of the actual use of DP for gene finding are legion, particularly in Marko-vian systems. It is standard to employ DP in both the training and application of Hidden Markov Models (HMMs). The Forward, Backward, and Baum-Welch algorithms for training an HMM involve matrices wherein each cell corresponds to a conditional or joint probability on sequences and their emission by particular states. The Viterbi decoding algorithm for parsing a sequence with an HMM likewise involves a matrix with cells denoting conditionally optimal paths through the states of the HMM and their corresponding conditional probabilities. The global optimum is identified by the cell that pairs the HMM's designated final state with the end of the sequence.

Other uses of DP for gene finding include the decoding algorithms used in applying Generalized Hidden Markov Models (GHMMs) and Nonstationary Markov Chains, and the procedures used to train and apply neural networks.

Practical Considerations

Various practical considerations can complicate the task of devising and implementing a DP algorithm. Among the most prominent are those involving space/speed trade-offs. The space requirements of multidimensional DP matrices can grow very quickly as the lengths of the dimensions increase, but often it is possible to eliminate portions of the matrix from consideration right at the outset, thereby permitting the adoption of a "sparse matrix" representation in which memory is allocated only for the portions of the matrix actually needed. Such a representation may or may not improve speed and memory efficiency, but it can also require significantly more effort during the development and maintenance of the software.

Even if the complete matrix is fully allocated in memory, it may still be advantageous to eliminate from consideration certain cells in the matrix that are unlikely to contribute to the optimal solution, similar to "banded" alignment techniques. When the probabilities of these eliminated cells are small but nonzero, the resulting procedure becomes a heuristic that is no longer guaranteed to find the optimal solution. In many cases this might be acceptable, but doing this typically involves empirical studies to establish an acceptable range of values for the cells being eliminated. This may need to be done every time the gene finder is trained for a new organism.

Devising the original recurrence relations can itself be a difficult task. For any given set of proposed equations, a worthwhile exercise is the derivation of a rigorous proof that the equations exhibit the intended semantics and do not permit greedy behavior. Unintended greediness could allow the algorithm to maximize the objective function as encoded without strictly adhering to the intended semantics, and could thereby compromise prediction accuracy. For example, failure to properly separate the inductive scores of the three coding phases until the end of a CDS in a Markov chain promotes greedy behavior, because the phase is not selected in a globally optimal manner.

Validation of the final software implementation is important as well, but can be very difficult when the expected predictions of a given DP formulation are not precisely known and would be impractical to produce manually. In these cases, subtle programming errors can go undetected unless one undertakes the time-consuming exercise of rigorously tracing through a number of sample computations to verify correct operation.

Another complication that not uncommonly arises in DP implementations applied to long sequences is the occurrence of numerical underflow, in which a value in the computation becomes so small that it cannot be represented by the host machine, thereby causing a floating-point exception or simply rendering gene models indistinguishable by assigning them all a score of zero. This is especially common in probabilistic formulations involving the multiplication of large numbers of probabilities. Several methods for avoiding underflow have been devised, such as arbitrarily rescaling the numbers or applying the log transformation, but some of these methods, such as rescaling, can significantly complicate the implementation and validation of the program, and generally must be derived anew for each gene finder.

In an attempt to counter some of these obstacles, several recent works have attempted to provide tools for the automatic construction of DP algorithms and software, though whether these techniques will see widespread adoption and tangibly impact the field remains to be seen.

Future Challenges

Gene-finding researchers now face an array of challenges for which new DP algorithms need to be developed. As more genomic information becomes available, the successful migration of gene-finding techniques into the realm of comparative genomics becomes increasingly important. The use of models such as Pair HMMs for gene finding entails a potentially significant increase in computational complexity that must be addressed.

Recent attempts at using these models have drawn on techniques such as the use of sparse matrices, heuristic optimization, and approximate alignments (themselves relying on DP methods), and generally have involved one or more simplifying assumptions, such as strict conservation of intron/exon structure.

Much current work now focuses on gene prediction in two species simultaneously; generalizing this to three or more species will require yet additional innovation to handle the enormous computational load. More generally, one might imagine more flexible DP frameworks in which suboptimal parses are made available in an efficient manner for perusal "on demand" by human annotators or for automatic integration with external evidence, perhaps in the context of a tightly coupled ensemble of separate gene-finding programs.

Gene Prediction

Gene prediction an important aspect of genome projects. Ineukaryotes, gene prediction and annotation is not a simple process due to the various sizes of introns (noncoding sequences) located between exons (coding sequences). In addition, many genes have alternative splice variants which make eukaryotic gene structure and length difficult to predict.

Many gene prediction programs have been developed for genome wide annotation. They are generally categorized into three groups. The first group uses an *ab initio* approach to predict genes directly from nucleotide sequences. Prediction programs in this group utilize statistical models to differentiate the promoter, coding or non-coding regions, as well as intron-exon junctions in genomic sequences. Hidden Marcov Models (HMMs) is a popular model used to make gene prediction programs, such as Grail, FGENESH, HMM gene, MZEF, and GENSCAN. The second group uses a similarity based approach to identify gene structure using a sequence alignment between genomic sequence and transcript (EST and cDNA) or protein databases. This approach has recently been expanded to genomic sequence comparison (comparative approach) between evolutionarily related species in order to identify functional regulatory elements which tend to be conserved through evolution. AAT, CRASA, and AGenDA belong to this group. The third group combines the *ab initio* method and similarity based approach. Procrustes, FGENESH+, GenomeScan, and Gene Wise are available for this approach.

Splicing site prediction is important in choosing the correct gene models on the basis of accurate intron-exon boundaries. Many programs use computational models based on consensus dimer sequences in donor sites, acceptor sites, and branch points (about 30bp upstream of acceptor site). They also use sequence alignments between transcripts and genomic sequences to predict splicing sites in genomic sequences. NetGene2, SplicePredictor, or GeneSplicer is used for splicing site prediction.

tRNAScan-SE identifies transfer RNA genes in genomic sequences by searching for conserved A & B box promoter sequences and progressively identifying various stem-loop-structures. It provides tabular and secondary structure as the standard output.

Although some areas of the genome rely only on *ab initio* or similarity based approaches due to prediction failure or lack of experimental data, a combined approach generally increases the accuracy of gene annotation.

Gene-prediction Algorithm

CONTRAST, a new gene-prediction algorithm that uses sophisticated machine-learning techniques, has pushed *de novo* prediction accuracy to new heights, and has significantly closed the gap between *de novo* and evidence-based methods for human genome annotation.

Gene prediction is one of the most important and alluring problems in computational biology. Its importance comes from the inherent value of the set of protein-coding genes for other analysis. Its allure is based on the apparently simple rules that the transcriptional machinery uses: strong, easily recognizable signals within the genome such as open reading frames, consensus splice sites and nearly universal start and stop codon sequences. These signals are highly conserved, are relatively easy to model, and have been the focus of a number of algorithms trying to locate all the protein-coding genes in a genome using only the sequence of one or more genomes. This technique, so-called *de novo* prediction, does not use information about expressed sequences such as proteins or mRNAs.

In this month's issue of *Genome Biology*, Gross and colleagues describe the gene-prediction program CONTRAST, the latest significant advance in *de novo* gene prediction. The program exploits patterns inherent in multiple sequence alignments while making few assumptions about evolutionary processes. Its accuracy is considerably higher than any other *de novo* prediction program and has significantly closed the gap between *de novo* and evidence-based methods for human genome annotation.

There have been two previous significant breakthroughs in *de novo* human gene prediction. The first was the identification and optimization of algorithms to effectively model the problem. The second was the use of an evolutionarily related genome sequence to reliably increase both the sensitivity and specificity of the predictions. Both advances are briefly discussed below.

Algorithms based on a generalized hidden Markov model (GHMM) framework have been particularly successful for gene prediction. A GHMM can be used to describe the relationship between the components of a protein-coding gene (such as exons and splice sites) and the sequence of genomic DNA in which the gene is found. The best-known example of this method is the program GENSCAN, which in 1997 was shown to be dramatically more accurate than the previous state-of-the-art prediction programs. GENSCAN was easy to use, very fast, and predicted genes in the long sequences of genomic DNA that would characterize the human genome project. Although subsequently shown to predict only 10-15% of genes correctly on realistic genome-wide datasets, GENSCAN remains a popular bioinformatics tool. GENSCAN predictions continue to be a standard feature for every genome released on both the University of California Santa Cruz (UCSC) and Ensembl genome browsers.

In 2002, with the publication of the mouse genome sequence, human gene prediction formally entered the era of comparative genomics. A number of programs were developed to exploit this new data source. In both human-mouse comparisons and across the tree of life, the most successful of these dedicated algorithms was TWINSCAN, a gene-prediction program that exploited the signature of evolution using a reimplementation and extension of the GENSCAN GHMM model. TWINSCAN's improved accuracy featured a dramatic reduction in false-positive predictions, while managing to predict about 25% of human protein-coding genes completely accurately. TWINSCAN itself was then extended with a more expressive model of evolutionary conservation derived from a multiple sequence alignment of several complete genomes. This extension, known as N-SCAN, predicts approximately 35% of human genes correctly, but is no more accurate with a multiple sequence alignment than it is with the most informative pairwise genome alignment. Thus, even though the N-SCAN model of evolutionary conservation is better than the one used by TWINSCAN, N-SCAN is not benefiting from the additional genome sequences used in the alignment.

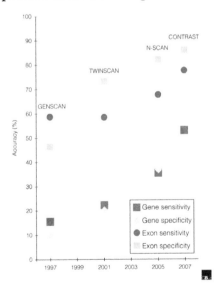

Increase in the accuracy of de novo gene prediction over time. The gene sensitivity and specificity and the exon sensitivity and specificity on the EGASP test set are shown for several programs by year of initial publication. Included are GENSCAN (1997), TWIN-SCAN (2001), N-SCAN (2005) and CONTRAST (2007). Note the significant decrease in false positive predictions (as measured by the rise in TWINSCAN's exon specificity) with the inital use of evolutionarily related genome sequences. By comparison, the accuracy of the Ensembl evidence-based gene predictions used in the EGASP experiment at the gene level were 71.6% sensitivity and 67.3% specificity and 77.5% sensitivity and 82.7% specificity at the exon level.

At the same time as these advances in *de novo* gene prediction, evidence-based gene prediction was also progressing rapidly. The best evidence-based systems integrate data from sources such as mRNA and protein sequences to predict specific genes that are supported by a variety of expressed sequences. These evidence-based gene sets are often used for other biological analyses such as.

CONTRAST is a dramatic advance on the previous state of the art. Using the Consensus CDS (CCDS) set as the gold standard, CONTRAST predicts nearly 60% of the genes correctly using only the human genome sequence and a multiple alignment with 11 so-called 'informant' genome sequences. This result is a stunning improvement on the previous state-of-the-art *de novo* gene-prediction algorithms both on the CCDS set and the gold standard manually annotated genes used for the ENCODE Genome Annotation Assessment Project (EGASP). Close examination of the EGASP results shows that CONTRAST compares very favorably with even the best evidence-based, expressed sequence prediction methods, especially for exon accuracy.

To achieve this, Gross *et al.* did something unconventional in the gene-prediction field. They ignored what is known about evolutionary relationships and assumed that there must be additional information in the multiple sequence alignment even if they could not exactly say what sort of information was there. Doing this required a switch from generative models such as HMMs, which have been used by essentially all previous *de novo* prediction programs, to discriminative models such as support vector machines and conditional random fields. A support vector machine (SVM) is an example of the machine-learning technique called 'supervised learning', in which the algorithm is able to classify new items based on rules it has discovered from a correctly labeled training set. A conditional random field (CRF) can be used to classify sequential data and is applicable to many of the same problems as an HMM. CONTRAST uses both SVM and CRF techniques for different parts of the gene-prediction problem. The SVMs are used for coding region boundary detection (splice sites, start and stop codons), whereas a CRF is used to model the gene structure (that is, how all the pieces fit together). Readers interested in more information about these machine-learning techniques may like to start with a recent biology-based primer on SVMs.

There are limits for biological understanding with these new techniques. A process of evolution resulted in the extant sequences that we see, and understanding this process would be immensely valuable. Generative models such as HMMs attempt to explicitly describe the evolutionary process by generating the multiple sequence alignment of an evolutionarily conserved exon. For example, a phylogenetic HMM may use separate models of molecular evolution for the first, second and third positions of each codon. Unlike phylogenetic HMMs, discriminative machine-learning techniques such as those used by Gross *et al.* do not model the complexities of the evolutionary process, but they are able to find the subtle differences in the alignments associated with real genes from other, very similar alignments in the genome.

In the current implementation, training CONTRAST requires the target genome to be at least reasonably well annotated at the start. It is not yet clear how well it will perform when annotating a genome with no high-quality training data, although unpublished results from the CONTRAST team demonstrate substantial accuracy with only a few thousand training genes . The situation where no training data is available could be simulated, at least for the case of human and mouse, by using one of the genomes as a well-annotated training set and the other to test predictive accuracy. As the most accurate *de novo* prediction program, CONTRAST will help complete the protein-coding gene set in well annotated genomes such as human and mouse, and may be vital for accurate annotation of complex genomes with informative sequence alignments to related species, but without significant expression data. Nevertheless, annotating a genome without the sequence of a closely related species is likely to remain a challenge.

CONTRAST is not the first program to apply these types of machine-learning technique to the problem of computational gene prediction. Bernal *et al.* recently introduced a gene-prediction program called CRAIG, which does not use any sequence alignments, but does use a semi-Markov CRF. CRAIG shows notable improvement over a large selection of other non-alignment-based programs. However, it performed less well than HMM-based multi-genome prediction programs such as N-SCAN. DeCaprio *et al.* developed Conrad, a comparative gene-prediction program that also uses semi-Markov CRFs. Conrad shows striking improvements on fungal genomes compared with other leading prediction programs, but its current implementation makes its application to large mammalian genomes computationally prohibitive.

It is still the case that the best full-length gene predictions are done by mapping expressed sequences to the genome assembly. CONTRAST finds the initial and terminal exons of a gene relatively difficult to predict and this somewhat limits exact gene prediction. However, Gross *et al.* show convincingly that there is complex information in the multiple sequence alignment of mammalian genomes and that this information can be exploited to create far more accurate gene predictions than those produced by the best HMM-based algorithms. The performance of CONTRAST suggests that the dominance of HMM-based programs in gene-prediction might be waning. Without doubt, further advances in machine-learning methods for large-scale biological analysis will help us integrate and understand complex biological data. A challenge for computational biologists is to transform the language of SVMs and discriminative learning techniques into biological models that will help us understand the complex processes of evolution that have created the extant species that we are now so busily sequencing.

The development of CONTRAST is a welcome result to those of us who believed that there must be additional information that could be used for gene prediction in multiple sequence alignments. Brent recently suggested a number of possible reasons why multiple sequence alignments had failed to increase the accuracy of comparative gene prediction. These included sequence quality, alignment methods, and lack of splice site and exon conservation in the mammalian lineage. It looks as though his final reason - that designers of *de novo* gene prediction algorithms had not yet been clever enough to come up with a solution - might well have been the right one.

BLAST Technique

An important goal of genomics is to determine if a particular sequence is like another sequence. This is accomplished by comparing the new sequence with sequences that have already been reported and stored in a database. This process is principally one that uses alignment procedures to uncover the "like" sequence in the database. The alignment process will uncover those regions that are identical or closely similar and those regions with little (or any) similarity. Conserved regions might represent motifs that are essential for function. Regions with little similarity could be less essential to function. In a sense, these alignments are used to determine if a database contains a potential homologous sequence to the newly derived sequence. Further, phylogenetic studies are necessary to determine the orthologous/paralogous nature of the two aligned sequences.

Two alignment types are used: global and local. The global approach compares one whole sequence with other entire sequences. The local method uses a subset of a sequence and attempts to align it to subset of other sequences. The output of a global alignment is a one-tocomparison of two sequences. Local alignments reveal regions that are highly similar, but do not necessarily provide a comparison across the entire two sequences. The global approach is useful when you are comparing a small group of sequences, but becomes become computationally expensive as the number of sequence in the comparison increases. Local alignments use heuristic programming methods that are better suited to successfully searching very large databases, but they do not necessarily give the most optimum solution. Even given this limitation, local alignments are very important to the field of genomics because they can uncover regions of homology that are related by descent between two otherwise diverse sequences.

Here are examples of global and local alignments. The global alignment looks for comparison over the entire range of the two sequences involved.

```
GCATTACTAATATATTAGTAAATCAGAGTAGTA
          |||||||||| ||
AAGCGAATAATATATTTATACTCAGATTATTGCGCG
```

As you can see only a portion of this two sequences can be aligned. By contrast, when a local alignment is performed, a small seed is uncovered that can be used to quickly extend the alignment.

The initial seed for the alignment:

```
              TAT
              | | |
AAGCGAATAATATATTTATACTCAGATTATTGCGCG
```

And now the extended alignment:

```
            TATATATTAGTA
            | | | | | | | | |  | |
AAGCGAATAATATATTTATACTCAGATTATTGCGCG
```

The most common local alignment tool is BLAST (Basic Local Alignment Search Tool) developed by Altschul et al.. The operative phrase in the phrase is local alignment. The BLAST is a set of algorithms that attempt to find a short fragment of a query sequence that aligns perfectly with a fragment of a subject sequence found in a database. That initial alignment must be greater than a neighborhood score threshold (T). For the original BLAST algorithm, the fragment is then used as a seed to extend the alignment in both directions. The alignment is extended in both directions until the T score for the aligned segment does not continue to increase. Said another way, BLAST looks for short sequences in the query that matches short sequences found in the database.

The first step of the BLAST algorithm is to break the query into short words of a specific length. A word is a series of characters from the query sequences. The default length of the search is three characters. The words are constructed by using a sliding window of three characters. For example, twelve amino acids near the amino terminal of the Aradbidopsis thaliana protein phosphoglucomutase sequence are:

```
NYLENFVQATFN
```

This sequence is broken down into three character words by selecting the first amino acid characters, moving over one character, selecting the next three amino acid characters, and so on to create the following seven words:

```
NYL YLE LEN ENF NFV FVQ VQA QAT ATF TFN
```

These words are then compared against a sequence in a database. Here is an example of a word match with rabbit muscle phoshoglucomutase (subject line):

```
Query              ENF
Subject        SSTNYAENTIQSIISTVEPAQR
```

This search is performed for all words. For the original BLAST search, those words whose T value was greater than 18 were used as seeds to extend the alignment.

The T value is derived by using a scoring matrix. The BLOSUM 62 matrix is the default for protein searches and will be discussed later. The alignment is extended in both directions until the alignment score decreases in value. As an example, consider the following alignment between the A. thaliana and rabbit muscle phophoglucomutase:

```
Query      NLYENFVQATFNALTAEKV
           NY ENF+Q+  +  +    +
Subject    NYAENTIQSIISTVEPAQR
```

The centerline provides the following information. A letter designates an identity (or high similarity) between the two sequences. A "+" means the two sequences are similar but not highly similar. If no symbol is given between the two sequences, then a non-similar substitution has occurred.

Those alignments whose T score does not decrease are then compared with scores obtained by random searches. Those alignments whose score is above the cutoff are called a *High Scoring Segment Pair* (HSP). Once this alignment process is completed for a query and each subject sequence in the database, a report is generated. This report provides a list of those alignments (default size of 50) with a value greater than the S cutoff value.

For each alignment reported, an *Expect (e) Value* is reported. This value is a function of the S value and the database size. An e value of 1 means that one alignment using a query of this size will by chance produce a S score of this value in a database of this size. As you can imagine an e value of -10 ($=1 \times 10^{-10}$) means that it is much more unlikely that random chance lead to this current alignment compared to an alignment with an e value of 1. The expect value is often considered to be a probability. In other words, the probability of achieving a score of this value using a sequence of this length against a database of this size is equal to the expect value.

Therefore, a lower e value means that alignment is significant at a specific probability level. It is important that you note that the expect value is specific to a database of a certain size. This means, that if you perform your BLAST alignment at a later date, you e value might change because the size of the database has changed.

In general, if you see an e value of -30, you can be assured that your sequence is homologous to the sequence to which aligned in this database. Furthermore, e values of -5 are often considered significant enough when annotating a genome.

The example above describes the process of using a protein query to search for alignments in protein database. Alignments are also possible between a nucleotide query and a nucleotide database. The entire BLAST process described above is the same for nucleotide searches except the default word size is eleven and a different scoring matrix is applied.

Scoring matrices are used to obtain the S value. For nucleotides, these are simple; each identical match is given the same score, and all mismatches are given a penalty (negative) score.

BLAST Nucleotide Matrix ("Ungapped Alignment")

	A	T	C	G
A	5			
T	-4	5		
C	-4	-4	5	
G	-4	-4	-4	5

BLAST Nucleotide Matrix ("Gapped Alignment")

	A	T	C	G
A	1			
T	-3	1		
C	-3	-3	1	
G	-3	-3	-3	1

The amino acid scoring matrix is more complex. Henikoff and Henikoff studied 2000 aligned blocks of 500 groups of related proteins. They determined the different types of amino acid substitutions that occurred in these proteins. From this study, they developed the BLOSUM 62 matrix. (BLOSUM = BLOcks SUbstitution Matrix) This matrix gives a score (positive value) or penalty (negative value) for each amino acid identity or substitution between two aligned sequences. From the table below, you can see that not all identities or substitutions are of equal value. This is because the comparison the authors did between the many proteins gave an indication of the likelihood that a specific substitution might occur.

	A	C	D	E	F	G	H	I	K	L	M	N	P	Q	R	S	T	V	W	Y
A	4	0	-2	-1	-2	0	-2	-1	-1	-1	-1	-2	-1	-1	-1	1	0	0	-3	-2
C		9	-3	-4	-2	-3	-3	-1	-3	-1	-1	-3	-3	-3	-3	-1	-1	-1	-2	-2
D			6	2	-3	-1	-1	-3	-1	-4	-3	1	-1	0	-2	0	-2	-3	-4	-3
E				5	-3	-2	0	-3	1	-3	-2	0	-1	2	0	0	-1	-2	-3	-2
F					6	-3	-1	0	-3	0	0	-3	-4	-3	-3	-2	-2	-1	1	3
G						6	-2	-4	-2	-4	-3	0	-2	-2	-2	0	-2	-3	-2	-3
H							8	-3	-1	-3	-2	1	-2	0	0	-1	-2	-3	-2	2
I								4	-3	2	1	-3	-3	-3	-3	-1	-1	3	-3	-1
K									5	-2	-1	0	-1	1	2	0	-1	-2	-3	-2
L										4	2	-3	-3	-2	-2	-2	-1	1	-2	-1
M											5	-2	-2	0	-1	-1	-1	1	-1	-1
N												6	-2	0	0	1	0	-3	-4	-2
P													7	-1	-2	-1	-1	-2	-4	-3
Q														5	1	0	-1	-2	-2	-1
R															5	-2	-2	-3	-3	-2
S																4	1	-2	-3	-2
T																	5	0	-2	-2
V																		4	-3	-1
W																			11	2
Y																				7

So why is it called BLOSUM 62? If you were to score an alignment between two amino acid sequences that were 62% identical, their BLOSUM 62 score would be 1. Similar matrices are also available if you require a higher or lower percent identity. These are BLOSUM 45 and BLOSUM 80. The BLOSUM 45 matrix should be used if you are looking for distantly related sequences, whereas the BLOSUM 80 matrix is appropriate for searches involving highly conserved sequences. For protein alignments, the BLAST algorithm uses BLOSUM 62 as the default matrix.

Using the BLOSUM62 matrix, we can then derive a score for the following alignment.

```
Query        NLYENFVQATF

NY           ENF+Q+

Subject      NYAENTIQSII
```

Going from left to right the score is summed as follows:

Query	N	L	Y	E	N	F	V	Q	A	T	F
Subject	N	Y	A	E	N	T	I	Q	S	I	I
Score	5		-1	-2	5	6	-2	3	5	1	-1	0

Score = 19

BLAST2 (1997. Nucleic Acids Research 25:3389-3402) takes a different (and three-times faster) approach than the original BLAST algorithm. As with the original BLAST it looks for matchs to the three character words, but the T value is lower. It then identifies two words that lie next to each other and uses those neighboring words as the seed to extend the alignment. As with the original BLAST procedure, S scores are obtained, and expect values are calculated.

Another feature introduced with BLAST2 was the ability to add gaps to the alignment.

Because gaps are evidence of evolutionary differences between sequences (assuming they are not sequencing errors), *gap penalties* are used to reduce the score value. The default for protein searches is a reduction of 11 for the introduction of a gap, and a reduction of 1 for each gap added at that same gap location. Gaps are useful because you can actually increase the score of a local alignment, even when gap penalties are included in the score.

As mentioned above, BLAST is actually a collection of algorithms. So when you do a BLAST search you actually need to specify the type of search that you will perform. The following table outlines each algorithm and the nature of the query and database used.

Search	Query	Database
Blastn	Nucleotide	Nucleotide
Blastx	Translated nucleotide in all six frames	Protein
Tblastx	Translated nucleotide in all six frames	Translated nucleotide in all six frames
Blastp	Protein	Protein

Basic Local Alignment Search Tool

Alignments

- Used to uncover homologies between sequences

- Combined with phylogenetic studies

- Can determine orthologous and paralogous relationships

Global Alignments

- Compares one whole sequence with other entire sequence

- Computationally expensive

Local Alignment

- Uses a subset of a sequence and attempts to align it to subset of other sequences

- Computationally less expensive

Global Alignment Example

```
GCATTACTAATATATTAGTAAATCAGAGTAGTA
          | | | | | | | | | |   | |
AAGCGAATAATATATTTATACTCAGATTATTGCGCG
```

Only a portion of this two sequences can be aligned

Local Alignment Example

A small seed is uncovered.

The initial seed for the alignment:

```
            TAT
            | | |
AAGCGAATAATATATTTATACTCAGATTATTGCGCG
```

And now the extended alignment:

```
TATATATTAGTA
||||||||| ||
AAGCGAATAATATATTTATACTCAGATTATTGCGCG
```

BLAST

Basic Local Alignment Search Tool

- Set of alignment algorithms
- Use the same search protocol to:
    - Find a short fragment of a query sequence
    - That aligns with a fragment of a subject sequence found in a database

General Concept for Original BLAST Program

- Sequence (query) is broken into words of *length W*
- Align all words with sequences in the database
- Calculate *score T* for each word that aligns with a sequence in the database using a substitution matrix
- Discard words whose T value is below a *neighborhood score threshold*
- Extend words in both directions until score falls by *dropoff value X*
- When compared to previous best score

BLAST Words

- Three characters in length
- Complied by using a sliding window

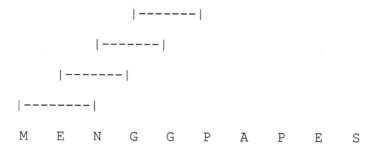

```
              |-------|
           |-------|
        |-------|
     |--------|
   M   E   N   G   G   P   A   P   E   S
```

Align All Words and Calculate T Score

```
                                   16
                               |-------|

                            18
                        |-------|

                   17
               |-------|

            19
        |-------|

      10
  |-------|

    3
|-------|

  -2
|--------|
M    E    N    G    G    P    A    P    E    S

1   -1   -2    6    6    7    4    7    5    4    BLOSUM 62 Score

I    P    A    G    G    P    A    P    E    S
```

Build Alignment

- Original alignment: T Score =19

```
                 G    G    P
1   -1   -2      6    6    7    4    7    5    4    BLOSUM 62 Score
I    P    A      G    G    P    A    P    E    S
```

- Extend one amino acid in each direction: T Score = 21

```
            N    G    G    P    A
1   -1   -2      6    6    7    4    7    5    4    BLOSUM 62 Score
I    P    A      G    G    P    A    P    E    S
```

- Stop when next extension drops off below value X compared to previous score

Points to Remember

- The T score is converted into a bits score by a complicated formula
- The X value is based on the bit score

Search Matrices

BLOSUM 62 matrix. (BLOSUM = BLOcks SUbstitution Matrix)

- Henikoff and Henikoff (1992. PNAS 89:10915-10919)

- Studied 2000 aligned blocks of 500 groups of related proteins

  - Determined the different types of amino acid substitutions that occurred in these proteins

  - Developed the matrix based on the study

  - Positive value

    - Identities or high similarities

  - Negative value

    - Penalty

    - Non similar substitutions

BLOSUM 62 Amino Acid Matrix

	A	C	D	E	F	G	H	I	K	L	M	N	P	Q	R	S	T	V	W	Y
A	4	0	-2	-1	-2	0	-2	-1	-1	-1	-1	-2	-1	-1	-1	1	0	0	-3	-2
C		9	-3	-4	-2	-3	-3	-1	-3	-1	-1	-3	-3	-3	-3	-1	-1	-1	-2	-2
D			6	2	-3	-1	-1	-3	-1	-4	-3	1	-1	0	-2	0	-2	-3	-4	-3
E				5	-3	-2	0	-3	1	-3	-2	0	-1	2	0	0	-1	-2	-3	-2
F					6	-3	-1	0	-3	0	0	-3	-4	-3	-3	-2	-2	-1	1	3
G						6	-2	-4	-2	-4	-3	0	-2	-2	-2	0	-2	-3	-2	-3
H							8	-3	-1	-3	-2	1	-2	0	0	-1	-2	-3	-2	2
I								4	-3	2	1	-3	-3	-3	-3	-1	-1	3	-3	-1
K									5	-2	-1	0	-1	1	2	0	-1	-2	-3	-2
L										4	2	-3	-3	-2	-2	-2	-1	1	-2	-1
M											5	-2	-2	0	-1	-1	-1	1	-1	-1
N												6	-2	0	0	1	0	-3	-4	-2
P													7	-1	-2	-1	-1	-2	-4	-3
Q														5	1	0	-1	-2	-2	-1
R															5	-2	-2	-3	-3	-2
S																4	1	-2	-3	-2
T																	5	0	-2	-2
V																		4	-3	-1
W																			11	2
Y																				7

So Why is it Called BLOSUM 62?

- Alignment between two amino acid sequences that were 62% identical.

- BLOSUM 62 score would be 1.

- BLOSUM 45:

  - 45% identical

  - distantly related sequences.

- BLOSUM 80:

  - 80% identity

  - Highly conserved sequences.

BLAST Statistics

Score (Bits)

- A statistical conversion of the score derived by summing using the substitution matrix.

Expect (e) Value

- Function of the S value and the database size.

- An e value of 1.

- One alignment using a query of this size will by chance produce a S score of this value in a database of this size.

E value of −10 (=1x10^{-10})

- Unlikely that random chance lead to this current alignment compared to an alignment with an e value of 1.

- Often considered to be a probability.

NOTE

- Expect value is specific to a database of a certain size.

  - Later searches may give different value

- Why?

  - Database size has changed.

Rules of Thumb

- E value of −30 or less
    ◦ Sequences are homologous
- E values of −5
    ◦ Often considered significant enough when annotating a genome

BLAST2

Takes a different (and three-times faster) approach than the original BLAST algorithm

- Same word search
- Lower T value
- Neighboring words discovered
    ◦ Must be at a distance less than A (default 40)
- Alignment extended from the neighboring words

Gap penalties

- New in BLAST2
- Allow for better alignments
- Default for amino acid search
- Introducing a gap
    ◦ -11
- Extending that gap
    ◦ -1

BLAST Algorithms

Search	Query	Database
Blastn	Nucleotide	Nucleotide
Blastx	Translated nucleotide in all six frames	Protein
Tblastx	Translated nucleotide in all six frames	Translated nucleotide in all six frames
Blastp	Protein	Protein

Nucleotide Scoring Matrices

BLAST Nucleotide Matrix ("Ungapped Alignment")

	A	T	C	G
A	5			
T	-4	5		
C	-4	-4	5	
G	-4	-4	-4	5

BLAST Nucleotide Matrix ("Gapped Alignment")

	A	T	C	G
A	1			
T	-3	1		
C	-3	-3	1	
G	-3	-3	-3	1

Bioinformatics vs. Computational Biology

The world of quantitative biology is large, diffuse and sometimes overwhelming. It's hard sometimes to even figure out what someone means when they say "bioinformatics". This can make it hard to figure out what part of the field someone works in.

One way to break it down is to describe bioinformatics as the building of tools and methods for the processing and management of biological data, and computational biology as the pursuit of biological sciences using computational methods. Therefore, bioinformatics is more of an engineering discipline and computational biology more a scientific discipline.

It's helpful to think about these distinctions, subtle as they seem. It takes a certain mindset and skillset to build a robust sequencing analysis pipeline that will serve the needs of a large group of scientists for years. That mindset and skillset may be very different from the one required to do a deep investigation of the variants that impact risk of heart disease.

We can argue about the naming conventions all we want, but the label we apply to these two types of specialist doesn't really matter. What matters is what they do; the person I would call a computational biologist writes code, yes, but does it in pursuit of a particular biological problem, and they would love to write less code and more manuscripts. The bioinformatician, on the other hand, wants to spend their time writing robust, high-quality code that does interesting and powerful computations. Papers are more of a nice side-effect.

The truth of the matter is that most programming biologists are a mix of the two disciplines.

When hiring for a small department or a startup, the distinction between these two caricatures becomes very important. Some people will be in the field for the biology specifically, and will choke when pressed to develop a tool for use by a team. Others will jump at the chance to write such a thing. Every group needs both of these. Consider the current needs; will this person be building a pipeline that will be re-used again and again? Or will they investigate particular variants, or particular compound response profiles? Fitting the right person to the job will ensure a happy employee and high productivity.

Figuring out what kind of background and preferences someone has can be as simple as asking them. Their resume or LinkedIn profile can also give clues. A software-focused person will tend to have one or more large, open-source bioinformatics software tools prominently listed. Their reference list may include a few papers describing this project and others (potentially many others) that use that tool. A manuscript-focused person will not be as likely to have a major tool-building segment of their resume. Instead, they will list a series of biology or dataset-focused projects, with manuscripts describing each.

Computational biology is the the study of biology using computational techniques. The goal is to learn new biology, knowledge about living sytems. It is about science.

Bioinformatics is the creation of tools (algorithms, databases) that solve problems. The goal is to build useful tools that work on biological data. It is about engineering.

References

- Bioinformatics, science: britannica.com, Retrieved 13 May, 2019

- Bioinformatics-Algorithms-Techniques-and-Applications: researchgate.net, Retrieved 23 January, 2019

- Bioinformatics-algorithms: bioinformaticsonline.com, Retrieved 28 March, 2019

- Hirschberg-s-algorithm, algorithms-and-methods: bioinfoguide.com, Retrieved 8 June, 2019

- Smith-waterman-algorithm, algorithms-and-methods: bioinfoguide.com, Retrieved 12 January, 2019

- Peitsch, M.C., and Schwede, T. (2008) Computational Structural Biology: Methods and Applications World Scientific, ISBN 978-9812778772, Retrieved 21 August, 2019

- Moody, Glyn (2004). Digital Code of Life: How Bioinformatics is Revolutionizing Science, Medicine, and Business. ISBN 978-0-471-32788-2, Retrieved 4 July, 2019

- Gusfield, Dan (1997). Algorithms on strings, trees, and sequences : computer science and computational biology (Reprinted (with corr.) ed.). Cambridge [u.a.]: Cambridge Univ. Press. ISBN 9780521585194, Retrieved 2 April, 2019

- Sequence_alignment: bioinf.comav.upv.es, Retrieved 28 August, 2019

- Dynamic-programming-for-gene-finders-bioinformatics: what-when-how.com, Retrieved 4 July, 2019

- Gene-prediction, medicine-and-dentistry: sciencedirect.com, Retrieved 14 May, 2019

- Blast-explanation-lecture-and-overhead: ndsu.edu, Retrieved 24 February, 2019

- Bioinformatics-vs-computational-biology: diamondage.com, Retrieved 13 March, 2019

- Bioinformatics-computational-biology-same-no: rbaltman.wordpress.com, Retrieved 3 June, 2019

Chapter 5
Databases and Software

Databases are an integral part of bioinformatics research and applications. Some of the software used in bioinformatics are Clustal, MUSCLE, Bowtie and HMMER. The topics elaborated in this chapter will help in gaining a better perspective about these software as well as the different types of databases such as primary and secondary databases.

Computational Analysis of Protein Structures

The Data

Nucleotide sequences contain the blueprints for the development of living organisms. They directly encypher the amino acid sequences of proteins, agents of biological structure and function. Once the amino acid sequence of a protein has been synthesized, it then spontaneously folds to create a unique three-dimensional protein conformation. It is at this point that the linear genetic code is translated into three dimensions.

Nucleic acid sequences, protein sequences, and protein structures are all collected and distributed by data banks.

Nucleic acid sequences are collected by a tripartite association of organizations: GenBank® in the United States of America, with scientists at Los Alamos National Laboratory and Intelligenetics, Inc.; The Nucleotide Sequence Data Bank at the European Molecular Biology Laboratory in Heidelberg, Federal Republic of Germany; and the DNA Data Bank of Japan, at the National Institute of Genetics, in Mishima. These groups collaborate in harvesting data from published journals, and in sharing the results. To an increasing extent, the data banks are receiving data in computer-readable form directly from scientists. The data are converted to standard formats, checked and annotated, and then exchanged among the databanks and distributed to scientists.

It may be interesting to have some standards of comparison for the amounts of data involved. If one base pair is stored as one byte, the genome of the Epstein-Barr virus has 172 kbytes, the genome of the much studied bacterium E. coli has 4000 kbytes, the genome of yeast is around 20,000 kbytes, and the human genome is a factor of 1000 above E. coli at 4×10^9 bases or 4×10^6 kbytes. The E. coli genome stored at 1 byte per base pair has approximately the same number of characters as the Cambridge, England telephone directory. A human genome has about an order of magnitude more characters than the Oxford English Dictionary. The Dictionary in its new printed form is a set of 16 large volumes, and also occupies an entire compact disc.

Protein sequences are collected by another triple partnership. For many years, the group at the National Biomedical Research Foundation in Washington, D.C. maintained the major computerreadable archive of protein sequence data. In addition to collecting, annotating, and distributing sequences, this group has developed a powerful information retrieval system integrated with the data in the Protein Identification Resource (PIR). This group has recently been joined by others in the Federal Republic of Germany and in Japan.

The archive of three-dimensional structures of biological macromolecules is the Protein Data Bank at Brookhaven National Laboratory in New York, U.S.A. It collects the results of structure determinations, primarily by x-ray crystal structure analysis, but with a soupçon of structures determined by neutron diffraction; these to be joined by structures determined by NMR, which has established itself as quite a fruitful source of structural information for relatively small macromolecules. The Crystallographic Data Center in Cambridge, England, maintains a database of small molecular structures determined by x-ray crystallography. This information is extremely useful in studies of the conformations of the component units of biological macromolecules, and for investigations of macromolecule-ligand interactions.

A Task Group of CODATA (Committee on Data of the International Council of Scientific Unions), chaired by Prof. B. Keil of the Institute Pasteur; secretary, Dr. A. Tsugita of the Science University of Tokyo, has been working to try to foster collaboration among data banks, and between the data banks and the scientific community.

Data Distribution

In the past, most of the data banks distributed their contents on magnetic tape or floppy disk, emitting successive releases at standard intervals, typically 3 months apart. Recently there has been some exploration of the use of computer networks for data distribution (as well as for submission of data), using the concept of a Netserver which responds to queries sent in over networks by returning a requested item as a reply (if possible). Other high-density storage media—notably CD-ROM—are also being explored; particularly exciting is the possibility of desk-top information retrieval systems self-contained in a personal computer-CD reader combination.

Information-retrieval Systems

To say that an understanding of the relationships among the data will provide the keys to breakthroughs in theoretical and experimental biology raises more questions than it answers. The availability of so much data, and the large number and incomplete definition of the relationships among them, create serious problems of data storage, quality control, and information retrieval. Plans for "mega-projects" such as the sequencing of the entire human and rice genomes will only intensify these challenges.

The rapid increase of computer power in recent years has begun to give us the tools to address these problems, and we must focus on the problems of design of a system to store, check, update, and distribute the incoming data, and then to provide the tools to produce new scientific results. These problems are common to many fields of science. Their general solution, based on an effective data base management system, has advantages that are well known: Applications programmers are relieved from standard management tasks, quality control is easier— redundancy and inconsistency in the data or in its formatting can be reduced, and the integrity of the data thereby more easily maintained.

A molecular biology information system must include both sequence and structural data, and the database management system must be able to answer, directly, most of the questions that investigators want to ask about the relationships among the data. It must also be flexible enough to accommodate new questions. Whether a commercial database management system can be used, or whether modifications or extensive redesign are required, depends on the structure and type of the information, on the manipulations to be performed on the data, and on the universe of user queries. Because the field is evolving with great speed intellectually, it is very hard to foresee the kind of questions we will come up with, even in the next few years. In the design of a database management system for molecular biology it would be fatal to sacrifice flexibility for efficiency.

It is necessary to present structural and non-structural data in the same framework. Inquiries such as "Is this sequence fragment present in other sequences?" and "Is this structural motif present in other structures?" should be asked by the user within a common framework of dialog. Of course the second type of question is more complicated, for it requires an interface general enough to define a structural motif. Thus the question "Is this new entry similar to any already-existing one?" is relatively well-defined if we are talking about linear (sequence) data, because the answer can be expressed in terms of the number of common residues and standard statistical parameters. In contrast, the same question, in the sense of structural similarity, requires further specification: For example, do we want to know about the overall shape of the molecule, about the relative positions of secondary structure elements, about the geometry of conserved residues in the active site? All these are legitimate inquiries, and such variations place great strain on a query interpreter.

Proteins exhibit both complex topological features and detailed local structural patterns. The careful observation of proteins, one at a time, can help us to define and propose some general principle of protein architecture; the comparative analysis of several structures probe the likelihood that our hypothesis is correct, and devising a general algorithm for testing the hypothesis with the entire available data set can confirm the proposed rule.

A problem facing those who would design a "packaged" system is the difficulty of defining a set of operations that encompasses the needs of the users. We ourselves, after having spent years in analyzing the operations useful in research (trying with only limited success to define a set of "elementary" operations in terms of which most manipulations might be defined) and in constructing software, find it frustrating that when a new project is undertaken it almost always requires the development of new tools.

Thus the database will have to cope with all the problems well-known from traditional "one-dimensional" databases, and also new ones specifically related to a "three-dimensional" database and a subject with widening intellectual horizons. The traditional problems include, for example, the problems of accommodating uncertain and partial data, of updating the system without loss of continuity, and most important of all, the problem of checking the data for consistency. Particular to chemical structural data is the need for a molecular graphics interface. Because features of the database entries must be presented graphically, in a consistent way, the design of the database must include a means of integrating the retrieval of information with molecular graphics packages.

A complete database should provide a flexible graphics interface allowing the user to visualize the atomic details of protein and nucleic acid structures, and some schematic view of their overall shape and secondary and tertiary structure. Whether the interface should include the graphics software or provide a way of interchanging information with the several existing graphics packages is not the most important question. The objection that in the first case the database would be more hardware-dependent will be overcome by the spread of graphics standards. What is needed in both cases is the availability of a clear definition of objects, representations and views applied to molecular objects.

Molecular Graphics

How do we go about analyzing protein structures? First, we make a general inspection of the structures, using computer graphics. Programs take a set of coordinates and create a visual image on some device. The system gives the user the facility of selecting a portion of the molecule to be shown, selecting the orientation of the picture, and selecting the representation of the structure.

Two basic representations are (1) to show each atom as a sphere, distinguishing different atoms by different colours or shades; (2) to show each bond as a line. The former requires what is called a "raster" device, giving an image with the appearance of a television screen. Typically the image can contain 512×512 or 1024×1024 "pixels," with each point chosen from one of 256 (or more) possible combinations of colour and intensity; thus one might have 16 intensity levels of each of 16 colours.

The second type of representation is called line or vector or calligraphic graphics. Here the technology exists to draw tens of thousands of lines, in different colours, at a refresh speed that does permit real-time rotation, which greatly enhances the observer's perception of the three-dimensional structural relationships. (Real-time rotation of raster pictures is possible in the new generation of graphics workstations, which are now being applied to molecular biology. This capacity has existed for some time, but until recently only in devices of such high cost that they were limited to special applications such as the training of aircraft pilots.) Other important methods of enhancing the perception of three-dimensional structural relationships include stereo, hidden-line removal, and depth cueing (that is, the diminishing of intensity of objects farther from the eyepoint.)

 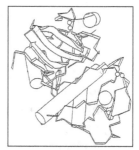

Two closely-related proteins; (a) actinidin and (b) papain. The amino acid sequences of these molecules have about 50% identical residues.

Because of the complexity of protein structures, pictures in which every atom or every bond is shown individually are often uninformative. People have therefore devised simplified or schematic representations. In these, a common grouping of atoms called an α-helix may be shown as a cylinder, and another common grouping of atoms called a strand of β-sheet may be shown as a large arrow.

Two quite distantly-related proteins: (a) sperm whale myoglobin and (b) lupin leghaemoglobin. In this case almost the entire chains have the same fold.

The analysis of a protein into helices, sheets, and other regions (often called loops) is part of the initial investigation of the structure and might be considered analogous to the parsing of a sentence, or at least to the identification of nouns and verbs. Helices and sheets are common arrangements of regions of proteins, stabilized by hydrogen bonds. They were predicted by Linus Pauling on the basis of physico-chemical principles before the discovery of the first protein structures, myoglobin and haemoglobin, in which the presence of helices was gratifyingly confirmed.

We can identify helices and sheets in proteins either visually, or by the detection of hydrogen bonds by purely numerical analysis of the coordinates, or by geometrical

analysis of the positions of the atoms. There exist programs that will take a set of coordinates and produce a set of helix and sheet assignments automatically. Because of
the not uncommon "fraying" of the ends of these regular substructures, these programs
work fairly well but not perfectly.

Two other distantly-related proteins: (a) poplar leaf plastocyanin and
(b) *A. denitrificans* azurin. In this case the double β-sheet portion of these molecules
retains the same fold, but the long loop at the left changes its conformation completely.

Knowing where in the structure the helices and sheets lie, we can create a variety of
representations of the structure. Protein structures have been classified into certain
basic types on the basis of the types of secondary structures they contain and the spatial
relationships between them. Such a diagram will be enough for an expert to place a new
structure in the current scheme, or to recognize a real novelty.

Storing images or the coordinates necessary to rebuild them could be transparent
to the user if a "molecular graphics metafile" is provided, where a clear definition
of the properties of the displayed object is stored. While standardizing the graphic
representation of a molecular object is relatively straightforward when dealing with
one molecule at a time, several problems arise when more than one molecule has to
be displayed in the same coordinate space. Showing two superimposed molecules,
or an enzyme together with its substrate, requires in both cases the visualization of
two molecules, but the physical meaning of the two double images is completely different. Some operations are allowed in one case (for example in the first case two
atoms occupy the same position in space) but forbidden in the other. In other words
the "metafile" should also define the possible operations that can be performed in
each case, so that the application program, whether it is a part of the database or not,
should treat the two cases differently providing the user with the appropriate functions for each.

Protein Modeling

The general ideas presented here can now be illustrated with an important example;
the question of modeling the structures of unknown proteins. In order to have a specific
framework for this discussion, let us consider a particular problem; one which in fact
arises in virtually this exact form.

Suppose we know the structures of two related proteins, for example, the sulphy-dryl proteases actinidin and papain, or the two electron-transport proteins plasto-cyanin and azurin, or sperm whale myoglobin and lupin leghaeraoglobin. Suppose someone shows up with a third sequence, of a natural protein of unknown structure related to the other two. What can we say about its structure? (The restriction to natural variants is now important because molecules synthesized in the laborato-ry have not undergone the trial of natural selection and may not follow the same rules.)

We must know how to align the sequences of the known proteins, we must be able to identify and describe the structural differences between the known proteins, and we must be able to know how the differences in the amino acid sequences are related to the structural differences. Deriving this insight from the known proteins we can extrapo-late to their unknown relative. Let us consider some of the computational steps we go through, and the nature of the software and hardware that have proved useful.

Let us first dispose of what we might with some temerity call a potential distraction: Someday it may be possible to ignore the fact that the unknown protein is related to others of known structure, and to predict its conformation from physical principles. This is just not possible today.

It follows that, given a new sequence, we must first try to find out whether it is related to proteins of known structure. There are now fairly standard techniques for screen-ing databases of sequences, to pick up many—but not all—relationships. Very distant relationships may elude these procedures, as it is a fact that structural relationships can exist when the overall sequence similarity has diverged so far as to conceal the ho-mology. There are more sensitive methods for picking up members of some individual protein families, by looking for a specific "fingerprint" or "signature" of a protein that may involve only a small fraction of the residues.

If we find that the unknown protein is related to other proteins of known structure, it is possible to draw two conclusions about its conformation:

1. The structure of the unknown protein is like the structure of the known proteins, and

2. The structure of the unknown protein is unlike the structure of the known proteins.

Although this sounds like something from Alice in Wonderland, both comments are true. The first is a statement that related amino acid sequences determine protein struc-tures that have the same general topology or fold, over at least 50% of the molecule. The second statement points out that amino acid sequence changes produce conformation-al changes, so that the structure of one of the proteins will be a distorted version of the structure of the other. The extent of the distortion, which limits the quality of the model of the unknown protein that we could build, depends on how far the amino acid sequences have diverged.

We have already discussed how we look at one protein structure at a time. To reason about an unknown protein from related known ones, we must now turn to the question of how we analyze the structural differences between two related proteins.

There is a basic computational tool in comparative structural analysis, which is the geometric superposition of a pair of structures. Given two lists of atoms, which may be regions selected from two proteins, the problem is to find a rotation matrix and translation vector that will optimally superpose the two structures, in a least-squares sense. We must know the proper correspondence of the atoms in the two structures, not a trivial question in the face of insertions and deletions of amino acids in the sequences of proteins.

Fortunately, this is a very simple problem to solve, and several fast and reliable algorithms are available. The result of such a calculation is the optimal geometric transformation, and the root-mean-square (rms) deviation of the atomic positions. It is also possible to list individual atomic deviations and thereby distinguish well-fitting regions from other regions in which structural change has occurred. The operation of performing superpositions of selected regions of proteins is the basic tool of quantitative structural comparison, akin to something as fundamental as pipetting in the laboratory.

What does such analysis tell us about the structural differences between pairs of related proteins? First, it shows that in a family of proteins there is a core of the structure that retains the same basic topology, or fold, and the rest can have a completely different conformation. (To explain the idea of the common core of two structures, look at the letters B and R. Considered as structures they have a common core corresponding to the letter P. Outside the common core they differ: at the bottom right B has a loop and R has a diagonal stroke.) In plastocyanin and azurin, the double β-sheet retains its fold but the long loop at a side of the sheet does not. Secondly, it shows that although individual helices and sheets tend to retain their structures fairly rigidly, there are changes in their relative geometrical relationship—shifts and rotations of one relative to another. Using superposition calculations we can measure the magnitude of these shifts and rotations.

What can we then say about the structure of a new protein? The general comment is that the common core that this protein shares with the known structures will have the same fold; but, except in special cases, we cannot predict the structure of the regions outside the core. More specifically, we can relate the fraction of the structure in the core, and the magnitude of the distortions of the core structure, to the divergence of the amino acid sequences. Note that these quantitative results required numerical superposition calculations, not merely looking at the structures. There are numerous program systems that combine interactive graphics with superposition facilities.

The basic rule-of-thumb that emerges from these results is that if the amino acid sequences are 50% identical, or more closely related, it will be possible to build a useful model, by transferring the side chains of the new sequence to the backbone of the most closely-related protein of known structure, retaining the side chain conformation whenever possible. In these circumstances, the model will be expected to have the correct fold in over 90% of the structure, and the overall rms deviation of the backbone will be no more than 1 Å. If the sequences are more closely related, the model will be correspondingly better. Such a model would be of a quality useful for interpreting changes in function.

If the amino acid sequences of the new protein and that of its closest relative of known structure have lower than 50% residue identify, we should be more discouraging about building a useful model. If the sequences have only 20% residue identity, the model might even have the correct fold in only half of the structure, and the atomic deviations of the remaining core might well be over 2 Å. Most people would feel that such a model would not be a useful guide to interpreting the properties of the unknown protein. However, often the binding site of a protein family is better preserved than the rest of the protein structure, and it may be possible to interpret changes in specificity in terms of mutations in and around the binding site itself.

It will have been noticed that our model building procedure has been the most naive and conservative possible: we identify the closest relative of the known structure, and retain as many structural features of this known structure as possible. Many people have suggested that this should be regarded as only a zero-order model, and that more powerful computational techniques might improve it. Such techniques might produce a quantitative improvement in the prediction of the conformation of the common core, or yield useful predictions of portions of the structure outside the core.

To achieve a global improvement in the structure, many people have tried to apply energy minimization or molecular dynamics. These are general methods, based on a detailed quantitative representation of the physical forces involved, to predict the conformations that these forces would create. It has been known for some time that these methods cannot fold up a protein "from scratch". It has more recently become clear that these methods cannot substantially improve a model of the type constructed as we have described. The problem seems to be, that if you take a native protein structure, just as determined by x-ray crystallography, and subject it to energy minimization, the program will find that the experimental structure is not at an energy minimum, and the minimum-energy conformation found will have an rms deviation from the correct structure of about 1 Å. But this is as large or larger than the deviation of the naive model, so significant progress has not been made.

Energy minimization is useful for "tidying up" a structure, for example, closing up gaps in the chain resulting from deletions in the amino acid sequence. But it does not give an effective way to move a model towards the correct structure.

The, question of modeling portions of the structure outside the core is one in which some progress has been made, at least for relatively short loops. We have faced the problem of modeling the antigen-binding loops of antibodies. Here and in related cases, the effective approach has been to look in the general corpus of known structures for a prefabricated piece that will fit. For hairpin loops between consecutive strands of a β-sheet, there are certain rules relating the conformation of the loops to the length and sequence of the loop. In favourable cases, these rules guide us in building the conformation of a loop by stitching in a piece from a known structure.

A more general approach, developed by T. Alwyn Jones and colleagues, is based on a general method of substructure search. This may be thought of as roughly analogous to a standard editing operation: that of identifying occurrences of a character string in text. The basic idea is that if one has fixed two points in the chain, perhaps as the ends of regions of secondary structure in the core, one can extract from a database of known structure examples of regions that match the structure of the two ends, and then can look at what appears in between. In favourable cases, it will emerge that there is a preferred way to connect the two regions and this can be applied to the modeling of the loops.

Databases and Software

Genome Assembly the genome assembly is simply the genome sequence produced after chromosomes have been fragmented, those fragments have been sequenced, and the resulting sequences have been put back together.

Each species in Ensembl has a reference genome assembly that is produced by an international genome consortium. (Ensembl does not produce genome assemblies.) The reference assembly can be compiled from the DNA of one individual, a collection of individuals, a breed or a strain. This depends on the species. Find the DNA source of each genome sequence in the More information and statistics link on each species home page.

Assembly Model

Most assemblies provided to Ensembl are 'haploid assemblies' and represent a single non-redundant path through the genome. Some assemblies, such as human and mouse, come with additional alternate sequences that represent additional paths through the genome. Examples of alternate sequences are:

- Haplotypes eg. MHC in human
- Novel patch
- Fix patch

These alternate sequences can be viewed in the Ensembl browser where available.

Updating a Genome Assembly

A genome assembly is updated when DNA has been sequenced that allows gaps to be filled. It may also be updated when a new assembling algorithm is released. This work is done by external groups, who submit the updated assembly to the INSDC.

A new genebuild may be performed by Ensembl when:

- A new assembly is submitted to the INSDC, and we decide to download and annotate the updated assembly, or

- When large amounts of new experimental data become available (for example, RNAseq, cDNA and protein sequences).

Assemblies are updated in Ensembl on the order of once every two years, or less often, depending on the species.

Older versions of genomic assemblies can be found in the archive sites.

Genome Coverage

Ensembl does not generate genome assemblies, but rather we download genome assemblies from the INSDC and annotate them. If you have any questions regarding the sequencing coverage of a genome assembly in Ensembl, please contact the original submitter. This information can be found by querying the assembly accession (eg. GCA_000208655.2) or WGS record (eg. AAGV00000000.3).

Genome Assemblers

The first sequence assemblers began to appear in the late 1980s and early 1990s as variants of simpler sequence alignment programs to piece together vast quantities of fragments generated by automated sequencing instruments called DNA sequencers. As the sequenced organisms grew in size and complexity (from small viruses over plasmids to bacteria and finally eukaryotes), the assembly programs used in these genome projects needed increasingly sophisticated strategies to handle:

- Terabytes of sequencing data which need processing on computing clusters;

- Identical and nearly identical sequences (known as *repeats*) which can, in the worst case, increase the time and space complexity of algorithms quadratically;

- Errors in the fragments from the sequencing instruments, which can confound assembly.

Faced with the challenge of assembling the first larger eukaryotic genomes—the fruit fly Drosophila melanogaster in 2000 and the human genome just a year later,—scientists developed assemblers like Celera Assembler and Arachne able to handle genomes of 130 million (e.g., the fruit fly Drosophila melanogaster) to 3 billion (e.g., the human genome) base pairs. Subsequent to these efforts, several other groups, mostly at the major genome sequencing centers, built large-scale assemblers, and an open source effort known as AMOS was launched to bring together all the innovations in genome assembly technology under the open source framework.

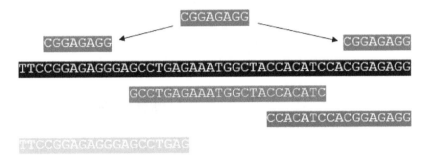

Sample sequence showing how a sequence assembler would take fragments and match by overlaps. Image also shows the potential problem of repeats in the sequence.

EST Assemblers

Expressed sequence tag or EST assembly was an early strategy, dating from the mid-1990s to the mid-2000s, to assemble individual genes rather than whole genomes. The problem differs from genome assembly in several ways. The input sequences for EST assembly are fragments of the transcribed mRNA of a cell and represent only a subset of the whole genome. A number of algorithmical problems differ between genome and EST assembly. For instance, genomes often have large amounts of repetitive sequences, concentrated in the intergenic regions. Transcribed genes contain many fewer repeats, making assembly somewhat easier. On the other hand, some genes are expressed (transcribed) in very high numbers (e.g., housekeeping genes), which means that unlike whole-genome shotgun sequencing, the reads are not uniformly sampled across the genome.

EST assembly is made much more complicated by features like (cis-) alternative splicing, trans-splicing, single-nucleotide polymorphism, and post-transcriptional modification. Beginning in 2008 when RNA-Seq was invented, EST sequencing was replaced by this far more efficient technology, described under de novo transcriptome assembly.

De-novo vs. Mapping Assembly

In sequence assembly, two different types can be distinguished:

1. de-novo: assembling short reads to create full-length (sometimes novel) sequences, without using a template.

2. Mapping: assembling reads against an existing backbone sequence, building a sequence that is similar but not necessarily identical to the backbone sequence.

In terms of complexity and time requirements, de-novo assemblies are orders of magnitude slower and more memory intensive than mapping assemblies. This is mostly due to the fact that the assembly algorithm needs to compare every read with every other read (an operation that has a naive time complexity of $O(n^2)$). Referring to the comparison drawn to shredded books in the introduction: while for mapping assemblies one would have a very similar book as template (perhaps with the names of the main characters and a few locations changed), the de-novo assemblies are more hardcore in a sense as one would not know beforehand whether this would become a science book, a novel, a catalogue, or even several books. Also, every shred would be compared with every other shred.

Handling repeats in de-novo assembly requires the construction of a graph representing neighboring repeats. Such information can be derived from reading a long fragment covering the repeats in full or only its two ends. On the other hand, in a mapping assembly, parts with multiple or no matches are usually left for another assembling technique to look into.

Influence of Technological Changes

The complexity of sequence assembly is driven by two major factors: the number of fragments and their lengths. While more and longer fragments allow better identification of sequence overlaps, they also pose problems as the underlying algorithms show quadratic or even exponential complexity behaviour to both number of fragments and their length. And while shorter sequences are faster to align, they also complicate the layout phase of an assembly as shorter reads are more difficult to use with repeats or near identical repeats.

In the earliest days of DNA sequencing, scientists could only gain a few sequences of short length (some dozen bases) after weeks of work in laboratories. Hence, these sequences could be aligned in a few minutes by hand.

In 1975, the *dideoxy termination* method (AKA *Sanger sequencing*) was invented and until shortly after 2000, the technology was improved up to a point where fully automated machines could churn out sequences in a highly parallelised mode 24 hours a day. Large genome centers around the world housed complete farms of these sequencing machines, which in turn led to the necessity of assemblers to be optimised for sequences from whole-genome shotgun sequencing projects where the reads:

- Are about 800–900 bases long

- Contain sequencing artifacts like sequencing and cloning vectors

- Have error rates between 0.5 and 10%.

With the Sanger technology, bacterial projects with 20,000 to 200,000 reads could easily be assembled on one computer. Larger projects, like the human genome with approximately 35 million reads, needed large computing farms and distributed computing.

By 2004 / 2005, pyrosequencing had been brought to commercial viability by 454 Life Sciences. This new sequencing method generated reads much shorter than those of Sanger sequencing: initially about 100 bases, now 400-500 bases. Its much higher throughput and lower cost (compared to Sanger sequencing) pushed the adoption of this technology by genome centers, which in turn pushed development of sequence assemblers that could efficiently handle the read sets. The sheer amount of data coupled with technology-specific error patterns in the reads delayed development of assemblers; at the beginning in 2004 only the Newbler assembler from 454 was available. Released in mid-2007, the hybrid version of the MIRA assembler by Chevreux et al. was the first freely available assembler that could assemble 454 reads as well as mixtures of 454 reads and Sanger reads. Assembling sequences from different sequencing technologies was subsequently coined hybrid assembly.

From 2006, the Illumina (previously Solexa) technology has been available and can generate about 100 million reads per run on a single sequencing machine. Compare this to the 35 million reads of the human genome project which needed several years to be produced on hundreds of sequencing machines. Illumina was initially limited to a length of only 36 bases, making it less suitable for de novo assembly (such as de novo transcriptome assembly), but newer iterations of the technology achieve read lengths above 100 bases from both ends of a 3-400bp clone. Announced at the end of 2007, the SHARCGS assembler by Dohm et al. was the first published assembler that was used for an assembly with Solexa reads. It was quickly followed by a number of others.

Later, new technologies like SOLiD from Applied Biosystems, Ion Torrent and SMRT were released and new technologies (e.g. Nanopore sequencing) continue to emerge. Despite the higher error rates of these technologies they are important for assembly because their longer read length helps to address the repeat problem. It is impossible to assemble through a perfect repeat that is longer than the maximum read length; however, as reads become longer the chance of a perfect repeat that large becomes small. This gives longer sequencing reads an advantage in assembling repeats even if they have low accuracy (~85%).

Greedy Algorithm

Given a set of sequence fragments, the object is to find a longer sequence that contains all the fragments:

1. Calculate pairwise alignments of all fragments.

2. Choose two fragments with the largest overlap.

3. Merge chosen fragments.

4. Repeat step 2 and 3 until only one fragment is left.

The result need not be an optimal solution to the problem.

Biological Database

Biological databases are libraries of life sciences information, collected from scientific experiments, published literature, high-throughput experiment technology, and computational analysis. They contain information from research areas including genomics, proteomics, metabolomics, microarray gene expression, and phylogenetics. Information contained in biological databases includes gene function, structure, localization (both cellular and chromosomal), clinical effects of mutations as well as similarities of biological sequences and structures.

Biological databases can be broadly classified into sequence, structure and functional databases. Nucleic acid and protein sequences are stored in sequence databases and structure databases store solved structures of RNA and proteins. Functional databases provide information on the physiological role of gene products, for example enzyme activities, mutant phenotypes, or biological pathways. Model Organism Databases are functional databases that provide species-specific data. Databases are important tools in assisting scientists to analyze and explain a host of biological phenomena from the structure of biomolecules and their interaction, to the whole metabolism of organisms and to understanding the evolution of species. This knowledge helps facilitate the fight against diseases, assists in the development of medications, predicting certain genetic diseases and in discovering basic relationships among species in the history of life.

Biological knowledge is distributed among many different general and specialized databases. This sometimes makes it difficult to ensure the consistency of information. Integrative bioinformatics is one field attempting to tackle this problem by providing unified access. One solution is how biological databases cross-reference to other databases with accession numbers to link their related knowledge together.

Relational database concepts of computer science and Information retrieval concepts of digital libraries are important for understanding biological databases. Biological database design, development, and long-term management is a core area of the discipline of bioinformatics. Data contents include gene sequences, textual descriptions, attributes and ontology classifications, citations, and tabular data. These are often described as semi-structured data, and can be represented as tables, key delimited records, and XML structures.

Types

There are three common concepts of biological databases: Primary Databases,Secondary Databases and composite databases. These three differ in their archive structure. Primary databases often hold only one type of specific data which is stored in their own archive. They upload new data explored in experiments and update entries to ensure the quality of the data.

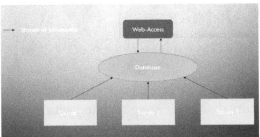
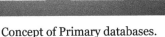
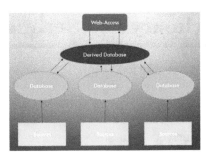

| Concept of Primary databases. | Concept of Secondary databases. |

Secondary databases are databases, which use other databases as their source of information, thus they get their data by requesting.

Nucleic Acids Research Database Issue

An important resource for finding biological databases is a special yearly issue of the journal *Nucleic Acids Research* (NAR). The Database Issue of NAR is freely available, and categorizes many of the publicly available online databases related to biology and bioinformatics. A companion database to the issue called the Online Molecular Biology Database Collection lists 1,380 online databases. Other collections of databases exist such as MetaBase and the Bioinformatics Links Collection.

Access

Most biological databases are available through web sites that organise data such that users can browse through the data online. In addition the underlying data is usually available for download in a variety of formats. Biological data comes in many formats. These formats include text, sequence data, protein structure and links. Each of these can be found from certain sources, for example:

- Text formats are provided by PubMed and OMIM.
- Sequence data is provided by GenBank, in terms of DNA, and UniProt, in terms of protein.
- Protein structures are provided by PDB, SCOP, and CATH.

Species-specific Databases

Species-specific databases are available for some species, mainly those that are often used in research (Model Organisms). For example, EcoCyc is an *E. coli* database. Other popular model organism databases include Mouse Genome Informatics for the laboratory mouse, *Mus musculus*, the Rat Genome Database for *Rattus*, ZFIN for *Danio Rerio* (zebrafish), PomBase for the fission yeast *Schizosaccharomyces pombe*, FlyBase for *Drosophila*, WormBase for the nematodes *Caenorhabditis elegans* and *Caenorhabditis briggsae*, and Xenbase for *Xenopus tropicalis* and *Xenopus laevis* frogs.

Primary and Secondary Databases

Primary Databases

In bioinformatics, and indeed in other data intensive research fields, databases are often categorised as primary or secondary. Primary databases are populated with experimentally derived data such as nucleotide sequence, protein sequence or macromolecular structure. Experimental results are submitted directly into the database by researchers, and the data are essentially archival in nature. Once given a database accession number, the data in primary databases are never changed: they form part of the scientific record.

Secondary Databases

By contrast, secondary databases comprise data derived from the results of analysing primary data. They are often referred to as curated databases but this is a bit of a misnomer because primary databases are also curated to ensure that the data in them is consistent and accurate.

Secondary databases often draw upon information from numerous sources, including other databases (primary and secondary), controlled vocabularies and the scientific literature. They are highly curated, often using a complex combination of computational algorithms and manual analysis and interpretation to derive new knowledge from the public record of science.

Secondary databases have become the molecular biologist's reference library over the past decade or so, providing a wealth of (often daunting) information on just about any gene or gene product that has been investigated by the research community. The potential for mining this information to make new discoveries is vast. It's our job in this course to reduce your activation energy to make more of these resources for your research.

Table: Essential aspects of primary and secondary databases.

	Primary database	Secondary database
Synonyms	Archival database	Curated database; knowledgebase
Source of data	Direct submission of experimentally-derived data from researchers	Results of analysis, literature research and interpretation, often of data in primary databases
Examples	• ENA, GenBank and DDBJ (nucleotide sequence) • ArrayExpress Archive and GEO (functional genomics data) • Protein Data Bank (PDB; coordinates of three-dimensional macromolecular structures)	• InterPro (protein families, motifs and domains) • UniProt Knowledgebase (sequence and functional information on proteins) • Ensembl (variation, function, regulation and more layered onto whole genome sequences)

Sequence Databases

Nucleotide and protein sequence databases represent the most widely used and some of the best established biological databases. These databases serve as repositories for wet lab results and the primary source for experimental results. Major public data banks which takes care of the DNA and protein sequences are GenBank in USA, EMBL (European Molecular Biology Laboratory) in Europe and DDBJ (DNADataBank) in Japan.

Gen Bank: The GenBank nucleotide database is maintained by the National Center for Biotechnology Information (NCBI), which is part of the National Institute of Health (NIH), a federal agency of the US government.

EMBL: The EMBL nucleotide sequence database is maintained by the European Bioinformatics Institute (EBI) in Hinxton.

DDBJ: DNA Data Bank of Japan Is a biological database that collects DNA sequences submitted by researchers. It is run by the National Institute of Genetics, Japan.

Ensembl: The Ensembl database is a repository of stable, automatically annotated human genome sequences. Ensembl annotates and predicts new genes, with annotation from the InterPro protein family databases and with additional annotations from databases of genetic disease-OMIM, expression-SAGE and gene family.

SGD: The Saccharomyces Genome Database (SGD) is a scientific database of the molecular biology and genetics of the yeast Saccharomyces cerevisiae.

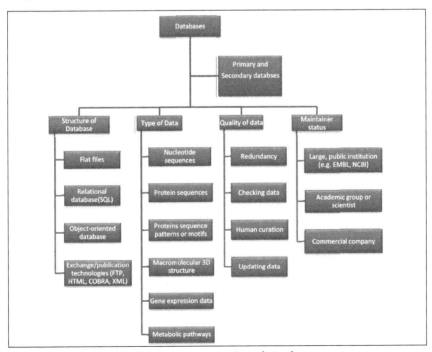

Schematic representation of Database.

dbEST: dbEST is a division of GenBank that contains sequence data and other information on short, "single-pass" cDNA sequences, or Expressed Sequence Tags (ESTs), generated from randomly selected library clones. Expressed Sequence Tags (ESTs) are currently the most widely sequenced nucleotide commodity in the terms of number of sequences and total nucleotide count.

PIR: The Protein Information Resource (PIR) is an integrated public bioinformatics resource that supports genomic and proteomic research and scientific studies. PIR has provided many protein databases and analysis tools to the scientific community, including the PIR-International Protein Sequence Database (PSD) of functionally annotated protein sequences. The PIR-PSD, originally created as the Atlas of Protein Sequence and Structure edited by Margaret Dayhoff, contained protein sequences that were highly annotated with functional, structural, bibliographic, and sequence data.

Swiss-Prot: Swiss-Prot is a protein sequence and knowledge database. It is well known for its minimal redundancy, high quality of annotation, use of standardized nomenclature, and links to specialized databases. As Swiss-Prot is a protein sequence database, its repository contains the amino acid sequence, the protein name and description, taxonomic data, and citation information.

TrEMBL: The European Bioinformatics Institute, collaborating with Swiss-Prot, introduced another database, TrEMBL (translation of EMBL nucleotide sequence database). This database consists of computer annotated entries derived from the translation of all coding sequences in the nucleotide databases.

UniProt: UniProt database is organized into three layers. The UniProt Archive (UniParc) stores the stable, nonredundant, corpus of publicly available protein sequence data. The UniProt Knowledge base (UniProtKB) consists of accurate protein sequences with functional annotation. Finally, the UniProt Reference Cluster (UniRef) datasets provide nonredundant reference clusters based primarily on UniProtKB. UniProt also offers users multiple tools, including searches against the individual contributing databases, BLAST and multiple sequence alignment, proteomic tools, and bibliographic searches.

Structure Databases

Knowledge of protein structures and of molecular interactions is key to understanding protein functions and com-plex regulatory mechanisms underlying many biological processes.

Protein Data Bank: The PDB (Protein Data Bank) is the single worldwide archive of Structural data of Biological macromolecules, established in Brookhaven National Laboratories in 1971. It contains Structural information of the macromolecules determined by X-ray crystallographic, NMR methods. PDB is maintained by the Research Collaboratory for Structural Bioinformatics (RCSB). It allows the user to view data both in plain text and through a molecular viewer using Jmol.

SCOP: The SCOP (Structural Classification of Proteins) database was started by Alexey Murzin in 1994. Its purpose is to classify protein 3D structures in a hierarchical scheme of structural classes.

CATH: The CATH database (Class, architecure, topology, homologous superfamily) is a hierarchical classification of protein domain structures, which clusters proteins at four major structural levels.

NDB: Nucleic Acid Database, also curated by RCSB and similar to the PDB and the Cambridge Structural Database, is a repository for nucleic acid structures. It gives users access to tools for extracting information from nucleic acid structures and distributes data and software.

Pathway Databases

Development of metabolic databases derived from the comparative study of metabolic pathways will cater the industrial needs in more efficient manner to further the growth of systems biotechnology. Some examples of the pathway databses are KEGG, BREN-DA, Biocyc.

Multiple sequence alignment of CDK4 protein generated with ClustalW.
Arrows indicate point mutations.

Clustal is a series of widely used computer programs used in Bioinformatics for multiple sequence alignment. There have been many versions of Clustal over the development of the algorithm that are listed below. The analysis of each tool and its algorithm are also detailed in their respective categories. Available operating systems listed in the sidebar are a combination of the software availability and may not be supported for every current version of the Clustal tools. Clustal Omega has the widest variety of operating systems out of all the Clustal tools.

Function

All variations of the Clustal software align sequences using a heuristic that progressively builds a multiple sequence alignment from a series of pairwise alignments. This method works by analyzing the sequences as a whole, then utilizing the UPGMA/Neighbor-joining method to generate a distance matrix. A guide tree is then calculated from the scores of the sequences in the matrix, then subsequently used to build the multiple sequence alignment by progressively aligning the sequences in order of similarity. Essentially, Clustal creates multiple sequence alignments through three main steps:

1. Do a pairwise alignment using the progressive alignment method
2. Create a guide tree (or use a user-defined tree)
3. Use the guide tree to carry out a multiple alignment

These steps are carried out automatically when you select "Do Complete Alignment". Other options are "Do Alignment from guide tree and phylogeny" and "Produce guide tree only".

Input/Output

This program accepts a wide range of input formats, including NBRF/PIR, FASTA, EMBL/Swiss-Prot, Clustal, GCC/MSF, GCG9 RSF, and GDE.

The output format can be one or many of the following: Clustal, NBRF/PIR, GCG/MSF, PHYLIP, GDE, or NEXUS.

Reading Multiple Sequence Alignment Output		
Symbol	Definition	Meaning
*	Asterisk	Positions that have a single and fully conserved residue
:	Colon	Conservation between groups of strongly similar properties with a score greater than .5 on the PAM 250 matrix
.	Period	Conservation between groups of weakly similar properties with a score less than or equal to .5 on the PAM 250 matrix

The same symbols are shown for both DNA/RNA alignments and protein alignments, so while * (asterisk) symbols are useful to both, the other consensus symbols should be ignored for DNA/RNA alignments.

Settings

Many settings can be modified to adapt the alignment algorithm to different circumstances. The main parameters are the gap opening penalty, and the gap extension penalty.

Clustal and ClustalV

The original program in the Clustal series of software was developed in 1988 as a way to generate multiple sequence alignments on personal computers. ClustalV was released 4 years later and greatly improved upon the original, adding and altering a few key features, including a switch to being written in C instead of Fortran like its predecessor.

Algorithm

Both versions use the same fast approximate algorithm to calculate the similarity scores between sequences, which in turn produces the pairwise alignments. The algorithm works by calculating the similarity scores as the number of k-tuple matches between two sequences, accounting for a set penalty for gaps. The more similar the sequences, the higher the score, the more divergent, the lower the scores. Once the sequences are scored, a dendrogram is generated through the UPGMA to represent the ordering of the multiple sequence alignment. The higher ordered sets of sequences are aligned first, followed by the rest in descending order. The algorithm allows for very large data sets, and works fast. However, the speed is dependent on the range for the k-tuple matches chosen for the particular sequence type.

Notable ClustalV Improvements

Some of the most notable additions in ClustalV are profile alignments, and full command line interface options. The ability to use profile alignments allows the user to align two or more previous alignments or sequences to a new alignment and move misaligned sequences (low scored) further down the alignment order. This gives the user the option to gradually and methodically create multiple sequence alignments with more control than the basic option. The option to run from the command line greatly expedites the multiple sequence alignment process. Sequences can be run with a simple command,

```
clustalv nameoffile.seq
```

or

```
clustalv /infile=nameoffile.seq
```

and the program will determine what type of sequence it is analyzing. When the program is completed, the output of the multiple sequence alignment as well as the dendrogram go to files with .aln and .dnd extensions respectively. The command line interface uses the default parameters, and doesn't allow for other options.

ClustalW

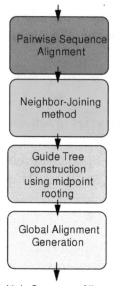

Depicts the steps the ClustalW software algorithm uses for global alignments.

ClustalW like the other Clustal tools is used for aligning multiple nucleotide or protein sequences in an efficient manner. It uses progressive alignment methods, which align the most similar sequences first and work their way down to the least similar sequences until a global alignment is created. ClustalW is a matrix-based algorithm, whereas tools like T-Coffee and Dialign are consistency-based. ClustalW has a fairly efficient algorithm that competes well against other software. This program requires three or more sequences in order to calculate a global alignment, for pairwise sequence alignment (2 sequences) use tools similar to EMBOSS, LALIGN.

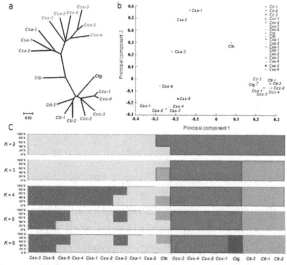

Diagram showing neighbor-joining method in sequence alignment for bioinformatics.

Algorithm

ClustalW uses progressive alignment methods as stated above. In these, the sequences with the best alignment score are aligned first, then progressively more distant groups of sequences are aligned. This heuristic approach is necessary due to the time and memory demand of finding the global optimal solution. The first step to the algorithm is computing a rough distance matrix between each pair of sequences, also known as pairwise sequence alignment. The next step is a neighbor-joining method that uses midpoint rooting to create an overall guide tree. The process it uses to do this is shown in the detailed diagram for the method to the right. The guide tree is then used as a rough template to generate a global alignment.

Time Complexity

ClustalW has a time complexity of because of its use of the neighbor-joining method. In the updated version (ClustalW2) there is an option built into the software to use UPGMA which is faster with large input sizes. The command line flag in order to use it instead of neighbor-joining is:

```
-clustering=UPGMA
```

For example, on a standard desktop, running UPGMA on 10,000 sequences would produce results in less than a minute while neighbor-joining would take over an hour. By running the ClustalW algorithm with this adjustment, it saves significant amounts of time. ClustalW2 also has an option to use iterative alignment to increase alignment accuracy. While it is not necessarily faster or more efficient complexity-wise, the increase in accuracy is valuable and can be useful for smaller data sizes. These are the various command line flags to achieve this:

```
-Iteration=Alignment
```

```
-Iteration=Tree
```

```
-numiters
```

The first command line option refines the final alignment. The second option incorporates the scheme into the progressive alignment step of the algorithm. The third specifies the number of iteration cycles where the default value is set to 3.

Accuracy and Results

The algorithm ClustalW uses provides a close-to-optimal result almost every time. However, it does exceptionally well when the data set contains sequences with varied degrees of divergence. This is because in a data set like this, the guide tree becomes less sensitive to noise. ClustalW was one of the first algorithms to combine pairwise alignment and global alignment in an attempt to be speed efficient, and it worked, but there is a loss in accuracy that other software doesn't have due to this.

ClustalW, when compared to other MSA algorithms, performed as one of the quickest while still maintaining a level of accuracy. There is still much to be improved compared to its consistency-based competitors like T-Coffee. The accuracy for ClustalW when tested against MAFFT, T-Coffee, Clustal Omega, and other MSA implementations had the lowest accuracy for full-length sequences. It had the least RAM memory demanding algorithm out of all the ones tested in the study. While ClustalW recorded the lowest level of accuracy among its competitors, it still maintained what some would deem acceptable. There have been updates and improvements to the algorithm that are present in ClustalW2 that work to increase accuracy while still maintaining its greatly valued speed.

Clustal Omega

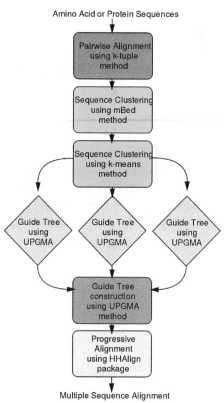

Flowchart depicting the step-by-step algorithm used in Clustal Omega.

ClustalΩ (alternatively written as Clustal O and Clustal Omega) is a fast and scalable program written in C and C++ used for multiple sequence alignment. It uses seeded guide trees and a new HMM engine that focuses on two profiles to generate these alignments. The program requires three or more sequences in order to calculate the multiple sequence alignment, for two sequences use pairwise sequence alignment tools (EMBOSS, LALIGN). Clustal Omega is consistency-based and is widely viewed as one of the fastest online implementations of all multiple sequence alignment tools and still ranks high in accuracy, among both consistency-based and matrix-based algorithms.

Algorithm

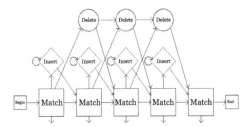

The structure of a profile HMM used in the implementation of Clustal Omega is shown here.

Clustal Omega has five main steps in order to generate the multiple sequence alignment. The first is producing a pairwise alignment using the k-tuple method, also known as the word method. This, in summary, is a heuristic method that isn't guaranteed to find an optimal alignment solution, but is significantly more efficient than the dynamic programming method of alignment. After that, the sequences are clustered using the modified mBed method. The mBed method calculates pairwise distance using sequence embedding. This step is followed by the k-means clustering method. Next, the guide tree is constructed using the UPGMA method. This is shown as multiple guide tree steps leading into one final guide tree construction because of the way the UPGMA algorithm works. At each step, (each diamond in the flowchart) the nearest two clusters are combined and is repeated until the final tree can be assessed. In the final step, the multiple sequence alignment is produced using HHAlign package from the HH-Suite, which uses two profile HMM's. A profile HMM is a linear state machine consisting of a series of nodes, each of which corresponds roughly to a position (column) in the alignment from which it was built.

Time Complexity

The exact way of computing an optimal alignment between N sequences has a computational complexity of O (L^N) for N sequences of length L making it prohibitive for even small numbers of sequences. Clustal Omega uses a modified version of mBed which has a complexity of O (N log N), and produces guide trees that are just as accurate as those from conventional methods. The speed and accuracy of the guide trees in Clustal Omega is attributed to the implementation of a modified mBed algorithm. It also reduces the computational time and memory requirements to complete alignments on large datasets.

Accuracy and Results

The accuracy of Clustal Omega on a small number of sequences is, on average, very similar to what are considered high quality sequence aligners. The difference comes when using large sets of data with hundreds of thousands of sequences. In these cases, Clustal Omega outperforms other algorithms across the board. Its completion time and overall quality is consistently better than other programs. It is capable of running 100,000+ sequences on one processor in a few hours.

Clustal Omega uses the HHAlign package of the HH-Suite, which aligns two profile Hidden Markov Models instead of a profile-profile comparison. This improves the quality of the sensitivity and alignment significantly. This, combined with the mBed method, gives Clustal Omega its advantage over other sequence aligners. The results end up being very accurate and very quick which is the optimal situation.

On bigger data sets Clustal Omega outperforms Probcons and T-Coffee which are both consistency-based algorithms, much like Clustal Omega is. On an efficiency test with programs that produce high accuracy scores, MAFFT is the fastest closely followed by Clustal Omega. Both were faster than T-Coffee, however, MAFFT and Clustal Omega require more memory to run. The general consensus is that BAliBASE remains the superior multiple sequence alignment tool, however for online resources, Clustal Omega is recommended especially for large datasets.

Clustal2 (ClustalW/ClustalX)

Clustal2 is the packaged release of both the command-line ClustalW and graphical Clustal X. Neither are new tools, but are updated and improved versions of the previous implementations seen above. Both downloads come precompiled for many operating systems like Linux, Mac OS X and Windows (both XP and Vista). This release was designed in order to make the website more organized and user friendly, as well as updating the source codes to their most recent versions. Clustal2 is version 2 of both ClustalW and ClustalX, which is where it gets its name. Past versions can still be found on the website, however, every precompilation is now up to date.

MUSCLE

MUSCLE uses two distance measures for a pair of sequences: a $k$mer distance (for an unaligned pair) and the Kimura distance (for an aligned pair). A $k$mer is a contiguous subsequence of length k, also known as a word or k-tuple. Related sequences tend to have more $k$mers in common than expected by chance. The $k$mer distance is derived from the fraction of $k$mers in common in a compressed alphabet, which we have previously shown to correlate well with fractional identity . This measure does not require an alignment, giving a significant speed advantage. Given an aligned pair of sequences, we compute the pairwise identity and convert to an additive distance estimate, applying the Kimura correction for multiple substitutions at a single site. Distance matrices are clustered using UPGMA, which we find to give slightly improved results over neighbor-joining, despite the expectation that neighbor-joining will give a more reliable estimate of the evolutionary tree. This can be explained by assuming that in progressive alignment, the best accuracy is obtained at each node by aligning the two profiles that have fewest differences, even if they are not evolutionary neighbors.

Profile Alignment

In order to apply pairwise alignment to profiles, a scoring function must be defined on an aligned pair of profile positions, i.e. a pair of multiple alignment columns. Let i and j be amino acid types, p_i the background probability of i, p_{ij} the joint probability of i and j being aligned to each other, f^x_i the observed frequency of i in column x of the first profile, and f^x_G the observed frequency of gaps in that column at position x in the family (similarly for position y in the second profile). The estimated probability α^x_i of observing amino acid i in position x can be derived from f^x, typically by adding heuristic pseudo-counts or by using Bayesian methods such as Dirichlet mixture priors. MUSCLE uses a new profile function we call the log-expectation (LE) score:

$$\text{LE}^{xy} = (1 - f^x_G)(1 - f^y_G) \log \Sigma_i \Sigma_j f^x_i f^y_j p_{ij}/p_i p_j$$

This is a modified version of the log-average function:

$$\text{LA}^{xy} = \log \Sigma_i \Sigma_j \alpha^x_i \alpha^y_j p_{ij}/p_i p_j$$

MUSCLE uses probabilities p_i and p_{ij} derived from the 240 PAM VTML matrix. Frequencies f_i are normalized to sum to 1 when indels are present (otherwise the logarithm becomes increasingly negative with increasing numbers of gaps even when aligning conserved or similar residues). The factor $(1 - f_G)$ is the occupancy of a column, introduced to encourage more highly occupied columns to align. Position-specific gap penalties are used, employing heuristics similar to those found in MAFFT and LAGAN.

Algorithm

The high-level flow is depicted in figure below:

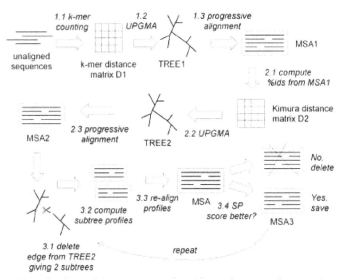

This diagram summarizes the flow of the MUSCLE algorithm. There are three main stages: Stage (draft progressive), Stage 2 (improved progressive) and Stage 3 (refinement). A multiple alignment is available at the completion of each stage, at which point the algorithm may terminate.

Stage 1, Draft progressive: The goal of the first stage is to produce a multiple alignment, emphasizing speed over accuracy.

- The $k$mer distance is computed for each pair of input sequences, giving distance matrix D1.

- Matrix D1 is clustered by UPGMA, producing binary tree TREE1.

- A progressive alignment is constructed by following the branching order of TREE1. At each leaf, a profile is constructed from an input sequence. Nodes in the tree are visited in prefix order (children before their parent). At each internal node, a pairwise alignment is constructed of the two child profiles, giving a new profile which is assigned to that node. This produces a multiple alignment of all input sequences, MSA1, at the root.

Stage 2, Improved progressive: The main source of error in the draft progressive stage is the approximate $k$mer distance measure, which results in a suboptimal tree. MUSCLE therefore re-estimates the tree using the Kimura distance, which is more accurate but requires an alignment.

- The Kimura distance for each pair of input sequences is computed from MSA1, giving distance matrix D2.

- Matrix D2 is clustered by UPGMA, producing binary tree TREE2.

- A progressive alignment is produced following TREE2 (similar to 1.3), producing multiple alignment MSA2. This is optimized by computing alignments only for subtrees whose branching orders changed relative to TREE1.

Stage 3, Refinement:

- An edge is chosen from TREE2 (edges are visited in order of decreasing distance from the root).

- TREE2 is divided into two subtrees by deleting the edge. The profile of the multiple alignment in each subtree is computed.

- A new multiple alignment is produced by re-aligning the two profiles.

- If the SP score is improved, the new alignment is kept, otherwise it is discarded.

Steps above are repeated until convergence or until a user-defined limit is reached. This is a variant of tree-dependent restricted partitioning .

Complete multiple alignments are available at steps 1.3, 2.3 and 3.4, at which points the algorithm may be terminated. We refer to the first two stages alone as MUSCLE-p, which produces MSA2. MUSCLE-p has time complexity $O(N^2L + NL^2)$ and space complexity $O(N^2 + NL + L^2)$. Refinement adds an $O(N^3L)$ term to the time complexity.

Bowtie

Bowtie is a software package commonly used for sequence alignment and sequence analysis in bioinformatics..The source code for the package is distributed freely and compiled binaries are available for Linux, macOS and Windows platforms. As of 2017, the Genome Biology paper describing the original Bowtie method has been cited more than 11,000 times. Bowtie is open-source software and is currently maintained by Johns Hopkins University.

Bowtie 2

On 16 October 2011, the developers released a beta fork of the project called Bowtie 2. In addition to the Burrows-Wheeler transform, Bowtie 2 also uses an FM-index (similar to a suffix array) to keep its memory footprint small. Due to its implementation, Bowtie 2 is more suited to finding longer, gapped alignments in comparison with the original Bowtie method. There is no upper limit on read length in Bowtie 2 and it allows alignments to overlap ambiguous characters in the reference.

HMMER

HMMER is used for searching sequence databases for sequence homologs, and for making sequence alignments. It implements methods using probabilistic models called profile hidden Markov models (profile HMMs).

HMMER is often used together with a profile database, such as Pfam or many of the databases that participate in Interpro. But HMMER can also work with query *sequences*, not just profiles, just like BLAST. For example, you can search a protein query sequence against a database with phmmer, or do an iterative search with jackhmmer.

HMMER is designed to detect remote homologs as sensitively as possible, relying on the strength of its underlying probability models. In the past, this strength came at significant computational expense, but as of the new HMMER3 project, HMMER is now essentially as fast as BLAST.

The goal of the HMMER project is to make advanced probabilistic methods for sequence homology detection available in widely useful tools. The HMMER software suite has been widely used, particularly by protein family databases such as Pfam and InterPro and their associated search tools. HMMER 3.0, released in early 2010, includes new technology producing roughly 100-fold speed improvements relative to previous versions of HMMER, such that HMMER3 search times are competitive with BLASTP search times. This new technology includes a combination of striped vector-parallelized alignment algorithms [using single instruction, multiple data (SIMD) vector instructions called SSE on Intel-compatible platforms and Altivec/VMX on PowerPC platforms]; a new heuristic acceleration algorithm; and a 'sparse rescaling' method enabling the Forward and Backward profile hidden Markov model (profile HMM) algorithms to be implemented using multiply/add instructions on scaled probabilities without numerical underflow. HMMER3 has now been adopted by most major protein family databases (1,2,6–9). In addition to speed improvements, HMMER also now uses log-odds likelihood scores summed over alignment uncertainty (Forward scores), rather than optimal alignment (Viterbi) scores, which improves sensitivity. Forward scores are better for detecting distant homologs as there can often be several possible ways of aligning a distantly related query to a target. By summing over all possible alignments, each alternative alignment contributes to the score, sufficient to indicate the similarity. However, by taking the best alignment, as in the case of Viterbi, from a set of poor alignments is often insufficient to distinguish the remote homolog from the noise. Furthermore, posterior probabilities of alignment confidence are reported, enabling detailed and intuitive assessments of alignments on a residue-by-residue basis.

Previous versions of HMMER have largely only been available as computationally intensive UNIX command-line applications requiring local installation and local computing resources. The greatly increased speed of HMMER3 makes it feasible to address this major usability hindrance with public HMMER web services. We have developed the HMMER web site to not only provide downloadable HMMER binaries, documentation and source code as it has done in the past, but now also to provide an interface for performing protein sequence searches with near interactive response times.

The hmmer Web Server

The HMMER 3.0 software suite includes four database search programs for protein sequence analysis: *phmmer, hmmscan, hmmsearch* and *jackhmmer*. The web site implements the first three of these search algorithms.

phmmer

The *phmmer* program is analogous to BLASTP. It takes a single protein sequence, in FASTA format, as an input query and searches it against a target sequence database. To perform the search, the query sequence is converted into a profile HMM. Traditionally, profile HMMs have been thought of only as position-specific models of an input multiple sequence alignment. However, in essentially the reverse of how the original position-independent scoring model in BLASTP was generalized to the position-specific scoring model in PSI-BLAST, profile HMMs can be devolved to simple position-independent probabilistic scoring models as a special case. Given a single query input sequence, profile HMM residue probabilities are set by deriving the implicit probabilistic basis of a standard score matrix such as BLOSUM62, plus empirically set insertion/deletion transition probabilities (parameters analogous to standard gap open, gap extend penalties).

The simple *phmmer* search submission form allows only the query sequence to be entered, in which case default search parameters are used. Clicking the 'Advanced' option, found in the top-right corner of the form, reveals more expert options for modifying the way that the search is performed. The default scoring matrix and gap parameters can be modified via the 'Advanced' form. It is also possible to set cut-off thresholds that sequence matches must achieve in order to be displayed (or reported) and for the match to be deemed significant (inclusion). HMMER reports both bit scores and *E*-values (expectation values). A bit score is a log-odds ratio score (base two) comparing the likelihood of the profile HMM to the likelihood of a null hypothesis (an independent, identically distributed random sequence model, as in BLAST). An *E*-value is the number of hits expected to achieve this bit score or greater by 'chance', i.e. if the search had instead been done on an identically sized database composed only of random non-homologous sequences. It is also possible to turn off the bias filter, used as part of the HMMER3 acceleration pipeline. Under certain circumstances, when the query contains a lot of low complexity, tandem repeats or trans-membrane regions, the bias filter may exclude homologous target sequences. Turning off the bias composition filter can increases sensitivity, but at a high cost in speed, as more sequences have to undergo more computationally expensive analysis, hence it is on by default.

In addition to running a *phmmer* search, a 'Pfam Search' is run by default. This triggers an inexpensive *hmmscan* search (described in the following section) against the Pfam library of profile HMMs, in parallel to the *phmmer* search.

Currently, the query sequence can be searched against one of six different target sequence databases: NR (14), UniProtKB (15), SwissProt, PDB (16), UniMes and the environmental division of NR. These target sequence databases have been chosen either because they represent large, comprehensive sequence collections (NCBI NR/UniProtKB), annotated or structurally characterized sequences (SwissProt and PDB) or metagenomic sequence databases (UniMes and env NR). On the web site, the default database is selected based on where the geographical location of the IP address found in the incoming HTTP request. Users from the USA have the NCBI NR database as default, whereas UniProtKB is the default database for users in Europe.

A *phmmer* search via the web can also take protein accessions or identifiers, found in one of the six underlying target sequence databases, as a query, instead of a sequence. An autocompletion provides suggestions of known accessions or identifiers after the first three characters of the name have been entered.

The number of results that are displayed per page and the columns that are included in the results table can also be configured. By default, '*Target*' (accessions and/or identifiers), '*Description*' (functional annotations), '*Species*' and '*E-value*' columns are displayed, with 100 results per page. This default view allows the results to be displayed even when the browser window is narrow (typically on mobile devices). However, the amount of data can be expanded, both in terms of additional columns and the number of rows per page in the table. The results can be customized either before or after the search is performed.

hmmscan

The *hmmscan* program (previously called *hmmpfam* in HMMER2) takes a query sequence and searches it against the Pfam profile HMM library as a target database. As with *phmmer*, significance and reporting thresholds can be defined either by bit score or *E*-value, and additionally, thresholds can be defined by the Pfam 'gathering threshold'. Each Pfam profile HMM has a specific, curated gathering threshold that sets the inclusion bit score cut-off. Pfam defines gathering thresholds conservatively, such that no known false-positive matches are detected for that family. Any match scoring above the gathering threshold is very likely to be a true positive. These thresholds are generally most useful in fully automated searches. However, using the conservative gathering thresholds may miss borderline matches that are true hits, so when trying to establish distant relationships in more manual searches, one of the alternative thresholding methods may be more appropriate.

hmmsearch

This program takes a profile HMM and searches it against a target sequence database, with the profile HMM being built from a query multiple sequence alignment. The web search allows either a HMMER3 formatted profile HMM or a multiple sequence alignment to be submitted as the query. A variety of different multiple sequence alignment formats are permitted (Clustal, MSF, SELEX, STOCKHOLM and aligned FASTA format). Once uploaded, the multiple sequence alignment is converted to a profile HMM using *hmmbuild* (in its default mode). The target sequence databases available for searching and cut-off settings are as with *phmmer* searches. A comparison of the HMMER program to their equivalents in BLAST is shown in Table.

Table: A comparison of HMMER and BLAST programs for protein sequence analysis

	HMMER	BLAST	Comments
Program	phmmer	blastp	Produces similar results in terms of homolog detection. Searching with the sequence from PDB ID 2abl, chain A against PDB yields 244 matches compared with 214 matches for phmmer and blastp, respectively, using an E-value threshold of 0.01 and default search parameters. The matches were inspected for the presence of an SH3 (Src homology 3) and/or SH2 (Src homology 2) domain(s). phmmer results have the added advantage of scoring each residue in the alignment, giving users an indication of the parts of the alignment that are trustworthy. HMMER web server allows configuration of the cut-offs and provides access to all matches.
Query	Single sequence		
Target Database	Sequence database		

Program	hmmscan	rpsblast	Typically used for detection of domains on a sequence. Profile HMMs are used by the majority of protein family databases. Both are run as by default as part of the phmmer/blastp web searches. Available as separate search on the HMMER web servers.
Query	Single sequence		
Target Database	Profile HMM database, e.g. Pfam	PSSM database, e.g. CDD	
Program	hmmsearch	Not applicable	There is no equivalent to hmmsearch in the BLAST suite. The web site uses hmmbuild to convert input alignments to a profile HMM. The command-line version psi-blast can be forced to perform a similar style of search by jump-starting it with a multiple sequence alignment.
Query	Profile HMM		
Target Database	Sequence database		
Program	jackhmmer	psi-blast	Both are used to iteratively search sequence databases. Subsequent iterations use the significantly scoring sequences from the previous round as input data. Jackhmmer is currently not supported on the HMMER web server. Gaps are weighted on observations for jackhmmer, rather than arbitrary open and extend penalties.
Query	Single sequence		
Target database	Sequence database		

All of these HMMER methods are run on a compute farm at Janelia Farm using a new program, *hmmpgmd*(the hmmer program daemon). *hmmpgmd* is a custom IP (Internet Protocol) socket-based parallel system that establishes persistent server and worker daemons to broker search jobs across 144 cores [12×12 2.67 GHz Intel(R) Xeon(R) CPU] as they are received from the web servers. We chose to implement a custom IP socket communication protocol rather than using an established message-passing system such as message passing interface (MPI) in order to minimize latency. Further optimizations in *hmmpgmd* include the persistent caching of the database in memory upon starting the daemon and a compact binary format protocol for returning results to the client, in this instance the web server. This program will be included in the next release of the HMMER3 software to aid the deployment of HMMER on other web sites or high-throughput pipelines.

TopHat

TopHat is an open-source bioinformatics tool for the fast and high throughput alignment of shotgun cDNA sequencing reads generated by transcriptomics technologies (e.g. RNA-Seq) using Bowtie first and then mapping to a reference genome to discover RNA splice sites *de novo*. TopHat aligns RNA-Seq reads to mammalian-sized genomes.

Uses

TopHat is used to align reads from an RNA-Seq experiment. It is a read-mapping algorithm and it aligns the reads to a reference genome. It is useful because it does not need to rely on known splice sites. TopHat can be used with the Tuxedo pipeline, and is frequently used with Bowtie.

Advantages

When TopHat first came out, it was faster than previous systems. It mapped more than 2.2 million reads per CPU hour. That speed allowed the user to process and entire RNA-Seq experiment in less than a day, even on a standard desktop computer. Trapnell_2009 Tophat uses Bowtie in the beginning to analyze the reads, but then does more to analyze the reads that span exon-exon junctions. If you are using TopHap for RNASeq data, you will get more read aligned against the reference genome.

A decent advantage for TopHat is that it does not need to rely on known splice sites when aligning reads to a reference genome.

Disadvantages

TopHat is in a low maintenance, low support stage. It has been superseded by HISAT2, which is more efficient and accurate and provides the same core functionality (spliced alignment of RNA-Seq reads).

Newer protocols are more efficient now, compared to TopHat such as cufflinks, STAR, and limma.

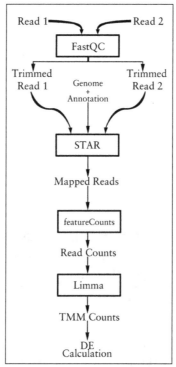

This is an example of a pipeline for RNA-seq workflow using STAR and Limma.
This particular pipeline is more efficient than one using TopHat.

MEGA

MEGA (Molecular Evolutionary Genetics Analysis) has been developed to facilitate statistical analyses of molecular evolution by using personal computers. Currently, there are many specialized programs for estimating evolutionary distances between nucleotide or amino acid sequences and reconstructing phylogenetic trees. However, they are usually written for specific methods of analysis and cannot be interconnected easily. MEGA is designed to conduct various statistical analyses in one program and to produce results in publication-quality outputs.

System and Requirements

MEGA, v. 1.0, is written and compiled in the Borland C^{++} and Applications Framework, v. 3.1. This program runs on all IBM personal computers and their compatibles with 640 kbyte RAM in DOS as well as in OS/2 and Microsoft Windows through DOS application capabilities. An event-driven user interface is implemented with menus and windows by using Borland Turbo Vision, v. 1.0. This interactive interface can be used on most color and monochrome monitors, and it responds to the keyboard as well as to the mouse. Graphics adapters, math coprocessors, and extended or expanded memory are not required to run MEGA, but a hard disk is essential.

MEGA does not limit the amount of data to be analyzed; the size of data is constrained only by the computer memory available from the basic 640k byte RAM.

Phylogenetic Inference

The Unweighted Pair Group Method with Arithmetic Mean, the neighbor-joining method and maximum parsimony methods are provided for phylogenetic inference. UPGMA and the neighbor-joining method require a matrix of pairwise distances. By contrast, maximum parsimony methods use information on evolutionary relationships of nucleotides at each site.

UPGMA assumes a constant rate of evolution for all different lineages, whereas the neighbor-joining method requires no such assumption and is known to be quite efficient in recovering true phylogenetic trees.

The maximum parsimony method for nucleotide sequences is included in MEGA. It treats all nucleotide changes as unordered and reversible (Eck and Dayhoff, 1966; Fitch, 1971). A new branch-and-bound and a new heuristic search algorithm are implemented. The branch-and-bound algorithm in MEGA reorders the sequences for maximum efficiency. Therefore, the input order of sequences is irrelevant. The heuristic search provided in MEGA is a relaxed version of the branch-and-bound algorithm where the minimum number of substitutions required to explain a part of the topology (partial-tree) is computed at every stage of sequence addition and a local upperbound is computed. A user defined search-factor is then added to the local upperbound, and all partial-trees that are shorter than the new local upperbounds are included in searching for maximum parsimony trees.

MEGA includes two different tests for evaluating the reliability of a tree obtained: the bootstrap test and the standard error test. The bootstrap test (Efton, 1982; Felsenstein, 1985) is provided for both UPGMA and the neighbor-joining methods. In this method, the same number of sites are randomly sampled with replacement from the original sequences, and a phylogenetic tree is constructed from the resampled data. This process is repeated many times, and the reliability of a sequence cluster is evaluated by its relative frequency of the appearance in bootstrap replications. No bootstrap consensus tree is constructed.

The standard error test is for evaluating the reliability of a neighbor-joining tree. In this method, once an NJ tree is obtained, the branch lengths of the tree are re-estimated by using the ordinary least-squares method, and the standard errors of these estimates are computed. To test the statistical significance of a branch with length b and standard error s(b), the /-test is used to obtain the confidence probability (CP).

Basic Statistical Quantities

MEGA has a feature to compute the nucleotide frequencies and codon frequencies (codon usage tables) for each or all nucleotide sequences used. Nucleotide frequencies can also be computed for the first, second and third nucleotide positions of codons. Numbers of 2- or 4-fold redundant codons in each sequence or all sequences can also be computed. In addition, nucleotide pair frequencies, transition/transversion ratios, the number of variable sites in specified segments, and the number of total variable and informative sites can be computed for sequence data.

Input and Output

Both sequence data and distance matrix data can be entered in MEGA as ASCII text files. Nucleotide and amino acid sequences must be written in IUPAC single-letter codes. Only aligned sequences are acceptable and they should be presented in either interleaved (block wise) or non-interleaved (continuous) format. Alignment gaps and missing data sites are also allowed in input sequences. Distance matrices can be presented either in the lower-left or in the upper-right triangular matrix. From the input data set, any subset may be selected for analysis. Some OTUs as well as some specific sites (domains) may be selected from the original data without modifying the input data file.

Nucleotide sequences can be translated into amino acid sequences, and both can be displayed on the screen. They can be written in files that can be directly used in other programs, such as PAUP and PHYLIP. The variable, informative, and 2- or 4-fold redundant sites can be highlighted in sequences displayed on the screen.

The phylogcnetic-tree editor facilitates the relocation of root, the adjustment of tree size, and the flipping and swapping of branches on the screen. The edited tree can be stored in text files, printed as graphic images on a wide range of printers (9-pin dot matrix to PostScript), and previewed on the screen with the EGA, VGA and Hercules graphics adapters.

References

- Steinegger, Martin; Mirdita, Milot; Söding, Johannes (2019-06-24). "Protein-level assembly increases protein sequence recovery from metagenomic samples manyfold". Nature Methods. doi:10.1038/s41592-019-0437-4, Retrieved 2 February, 2019

- Altman RB (March 2004). "Building successful biological databases". Brief. Bioinformatics. 5 (1): 4–5. doi:10.1093/bib/5.1.4. PMID 15153301, Retrieved 12 April, 2019

- Primary-and-secondary-databases, bioinformatics: ebi.ac.uk, Retrieved 22 June, 2019

- Biological-databases-integration-of-life-science-data: omicsonline.org, Retrieved 29 August, 2019

- Van Noorden R, Maher B, Nuzzo R (October 2014). "The top 100 papers". Nature. 514 (7524): 550–3. Bibcode:2014Natur.514..550V. doi:10.1038/514550a. PMID 25355343, Retrieved 9 May, 2019

- "CummeRbund - An R package for persistent storage, analysis, and visualization of RNA-Seq from cufflinks output". Retrieved 11 August 2015, Retrieved 11 July, 2019

Permissions

All chapters in this book are published with permission under the Creative Commons Attribution Share Alike License or equivalent. Every chapter published in this book has been scrutinized by our experts. Their significance has been extensively debated. The topics covered herein carry significant information for a comprehensive understanding. They may even be implemented as practical applications or may be referred to as a beginning point for further studies.

We would like to thank the editorial team for lending their expertise to make the book truly unique. They have played a crucial role in the development of this book. Without their invaluable contributions this book wouldn't have been possible. They have made vital efforts to compile up to date information on the varied aspects of this subject to make this book a valuable addition to the collection of many professionals and students.

This book was conceptualized with the vision of imparting up-to-date and integrated information in this field. To ensure the same, a matchless editorial board was set up. Every individual on the board went through rigorous rounds of assessment to prove their worth. After which they invested a large part of their time researching and compiling the most relevant data for our readers.

The editorial board has been involved in producing this book since its inception. They have spent rigorous hours researching and exploring the diverse topics which have resulted in the successful publishing of this book. They have passed on their knowledge of decades through this book. To expedite this challenging task, the publisher supported the team at every step. A small team of assistant editors was also appointed to further simplify the editing procedure and attain best results for the readers.

Apart from the editorial board, the designing team has also invested a significant amount of their time in understanding the subject and creating the most relevant covers. They scrutinized every image to scout for the most suitable representation of the subject and create an appropriate cover for the book.

The publishing team has been an ardent support to the editorial, designing and production team. Their endless efforts to recruit the best for this project, has resulted in the accomplishment of this book. They are a veteran in the field of academics and their pool of knowledge is as vast as their experience in printing. Their expertise and guidance has proved useful at every step. Their uncompromising quality standards have made this book an exceptional effort. Their encouragement from time to time has been an inspiration for everyone.

The publisher and the editorial board hope that this book will prove to be a valuable piece of knowledge for students, practitioners and scholars across the globe.

Index

CPSIA information can be obtained
at www.ICGtesting.com
Printed in the USA
BVHW011522190820
586704BV00026B/346

9 781647 400149